Developing Teaching Style
in Adult Education

Developing Teaching Style in Adult Education

Joe E. Heimlich
Emmalou Norland

Jossey-Bass Publishers · San Francisco

Substantial discounts on bulk quantities of Jossey-Bass books are available to corporations, professional associations, and other organizations. For details and discount information, contact the special sales department at Jossey-Bass Inc., Publishers. (415) 433-1740; Fax (415) 433-0499.

For international orders, please contact your local Paramount Publishing International office.

Manufactured in the United States of America. Nearly all Jossey-Bass books and jackets are printed on recycled paper that contains at least 50 percent recycled waste, including 10 percent postconsumer waste. Many of our materials are also printed with vegetable-based ink; during the printing process these inks emit fewer volatile organic compounds (VOCs) than petroleum-based inks. VOCs contribute to the formation of smog.

Library of Congress Cataloging-in-Publication Data

Heimlich, Joe E., date.
    Developing teaching style in adult education / Joe E. Heimlich, Emmalou Norland. — 1st ed.
      p.   cm.—(The Jossey-Bass higher and adult education series)
    Includes bibliographical references (p.   ) and index.
    ISBN 0-7879-0013-3
    1. Adult education—United States. 2. Adult education teachers —United States. 3. Teaching   I. Norland, Emmalou, date.
    II. Title III. Series.
    LC5251.H383   1994
    374.13—dc20   94-8094
                                             CIP

FIRST EDITION
HB Printing   10 9 8 7 6 5 4 3 2 1   *Code 9491*

The Jossey-Bass
Higher and Adult Education Series

Consulting Editor
Adult and Continuing Education

Alan B. Knox
University of Wisconsin, Madison

This book is dedicated to our families:
Mark, Heather, Eric, Mike, and Jenny

Contents

Preface

Developing Teaching Style in Adult Education is for adult educators in various settings who are seeking to improve as teachers. It describes a process adult educators can use to examine their beliefs about teaching and current teaching behavior in depth. It is intended to guide them through an exploration of who they really are as teachers, and then, through experiential exercises, to help them grow toward becoming the teachers they want to be.

Purpose

Because teacher education courses have focused more on learners than on teachers, we wanted to provide an opportunity for teachers to stop and take a long, hard look at themselves as individuals and, more specifically, as adult educators. We also felt it was crucial to professional growth for teachers to examine their beliefs, values, attitudes, and total philosophy about teaching, learning, content, environment, the teacher, the student, and the many other components of the teaching-learning exchange. We believe that teaching style is illustrated in all aspects of teaching: in thought, feeling, approach, and action. Consistency in these attributes is the key to growing and improving as a teacher.

Even though the book reflects historic and current scholarship in adult education, we have written it specifically for teachers of adults to use in their everyday work. Our target audience is practitioners, not the academy, although the ideas put forth should be helpful for any adult educator, including the university professor.

Our attempt to provide a theoretically grounded yet user-friendly process should help teachers of adults and teachers of adult educators develop their teaching styles. We know by the very nature of the cultural systems in which we have grown and continue to interact that the focus is on the product, not the process; the end, not the means. For us, this book represents a lifelong journey of exploring the process of our growth as teachers.

Because this book describes a process to use, the goal of many of the suggested activities throughout is movement, however slight, toward a greater understanding of oneself as teacher. Some of the activities may focus on simple exploration, others on reflection, and still others on application. We have included some reflections on our own journey toward becoming better teachers as well as reflections borrowed from other adult educators.

Overview of the Contents

The book is organized into three parts. Part One, which covers exploration, includes the concepts of growth and style (Chapter One), the historical and current perspectives on and definitions of teaching style and other key concepts (Chapter Two), and a description of the elements of the teaching-learning exchange and their relationship to one another (Chapter Three). Based on these initial presentations, Part Two, whose subject is reflection, examines the five primary elements of the teaching-learning exchange: content (Chapter Four), environment (Chapter Five), the teacher (Chapter Six), the learning community (Chapter Seven), and the learner (Chapter Eight). Finally, Part Three, which is concerned with application, suggests approaches for matching methods to style (Chapter Nine) and developing a personal style of teaching (Chapter Ten). Additional resources for readers—a teaching beliefs scale, several versions of a teaching values scale, an activity about culture as a characteristic of the learner, and a matrix of representative teaching methods—are also included.

Acknowledgments

We would like to acknowledge our friend and editor Martha Carroll, who helped our two voices sound more like one. Additionally, we appreciate all the help that Kathy O'Brien and Sylvia Carter provided. Also, thanks to Alan Knox, Jane Vella, and Gale Erlandson for the invaluable feedback they gave us throughout the writing process. Finally, we thank our families and friends for putting up with three years' worth of procrastinatory behavior.

Columbus, Ohio Joe E. Heimlich
June 1994 Emmalou Norland

The Authors

Joe E. Heimlich is leader of environmental sciences for Ohio State University Extension and assistant professor of environmental education, School of Natural Resources, at Ohio State University (OSU). He is also the environmental education associate on science, mathematics, and environmental education for the ERIC Clearinghouse. He received his B.A. degrees (1979) in communication arts and theater from Capital University. Both his M.A. degree (1989) in public policy education and his Ph.D. degree (1990) in adult education are from OSU. Earlier, he had been a singer, dancer, choreographer, and presentation consultant.

Heimlich is responsible for education about environmental issues for OSU Extension and works nationally to develop both education for adult audiences and programs for youths on environmental issues.

Current research focuses include constructs of "fun" in teaching-learning and affective alignment to environmental issues. Heimlich has written more than forty refereed papers and presentations and more than sixty extension publications.

Heimlich serves on numerous boards, committees, and task forces locally and nationally. Many of the educational tools he has developed in Ohio are used nationwide. He has been recognized with an early career award, a State Personnel Service Award, and the James D. Utzinger Extension Teaching Award.

Emmalou Norland is associate professor in the Department of Agricultural Education at Ohio State University. She received her B.E. degree (1981) in public affairs and community service from the University of Toledo and both her M.S. degree (1984) and her Ph.D. degree (1985) in agricultural and extension education from OSU. From 1985 to 1990, she served in a joint position as Ohio Cooperative Extension Service State Leader for Program Evaluation and assistant professor in the OSU Department of Agricultural Education.

Her current scholarly work, and her personal interests, focus on education for homeless adults. She has written more than sixty refereed papers and book chapters and also participated as a community volunteer in the areas of rural adult education, empowerment education, and religious adult education, to name a few. She has served as regional editor for the *Journal of the American Association of Agricultural Educators* and as chair of the editorial committee and member of the board of directors for the *Journal of Extension*.

Her professional awards include the Ohio State University Alumni Distinguished Teaching Award (1993), the Ohio State University College of Agriculture Pomerene Teaching Enhancement Award (1988), appointment as the Ohio State University Academic Leadership Program fellow to the Committee on Institutional Cooperation (1990), the Outstanding Young Agricultural Educator award from the central region of the American Association of Agricultural Educators (1991), and the Outstanding Young Agricultural Educator award from the National American Association of Agricultural Educators (1991).

Developing Teaching Style
in Adult Education

Part One

Exploring the Personal Side of Teaching

Chapter One

Relating Personal Growth and Teaching Style

Most adult educators want to be the best they can be and are willing to work to improve. They can do so by understanding how their beliefs and behaviors relate to teaching and learning. The purpose of this book is to help adult educators do just that.

The Process

Improvement can come by trial and error, by watching others, or by formally studying about teaching (Knox, 1986). This book proposes a process by which teachers can improve by making specific choices only after studying themselves. The overall purpose of the process is to provide individuals the opportunity to gather information about themselves, to assess that information, and to act upon that assessment in such a way as to become more internally consistent or *congruent*. The process includes the steps of exploration, reflection, and application.

Exploration

Exploration encompasses a wide variety of activities, including discovering, naming, creating, defining, placing, and categoriz-

3

ing. Much of what is done in exploration is the gathering of information and to a lesser extent, the interpretation of that information. For example, an adult educator exploring beliefs about the role of the teacher in the educational process might list, name, and group those beliefs and perhaps describe where each belief originated, but would not place a value—for example, right or wrong, good or bad or outdated—on those beliefs. Exploring actual teaching behavior would involve similar kinds of activities: describing, listing, naming and so on. Again, no value would be placed on the behavior.

Reflection

The next step, reflection, involves examining all the information gathered about both beliefs and behavior. Activities such as questioning, comparing, experimenting, considering, assessing, and valuing help the educator make intuitive sense of beliefs and behavior. Reflection provides the opportunity to assess the match, or "congruence," of belief and behavior: Am I thinking one thing but doing another? Do I believe, value, and react consistently?

Reflection takes time and assumes prior experience—in this case, prior experience with teaching adults. Without experience, reflection takes on the appearance of an academic exercise comparing theory to theory. The aim of reflection is to offer the opportunity to compare theory to practice, belief to behavior, understanding to doing. Reflection can provide the "bridge" from an educator's technical knowledge to professional competence (Schön, 1987).

Application

Finally, application suggests that any inconsistencies have been reconciled and that either the belief or the behavior has been changed to provide a "match." The teacher is ready to integrate a new position or new behavior into the teaching repertoire. A new stance or a new action has been explored and reflected upon and is now a part of that individual. This process as described may sound linear, but we don't mean it to be. Figure 1.1 shows how this process is in fact cyclical and dynamic.

Figure 1.1. The Cycle of Movement Toward Congruence.

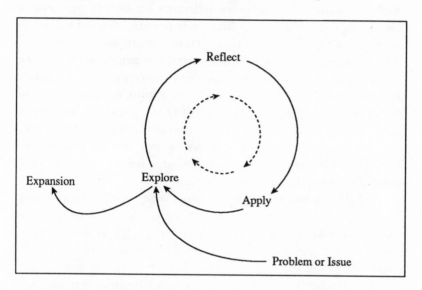

A Familiar Process

This concept of growth through reflection is not new for adult educators. In fact, most teachers have frequently employed the process of "reflection-in-action" (Schön, 1987, p. 26), that is, immediate thinking while acting to reshape the current action to address an unexpected problematic situation. Similarly, "the interplay between action and reflection" (Brookfield, 1990, p. 50) is a familiar process used by teachers in many adult education settings to facilitate learning.

For information to become knowledge, reflection time is necessary. "Knowledge is a structure of concepts and relationships built by reflective thought out of information received. Any experience of participation, observation, reading, or thinking can become part of a person's knowledge. It will become part of that knowledge if he or she thinks about it, and understands it" (Ebel, 1965, p. 377). If we are speaking about knowledge of self, the definition still holds: time for reflection is required before experience becomes knowledge.

Even though teachers may be familiar with and supportive of the *concept,* the *practice* of reflecting on oneself may not be something regularly or even frequently performed. Barriers such as time ("I can't get everything done as it is"), multiple responsibilities ("I'm on three committees, I teach several evening classes each week, and I regularly do outside workshops for other adult education agencies"), outside expectations ("the administration has made clear to me what my paid responsibilities are"), and limited "know-how" ("I'd appreciate some help to get me started on the process") may explain why so many teachers operate from a professional knowledge base without the "professional artistry" (Schön, 1987, p. 22) developed through self-reflection.

In other words, adult educators may possess the technical knowledge gained through study of theory. They may also conceptually understand how to apply that knowledge in the "typical" situation and perhaps have done so. But rarely do they have the luxury of facing the "typical" situation on a regular basis. Thus, when an unfamiliar situation arises, most educators may not have "an art of problem framing, an art of implementation, and an art of improvisation," all of which are "necessary to mediate the use in practice of applied science and technique" (Schön, 1987, p. 13). Through the process of exploration, reflection, and application, adult educators can gain necessary information about themselves. They can then use this insight to blend professional knowledge with "a core of artistry" (Schön, 1987, p. 13) to become the best they can be.

Teaching Style and the Growth Process

The concepts of teaching style and growth are inextricably linked. Teaching style has been referred to in many different ways: as a hypothetical construct; as "a classroom mode" (Fischer & Fischer, 1979, p. 251); as "a pattern composed of classroom behaviors" (Solomon & Miller, 1961, p. 12); as a complex of personal attitudes, traits, and behaviors, and the media used to transmit . . . data" (Huelsman, 1983, p. 15); and as "overall traits and qualities that a teacher displays in the classroom and that are consistent for various situations" (Conti, 1990, p. 3). Looking beyond the full definitions

above and focusing specifically on some of the words within them—
construct, mode, pattern, paradigm, approach, traits, and *qualities*—we can see that these definitions refer to teaching style as
something multidimensional, dynamic, and containing a planned
logic of organization.

Such "style" is not unique to adult educators. The following
description of the "style" of a British entertainer and writer, Quentin
Crisp, illustrates how people can consciously mold their own style:
"Mr. Crisp's style and personality are the results of a lifetime of
conscious choice and meticulous honing. He has created himself. . . . Mr. Crisp believes that by nature we are nothing, by nurture
everything. . . . He is a most vivid example of how fully developed
a human being can become through careful self-nurturing" (Kettelhack, 1984, p. xi). Crisp himself is fully aware of his own process of
developing style. In his words, "Style, in the broadest sense of all,
is consciousness. Most people are at present content to cherish their
mere identity. This is not enough. Our identity is just a group of ill-
sorted characteristics that we happen to be born with. . . . You have
to polish up your raw identity into a life-style. . . . The search for
a life-style involves a journey to the interior" (Kettelhack, 1984, pp.
3-4).

When we, as educators, begin to "polish up our raw identities" in the search for our style, we may discover that the journey
does indeed involve many side-trips to the interior. What we find
during interior exploration are those deeply held values, beliefs, and
attitudes that influence our very being. Apps (1989a, p. 17) described
the results of these "side-trips" as "knowing our foundations" and
suggested that "becoming conscious of what we believe and value
can help us" to make a variety of teaching decisions. Where do these
foundations come from? "We all have some foundation for what we
do. It comes to us from our childhood, from our schooling, from
the community in which we grew up, and from authority figures
with whom we have come in contact" (Apps, 1989a, p. 17).

So what can be said about the idea of growth as a teacher and
teaching? If, in fact, adult educators are interested in becoming the
best they can be, then it is important to discover just exactly what
they have to work with before planning and moving ahead in the
growth process. Identifying values, beliefs, attitudes, and behaviors

that together comprise a teacher's style can provide insight into where to begin.

Self-examination not only is an important ongoing process for an individual teacher's growth but also has implications for educators as a group (Conti, 1990). One major reason the profession of education is under constant attack is that "teachers, as a group are not able to clearly state their beliefs about teaching" (Conti, 1990, p. 79). Some of the questions to be used as a starting point for educators to build a philosophy upon which style emerges are: "What is our [my] view of the nature of the learner? What is the purpose of the curriculum? What is our [my] role as a teacher? What is our [and my] mission in education?" (Conti, 1990, p. 79). We will struggle with such question: throughout the remainder of this book.

Two Kinds of Growth for Adult Educators

Two specific types of growth relate to teaching style and can provide a lifetime of inward self-discovery and outward movement. The terms for these two kinds of growth are *movement toward congruence,* the internal alignment of values, beliefs, attitudes and behavior, and *expansion,* stretching beyond current beliefs, skills, abilities, habits, and preferences toward a more desired state. Movement toward congruence comes with introspection and purposeful change (to be the best adult educator one can be at this point in time). Expansion comes from the comparison of one's characteristics with a set of current, state-of-the-art principles of teaching and learning or desirable attributes of other adult educators, and then purposeful change (toward being the greatest adult educator one can ever be). Figure 1.2 presents a view of the relationship of movement toward congruence and expansion.

The two types of growth awaken, support, and strengthen each other, and their internal/external relationship represents a certain kind of harmony or rhythm. Rhythms of the growth process are what allow teaching style to be a dynamic, living thing. Even though movement toward congruence and expansion work together, occurring simultaneously, they can be understood as distinct processes. What follows is a brief discussion of each.

Figure 1.2. The Relationship of Congruence and Expansion.

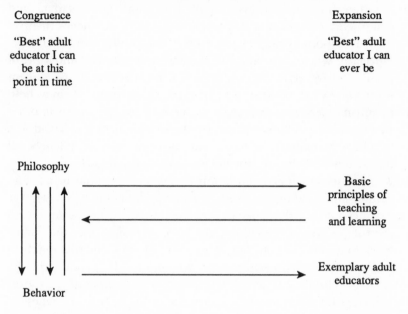

Congruence   Expansion

"Best" adult educator I can be at this point in time   "Best" adult educator I can ever be

Philosophy

Basic principles of teaching and learning

Exemplary adult educators

Behavior

Movement Toward Congruence

The concept of congruence suggests that the more closely one's values, beliefs, and attitudes are aligned to behavior, the more congruent the style and thus the better the teacher. This alignment is what makes a teacher the best teacher that individual can possibly be *at that particular time in the history of that teacher.*

Movement toward congruence is a kind of synergy, the coming together of separate parts that when joined become a distinctly different and greater whole than the sum of the parts. Individual parts seen separately can appear deficient, as Prather (1980, p. 123) asserts: "Any part of a body, if looked at separately, appears to need correction." Thus the whole teaching style is created by a cluster of human attributes that when combined is greater than the sum of individual attributes.

It is through the process of examination and meshing of values, beliefs, attitudes, and behavior that individual teaching style evolves. When attributes conflict, teaching style stagnates.

Recounting a conversation with a colleague may help to illustrate how the process of growth through movement toward congruence can occur. Many teachers profess that student involvement is important to every part of the teaching-learning exchange, especially when their students are adults. Yet an examination of those teachers' styles may not reveal behaviors that allow student input in any meaningful way, for example, by asking them to help establish objectives, select teaching methods, or participate in other planning issues. This was exactly the predicament our friend was in. Once the realization struck that one of her professed beliefs did not match her behavior, she knew something had to change.

After much contemplation of her own personal beliefs and values, she found that one reason behavior did not match belief was that deep down, she looked upon the role of teacher as similar to the role of parent. She had been raised to believe that the parent always knows what is right and good for the child and that the child really doesn't need opportunities for input. The parent provides what the child needs because the parent knows best and also loves and cares for the child. Thus when she found herself in a relationship in which she emulated the role of the parent, even when it was an adult-adult relationship, how better to show love and concern than by providing students with what she thought they needed? In fact, she discovered that her behavior really did match her deeply held inside beliefs but not what she claimed she believed.

Apps, citing Bem, touched on the phenomenon of the hidden dimensions of our values, beliefs, and attitudes when he suggested that these "zero-order beliefs influence what we do, but [that] we are not aware" of those hidden influences (Apps, 1989a, p. 17).

Of course, adult educators (like our colleague) realize they are not the parents of each student in class, especially when many of those students are older than the teacher! So why do they sometimes feel and act like it? For our friend, stepping into the role of teacher automatically caused her to step out of the culture of the student (Chapter Seven). She was still in a relationship with another human being, but when she found herself as the teacher, that relationship (by the very nature of the teaching-learning exchange) became hierarchical, with the teacher playing the dominant role. This hierarchy is very much like the parent-child relationship, one in which we have all participated. For most of us, this dominance does not have to mean "better than" but does indicate a condition of assumed power or control.

The question, then, is what needs to be changed: behavior, deeply held "zero-order beliefs," or profession of beliefs? As she struggled with that question, our friend decided that perhaps her parents didn't have "the corner on the market" of knowledge about her needs *and* that maybe she didn't know everything about her students' needs either. Apps (1989a) allowed that educators are free to analyze beliefs and to make judgments about them; in this instance, the educator's conclusion was that her deep-down beliefs— not her behavior—needed realignment.

Realigning beliefs and then changing behavior to fit the new alignment is very difficult. In this case, our colleague has started releasing control in the classroom one tiny step at a time, with the goal of sharing power with the learners as she would prefer such power to be shared with her. Since belief in sharing power is fundamental, underlying an entire life philosophy, surely teaching styles should reflect that belief.

Adult educators who do not allow their behavior to represent their values and attitudes undermine the potential for their style to become more than the sum of the parts. Teachers who uncover their underlying beliefs, recognize their own behaviors, and work to make the two congruent will experience a freedom that allows them to explore, reflect, apply, and grow in ways that they may never have experienced before.

The alignment of values, beliefs, attitudes, and behavior should not be confused with rigidity. As M. C. Richards explains in her book *Toward Wholeness* (1980) about Rudolf Steiner education in America, "Wholeness is not uniformity. It is a universe, that is, a way which is both a oneness (uni) and a movement or a turning (verse). How close to a potter's image this is! A turning oneness!" (Richards, 1980, p. 147).

Richards further describes wholeness as being "a living organism made up of many moving parts. And because wholeness lives, it follows the rhythms of growth and decline which characterize all living forms" (p. 147). Growth and decline, then, refer to the process of exploration, reflection, and the final decision that pulls the educator in a certain direction, toward either application and growth or stagnation and decline.

Expansion

As mechanical as it sounds, expansion really represents an organic process of growth through a spiral of inward introspection and outward comparison. Once a teacher knows enough about his or her beliefs, values, attitudes, and behavior and reaches a level of internal consistency and comfort, the next challenge toward growth in teaching style requires an evaluation of that teaching style using a set of external standards of comparison.

For a lifetime of growth, it is not enough to possess a congruent teaching style. The teacher must also like and accept that style even when comparing it to styles of others or accepted principles of teaching and learning. Expansion of style comes when the teacher examines a variety of possibilities for change and decides to try a new belief and accompanying behavior.

Teachers often find themselves competent in a particular skill but not completely satisfied with the outcome of it. When this situation arises, it very well may be that the teacher is congruent within but is also ready to try something new, different, and challenging. *New* might mean rethinking the reasoning behind performing the skill. *Different* might mean trying a completely different technique in a similar situation. *Challenging* might mean questioning the entire approach to the situation.

Here is a story about expansion from a good friend's teaching diary. An Adult Basic Education (ABE) instructor in a large public school system continuing education program, he has a wide variety of students. His classes tend to be stable in enrollment, so he sees the same individuals for several months at a time. His "problem," which really was not a serious problem per se but something that he was wanting to change, was the way he actually began each class. A shy person, he was not comfortable using a conversational tone such as "Good evening, welcome to class. How is everyone?" His typical beginning was "OK, let's get started." His belief matched his current behavior (we are here to accomplish something, let's get going), but after a while, the bluntness of this type of beginning just did not feel right anymore. What he needed was a new skill; he needed to expand his choices. A conversation with his supervisor (How do *you* begin class? May I come and watch?) and an afternoon in the library looking through some teaching methods books provided our friend some new skills to help him *expand* his teaching repertoire.

Expansion can only come from within. Teaching style is not like clothes—it is more than the trappings. Teaching style comes from "who I am" and therefore must grow from "all I've been" toward "all I could ever be." Expansion assumes experience with teaching. The impetus to expand teaching style boundaries is wisdom. Wisdom is the combination of knowledge and the filtering of that knowledge through experience.

Expansion assumes that the educators are looking outside themselves at a more desirable state of affairs and that wisdom suggests a change is in order. The accepted theories of quality adult education (much information found in Merriam & Caffarella, 1991, for example), "tried and true" principles of teaching and learning (such as presented in Brookfield, 1986), a mentor or role model, an exemplary educator, or even a past teacher of the educator could serve as that outside comparison. Through the process of knowing oneself (matching beliefs and behavior) and then comparing oneself to others (looking outside oneself and placing a value on change), educators can make informed decisions.

Beginning the Growth Process

Continuing education for teachers is important to morale, improvement of skills, updating of content, and avoidance of burnout (Bowes & Smith, 1986, p. 8). However, formalized opportunities for continuing teacher education tend to be "haphazard, undersupported, and poorly correlated with the individual's pressing needs, concerns and problems" (p. 8). But "both the quantity and quality of [continuing education] can be increased by encouraging adult educators to direct their own continuing learning" (p. 8). That is, continuing education teachers must also be continuing education students.

For the process of growth to become a formalized activity,

teachers of adults must first agree that they are in charge of their own destinies, recognize what specifically needs to be addressed, and be supported by administrators and others (Bowes & Smith, 1986). Among other suggestions, Bowes and Smith (1986, p. 10) advocate "the integration of self-knowledge as a learner, readiness for this type of activity and the availability of adequate support levels." When teachers have the first two of these under control, they can begin seeking the third.

Florini (1989), Brookfield (1990), and others have provided some suggestions for the initial exploration of teaching style. Florini states that "self-reflection, student evaluations, videotapes of one's teaching, and colleagues' observations are all worthy sources for the data needed to articulate one's teaching style" (p. 51). Notice that these techniques relate mostly to observable *behaviors* in the classroom—essentially representing just one piece of the picture of teaching style.

Conti (1990) discusses the familiar reflection-in-action approach, which is premised on a basic "reflect on the known to know more" idea of knowledge. As discussed earlier, this approach is an alternative to "technical rationality" (Schön, 1987, p. 3), which is the kind of knowledge gained from basic and applied university research. The kind of knowledge gained by reflection-in-action, initially described by Schön (1987), is articulated by Conti in this way: "Unexpected situations force practitioners to think in novel ways. They have to reframe the problems they face daily and construct a new reality for dealing with them. By using their prior knowledge and experiences, they are able to deal with new situations as they arise. As they reflect upon their responses to these situations, they acquire new knowledge for future action" (p. 80).

This description represents a kind of spiraling of growth in teaching style (Figure 1.3). The exploration, reflection, application, and growth provide the educator with the vehicle to move to the next plane of knowledge about self. Using this process, teachers can examine values, beliefs, attitudes, and behaviors related to specific teaching-learning exchanges, reflect upon them, draw conclusions, and take those conclusions into their teaching styles (movement toward congruence). Then, by making a judgment on those conclu-

Figure 1.3. The Spiral of Expansion.

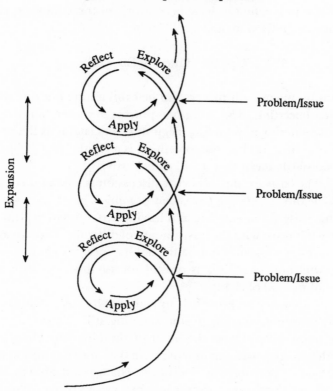

sions and taking action to change if desired, they can grow both within their previously held knowledge and beyond it (expansion).

This book—indeed, each chapter within the book—has been organized by the three steps of exploration, reflection, and application. We have limited our discussion, by necessity, to the process of movement toward congruence even though it has been suggested that movement toward congruence and expansion both occur simultaneously. Users of this book will find that the concept of "growing through congruence" is illustrated throughout the book by the presentation of material to aid in (1) exploring values, beliefs, attitudes, and behavior, (2) reflecting on the match of those attributes *within* the individual adult educator, and (3) then applying new behavior (or new beliefs) in the teaching-learning exchange. Some learning activities have been provided throughout to aid in exploration, reflection, and application.

Tips for "Entering Growth"

Beginning the growth process can be exhilarating but can also be very disconcerting. Beginning one process means ending another. Just like entering and leaving, beginning and ending is the natural pattern of life. Just because something is a regular part of life does not necessarily mean that it will come easily.

The basis for the following discussion is a pamphlet by Edwin Cole called *Entering Crisis and Leaving.* Cole (1987) suggested that his ten steps to entering and leaving crisis situations can help individuals do so with the least amount of difficulty. Perhaps avoiding "difficulty" should not be the adult educator's chief objective in growth, but it certainly is possible to use these tips to increase the comfort level of change.

A first step in growth is to realize and accept that to move in any direction, one has to stop standing still. Simple as it may seem, many people have the habit of thinking that change and growth will come without moving from the "at rest" position to the "in motion" position. By definition, change and growth imply movement. When one is riding in a car, views change. When one is growing, perspectives will also change. Adult educators can realize that those changes are natural and indicate progress. Ending is a necessary condition of beginning. Feeling assured that growth can be a product of choices helps one move more smoothly from the ending toward another beginning.

A planned series of choices related to change and growth can help assure some control in choice. Compare an English garden with a vacant urban lot. One is controlled growth, the other a rampage. Someone had a plan for the growth in the garden. Someone managed that growth and molded the resulting whole by integrating the various parts (plants, trees, brickwork). To be successful, that gardener needed information about all the parts as well as their potential relationships. An important thing teachers of adults can remember is that continuing development of teaching style can be managed with a pattern or plan just as adult learners develop a plan for their own growth.

Growth takes time, work, and persistence. It is also never-ending. Growth in teaching style sounds a lot like what nutritionists say about eating habits: You must develop a plan to change and then work toward that change for the rest of your life. You never arrive! What the final goal might really be is the perfecting of the plan.

Many times the beginning of a growth process is initiated by a crisis. Think about the law of inertia. Anything at rest stays at rest until something crashes into it and gets it moving! "Panic and productivity are opposites. Panic is always counter-productive" (Cole, 1987, p. 13). Being productive disallows panic. A clear example of productivity versus panic is the writing of a book. Panic does not help a writer meet a deadline. Productivity does.

A plan or pattern provides a structure for controlled growth, but it helps to "leave the top off and use expandable sides" so that the plan provides a structure to facilitate growth rather than to limit it. "Tunnel vision" is "the inability to see anything peripherally" (Cole, 1987, p. 16). Educators will want to check out the plan to see if it resembles peering through a tunnel or standing on a mountaintop.

Teachers many times feel powerless. Students, administrators, even entire systems, selectively ignore teachers, bringing them to the point of questioning their own worth. This perception of self-worth, created by a unique set of experiences and interpretations, plays an important part in establishing and maintaining the base upon which teacher beliefs, attitudes, and behavior are built. Gaining a voice can serve as what Giroux and Freire call "the means whereby teachers [and students] attempt to make themselves present in history and to define themselves as active authors of their own worlds" (quoted in Weiler, 1988, p. xiii).

For the plan to work, teachers must trust the process—something many educators encourage their learners to do. When meeting a person for the first time, trying a new activity, or learning a new skill, we need time to become accustomed to whatever it is that is new. Through time and experience, trust builds. If it does not, then there are usually two reasons why: (1) not enough time has been allowed to build trust, or (2) experience suggests not to invest additional time or to begin trusting. Trusting the process of growth, like anything new, will take time and experience.

Seek the wisdom of others who have been successful with the growth process. Share your thoughts and feelings with yourself as well. When asked what kept them from dropping out of school, some ABE students in London said, "I talk to myself" and "I just say to myself, 'I must do it, I've got to do it, I've started it, I've just to finish'" (Van Tilburg & DuBois, 1989, p. 3). That communication with self is a technique that most of us use a lot but probably don't even recognize. Keeping a journal, on the other hand, provides a visual experience with our own thoughts. That experience can be very powerful, providing an inside glimpse of our psyche. With such methods, you can say things to yourself that you could never say to anyone else. If you communicate with yourself as well as with others, there is virtually no thought or feeling that cannot be shared.

The process of "growing" in teaching style can be an exciting experience. All that is needed is a plan, some friendly support, and an interest in improving. As an individual seeking to become more congruent in your teaching style, what are you concerned about? What additional resources or information might you need as you begin? A teaching style journal or notebook of ideas might be an excellent place to begin recording the journey.

Another question to ponder when beginning the growth process might be: which of the following "beginning locations" best represents where you are now, as you prepare to go on your journey—A rocky mountaintop, the bottom of a glacier, a wooded path by a stream, outside your own front door, a dot on a road map, an entrance to a cave, in your car at a stoplight? or perhaps another spot that suits you better? Examine why you have chosen this location to illustrate where you are now. What is it about the beginning point that represents your values, beliefs, attitudes, and philosophy about growth? Where does it appear that your beginning location will lead you if you begin? What does it mean in terms of where you have been and what you have been doing? After thinking through these questions, individuals may want to further explore any concerns, questions, or issues still looming about beginning the growth process. The following discussion on dealing with self-knowledge will add yet another dimension to beginning growth.

The Relationship of Knowledge and Responsibility

One typical concern of many teachers related to growth is the responsibility accompanied by increased self-knowledge. Knowing requires acting. Later in the book, we will discuss the experience of reading assigned work of some adult students and then "dealing with what was read." This painful but enlightening process revealed the injunction: "Don't ask what you don't want to know because then you have to deal with it!" Once knowledge is gained, it demands to be used. As teachers pursue the development of teaching style, there will be the need to gather much new knowledge about beliefs and behavior that will then have to be acted upon. This gathering of knowledge creates a kind of responsibility to house, care for, or otherwise use that knowledge wisely.

Sharing knowledge about ourselves is sometimes called "self-disclosure" and generally refers to sharing personal information with *others*. However, the growth process of exploration, discovery, and reflection can be a kind of self-disclosure to *self* about self.

Kern (1990), in his book *Build the Fort . . . Today!*, shares a story about self-disclosure. His young daughter didn't like her third-grade teacher at all. She described her teacher as "mean, old, fat, ugly Mrs. Brown" (p. 14). Upon meeting Mrs. Brown early in the school year, Kern had to agree with his daughter's description. The last day of school, however, his young daughter came home elated. She said that Mrs. Brown had worn jeans and gone down the slide "just like us other kids" (p. 14). Kern's observation was that on "the last day of the school year, the kids learned who Mrs. Brown was and they liked her" (p. 14). With our process of self-disclosure to self, we make sure that we don't "wait until the last day of school" to learn who we are and miss out on all those years of "liking ourselves."

Fears of self-disclosure to self are very similar to the ones listed by Hagan (1990) as she described why people stop keeping journals or never really begin: "I am afraid if I find out who I really am, I'll hate myself"; "I am afraid that I am unimportant and uninteresting"; "I fear my lies would become apparent"; "I fear finding out something terrible about myself"; "I am afraid I will see how shallow and worthless I am"; "I fear if I listen to myself, there will be nothing to hear" (p. 2).

Her contention is that before we can fulfill our yearnings to have intimate relationships with others, we must first become intimate with ourselves. That process is hindered or stopped, however, by the fear of disappointment in what we will find if we look deep and take those side-trips to the interior. This may very well be a fear of being responsible for our knowledge.

There really is power in possessing information. The more you know about yourself, the more power you have—not over your environment, necessarily, but over your perceptions of it and your reactions to it. This is the phenomenon Crisp was referring to as "polishing up your raw identity": combining all the parts to make the whole.

Conclusion

An educational campaign for the staff of a large hospital used mobiles to represent the interconnectedness of things (interview with Robert L. Davis, vice president, Riverside Methodist Hospitals, Columbus, Ohio, September 1991). At the hospital, the mobile represents the relationship among the various components of the patient as a human being. It also represents the many staff members and departments who work together in that organization. When a force affects one part of the human being or organization, the rest of the parts react, and not necessarily in any recognizable, logical, or organized fashion.

When thinking about yourself as a teacher, picture the mobile. The multitude of personal characteristics dangle around a central point. When one characteristic is altered, or even slightly nudged, the entire entity moves, each part reacting to the force of the others. When we, as teachers, begin a growth process, we "wiggle different parts of our mobile." In reaction to that initial force, even if it is ever so gentle, we may experience a confusion that, if visible, might look like the swirling mobile.

To know others, we have to know ourselves first. To love,

care for, and nurture others, we have to have been loved, cared for, and nurtured ourselves. We can do that for ourselves if we spend the time "getting to know who we are." Purkey and Novak (1984) described the role of the teacher as "inviter." They suggested that "good teaching is the process of inviting students to see themselves as able, valuable, and self-directing and of encouraging them to act in accordance with these self-perceptions" (p. xiii). Borrowing their advice and redirecting it back to ourselves as teachers of adults, we must see ourselves as "able, valuable, and self-directing." To do this, we have to really know who we are: what are our values, beliefs, attitudes, philosophies, and behaviors? How are they congruent? Where did they come from? Do we approve of them? If not, what do we want to change? How will changing that element affect all the others? And finally, what does this process mean to our success as teachers?

Adult educators ready to begin the process of improving teaching style through moving toward congruence may want to begin with this approach to "testing the water." Hagan (1990) calls it "mirroring."

Write an introduction about yourself highlighting your personal values, beliefs, attitudes, and philosophy. Keep the introduction general. Now write an introduction about yourself that you would use in an employment interview for a teaching job. Be sure to include your values, beliefs, attitudes, and philosophy about the teaching-learning exchange. Are the introductions similar? What is in the general introduction that is not in the teaching-specific one and vice versa?

Try rewriting these introductions several weeks or months later. What has changed? Why? Can you see growth? Your own perceptions of what you would choose to say about yourself may have changed. Are your introductions more in depth, more personal, more positive, more clarified? Are you pleased with the differences? Would you say that you have actually changed, or have you just gained more information about yourself? Whatever the answers are is not as important as the process of asking them. In this case, the process *is* more important than the product.

Throughout this book, the concept of growth is illustrated using the simple process of exploration, reflection, and application.

Two kinds of growth, movement toward congruence and expansion, have been suggested, and congruence has been identified as the focus of this book on developing teaching style. But as more than one of our fellow teachers has asked us, "So what?" In nicer language, "How do adult educators know when they want (need) to enter the growth process?" The answer may lie in three simple statements educators often make: (1) "I don't understand what is going on here," (2) "This doesn't feel right," or (3) "I don't know how to do this." Whether the initial problematic situation is affective, cognitive, or behavioral, this book challenges teachers to begin the growth process: explore, reflect, apply, and grow!

Chapter Two

Understanding Basic Concepts
of Teaching and Learning

What is my teaching philosophy? Are my beliefs about teaching
and learning clearly illustrated in the teaching methods I use? Do
adults really differ from children in motivation to learn? How do
I really feel about including the learners in the planning for instruction? Who should be in control of decisions about content? Before
going further in the investigation of these and other questions, this
chapter introduces the basic concepts regarding teaching style of the
adult educator.

More than just a recitation of definitions, this chapter draws
on other writers and experts for insight into teaching, learning, the
teacher, the student, content, and other key ideas. Readers are chal-
lenged to begin to explore and reflect on their own set of beliefs,
attitudes, and values and to formulate personal working definitions.

What Is Teaching?

A search for the definitive meaning of the word *teaching* could
quickly become exhausting, for there are as many definitions of

teaching (particularly "good" teaching) as there are writers about the subject. Here are a few ideas that may stimulate readers to contemplate just what teaching does mean in their own unique circumstances in the world of adult education.

Some experts agree that teaching is "guiding and directing the learning process such that those who are learners acquire new knowledge, skills, or attitudes; increase their enthusiasm for learning; and develop further their skill as learners" (Newcomb, McCracken, & Warmbrod, 1986, p. 21). Others suggest that teaching is more like "a process of deliberate decision-making and action that makes learning more probable and more predictably successful than it would be without teaching" (Hunter, 1976). Notice the difference between the verbs in each definition. *Guiding and directing* projects a very different picture of teaching than does *deliberate decision-making and action.*

The use of role metaphors is one way that teachers can identify their own beliefs, attitudes, and values about teaching (Briscoe, 1991). In the first definition of teaching above, what might come to mind as a role metaphor for the teacher? How about a football coach calling the plays to the team from the sidelines (guiding and directing)? What metaphor could represent the teacher in the second definition of teaching? We thought maybe a chess player, making deliberate decisions and taking specific actions to move the pieces around to structure the best possible situation for success. The contrast between an athletic coach and a chess player suggests some very important differences in how the teacher and teaching are understood.

Teachers seeking to clarify their definitions of teaching may want to reflect on the following questions as they employ role metaphors. What is the role metaphor that best suits your definition of teaching? What is it about that metaphor that fits with your ideas about teaching? What are the underlying values, beliefs, and attitudes that support that metaphor? Are you comfortable with this role metaphor? Is there a metaphor that better represents the teacher you would like to be? Changing from a current to a more desired metaphor can actually help teachers to implement new and more desired teaching practices (Briscoe, 1991).

Bugelski's interesting definition of teaching suggests that

teaching is actually just a myth and that "there is no such operation as teaching in and of itself. No one can teach anyone anything; he can only arrange conditions whereby a learner might learn. Among such conditions are showing and telling, but whether or not learning goes on depends more on the learner than the teacher" (Newcomb et al., 1986, p. 21). Compare the previous definitions to this one; what differences in behavior would you expect to see among teachers espousing the varying definitions? In which teaching-learning setting would you expect learners to be most or least active?

Consider yet another definition. Teaching can be and generally is a "complex, intellectually demanding, socially challenging task which consists of a set of skills that can be acquired, improved, and extended . . . providing opportunities for students to learn." Learning implies "gains in knowledge and skills, the deepening of understanding, the development of problem-solving or changes in perceptions, attitudes, values, and behavior" (Brown & Atkins, 1988, pp. 1-2). In this definition, the preparation of the teacher seems to be highlighted—particularly skills needed to deal with complexity, intellectual ability, and social commitment.

Does your definition of teaching imply certain personal and professional characteristics of a teacher? How does your definition suit your own qualities and attributes? In other words, does your definition of teaching preclude your chance of being an effective teacher? And just how is effective teaching defined?

In making the distinction between bad and effective teaching, Brown and Atkins (1988) suggest that "bad teaching reduces motivation, increases negative attitudes to learning, and yields lower achievement," whereas "effective teaching is systematic, stimulating, and caring" (p.5). Good teaching brings about relatively permanent desirable changes in students' judgment, reasoning, thinking, creativeness, communication, attitudes, appreciation, understanding, and manipulative skills.

Describing good teachers is really creating a fictional ideal: good teachers are calm and never lose their cool; they have no biases; they can and do hide their feelings from students; they never play favorites; they can provide the perfect learning environment; they are consistent; they always know the answers, and certainly know more than the students; they support all other teachers. "In short, good teachers must be better, more understanding, more knowledgeable, more perfect than average people" (Gordon, 1974, p. 22). A question for us all might be: Should teachers "deny their humanity"? If not, then why do so many of us buy into "the myth of the perfect teacher" (Brookfield, 1990, p. 7)? Being the best teachers we can be means accepting, even honoring our humanity.

If we reject the idea of a perfect teacher, what, then, are the characteristics of an effective teacher? For adult educators, a good place to begin exploration might be Brookfield's discussion of "principles of effective practice" (1986, pp. 9–11). Effective facilitators need to know about and react to the nature of voluntary learning, create a climate of mutual respect, operate within a collaborative mode, foster a spirit of critical reflection that helps learners question cultural constructs, and, through praxis, nurture adults toward self-directedness and empowerment. Learning activities that are used by an effective adult educator might include learning contracts (p. 81) and peer learning groups (p. 83).

Now might be an opportune time to reflect upon our own beliefs about good, effective teaching. One premise of this book suggests that there are many "right" answers to that question. Our individual perspectives, formed from our experiences, provide the realities from which we operate. Educators are encouraged, however, to study and synthesize others' ideas and to "try some on for size" if appropriate. Empirical research results presented in journals and magazines and at conferences, opinion papers shared in adult education forums, and books and other written materials targeted at practitioners can serve as good stimuli for growing.

What Is Learning?

Inherent in most of the definitions of teaching is the outcome: learning. Revisit the definitions of teaching presented above and notice that everything a teacher does in teaching is directed toward facilitating learning. But what is learning? More important, what ideas surrounding *adult* learning can help teachers as they search for a deeper understanding of their beliefs, values, attitudes, and behavior related to teaching and learning?

Several issues aimed at clarifying beliefs about learning are presented below for consideration. Colleagues of ours find that issues like these make interesting table talk at lunch. In fact one favorite question of the lunch bunch resurfaces about every other week: "If the learner does not learn, then did the teacher teach?" We have not yet come to consensus, but if lunch talk gets dull we can always ask it again. We have also participated in roundtable discussions with other teachers of adults in the community concerning relevant issues for all types of adult learning situations. These regular discussions provide a sort of "sharing group" of adult educators with similar interests but diverse contexts. If not involved in some type of professional sharing group, educators seeking to grow and improve might want to identify others who have similar goals and begin a group.

Learning Might *Be Different for Adults Than for Children*

Knowles (1980, pp. 43–44) lists four features that distinguish adults from children in their learning: self-directedness, a rich experience base, the need to address real-life problems, and the need to apply learning immediately. Darkenwald and Merriam (1982, pp. 110–111), in a presentation of "principles of learning relevant to adult education," state that learning is affected by the amount of past learning of the learner, intrinsic motivation of the learner, positive reinforcement by the teacher, an organized presentation of material, repetition of concepts, the perceived meaningfulness of tasks and material, active participation by the learner, and physical and emotional environment created by the teacher.

Whether learning differs between children and adults is a question for exploration and thoughtful reflection. However, it is most important for educators to consider their own beliefs about how children and adults differ (or do not differ) in their learning and what effects those beliefs should have on teaching behavior.

Learning Implies Change; Who Decides What Change?

If the learner does not change, learning has not taken place. What kind of change needs to take place for learning to have occurred? Hedges (1989) describes learning as being "able to do something you have never done before and to remember it so you can do it again." For educators, the change is assumed to be positive: an increase in knowledge, a more positive attitude, acquisition of new or improved skills. It is also assumed to be permanent: the learner has adopted the change into the knowledge or attitude or behavior repertoire. The change will remain a part of the learner until he or she learns something new to replace the original learning.

Even though changes can occur in the affective, cognitive, and psychomotor domains, a teacher or learner might not initially identify all three domains as areas for change. The potential is always there, however, for learning to encompass what a learner can feel, think, and do.

What kinds of changes do you believe are important for the learners with whom you work? Is one domain—say, the affective—as important or more important for learners as another—for example, the cognitive? This question causes great controversy among a group of teachers who work with an education program for homeless adults. During staff meetings, loud discussions sometimes erupt when the topic of student outcomes is raised. "How can we waste our time on attitudinal changes in our folks—they need a job and they need it now!" "Okay, but how can they learn new skills if their self-esteem is so low that they won't even try?" And so it goes.

Mezirow (1978) has suggested that perspective transformation is the ultimate goal for change in adult learners. In addition to skills and knowledge acquisition and affective change (focused on self and on others), learners acquire the ability to purposefully shift from one paradigm to another. To put it simply, learners facing a new problem realize that their old perspectives do not work any longer. In an attempt to solve the problem, they try on different perspectives and select one that seems to work better than the old perspective. Full transformation requires close association with others who share that new perspective.

What are your beliefs, values, and attitudes toward the desired changes in learning? Does your behavior reflect those philosophical tenets? Who decides learner outcomes in your educational programs? Our friends in the staff meeting described above need to address not only learner-identified and organization-identified outcomes but funder-identified and society-identified outcomes as well. What does the teacher contribute to learner outcomes decisions in your situation? How does that situation work for you?

Who Does the Motivating in Learning?

Why do adults participate in learning situations? Answers from a group of extension educators reflecting upon their most recent teaching experience suggest a great diversity of motivational factors. "They came for the food." "I really believe they come because they like me and want to support me as an extension agent." "Several people came because their friends came." "I get this one guy who always comes whenever we offer anything in his part of town." "Most people came because they wanted to learn about the topic." "I wonder sometimes just why people do come out—at night, in the rain, clear across the county. I guess they really value the information we can provide."

Consider two basic orientations to learning: knowledge seeking and understanding seeking. Learning can be conceived as "a continuous process of development backwards and forwards between the two orientations" (Brown & Atkins, 1988, p. 156). The two processes are interrelated in that an increase in understanding most likely will result in an expansion of knowledge, and the expansion of knowledge can lead to reconceptualization of the topic to deepen understanding. What part can a teacher play in seeking and attaining knowledge and understanding?

For adult learners, most formal education is by choice, not requirement or chance. Motivation to learn is illustrated by their choices of how and when they participate and whether they persist. Even the process of learning during participation, Bender and Boucher say, "is a self-active, personal, choice making process—a person learns what he or she wants to learn" (quoted in Newcomb et al., 1986, p. 21).

What are some of the motivating factors for your own learners? Are your adult students goal oriented, activity oriented, or learning oriented? (Houle, 1961). Does the nature of learner motivation make a difference for you as the teacher? Is it important for the instructor of an evening "return-to-study" course in floriculture to know whether the students in the course are there for social relationships, are attending in compliance, have an altruistic orientation, are there for professional advancement, are seeking escape or stimulation, or have a real interest to learn the content (Merriam & Caffarella, 1991)?

Whether considering beliefs about initial participation, continued persistence, or student motivation during participation, educators will want to take note of how they understand motivation. How much control do you believe the educator has over motivation—some, a little, a lot, none? The final answers to these questions will help shape teacher behavior before, during, and after the teaching-learning exchange.

Learning Can Be Understood from a Variety of Perspectives

Psychological approaches to explaining learning each contain general assumptions about what learning is and is not. Behaviorist, cognitivist, humanist, motivationalist, personality, and social psychology theories all approach learning from different perspectives (Beard & Hartley, 1984). When thinking about how people learn, do you as an educator believe that if you present the information in a logical organized manner, learning will take place (cognitivist)? Or do you view the learner as already having the knowledge and your role as facilitating its discovery (humanist)? Or, as many of our previous teachers believed, do you think that learning occurs by reinforcement of response (behaviorist)? Many theories of learning exist. By examining and refining one of these theories, educators can frame their teaching approach to match what they truly believe about learning.

Similarly, reviewing popular literature that synthesizes empirical research results can provide many principles to be examined. Synthesis of prior research led to the identification of these six principles about learning: learning is lifelong, is personal, involves change, is a function of human development, relates to experience, and involves intuition (Brookfield, 1986).

In a recent approach to school redesign and reform, the American Psychological Association Task Force on Psychology in

Education (1991) designed a fairly comprehensive list of learner-centered principles to describe how learning takes place. Even though these ideas were put forth from a group addressing pedagogy, adult educators will want to do more than sift through them. We have found them to be true in a variety of adult education contexts.

For example, the task force suggests that learning is "naturally an active, volitional, internally mediated, and individual process of constructing meaning from information and experience, filtered through each individual's unique perceptions, thoughts, and feelings" (p. 1). An adult educator making decisions based upon this principle would encourage active involvement of students. Methods selected would most likely include small and large group discussion and perhaps individual reflection and writing during class. The teacher would work to help students link prior knowledge and experiences with new information. The verbal sharing of experiences would help those experiences come to life for all. In addition to preorganized activities, self-directed learning options would definitely be a major part of the curriculum.

This description is conspicuous in its generic adult education methodology. In other words, we all could have written what we would expect to see in a classroom of a teacher who agreed with the task force because our experiences with adult education and adult education theory have taught us these very principles. However, many teachers and learners can recount experiences where this description did not apply—where there was no self-directed learning activity, no small group or large group discussion, no discussion at all. If adult educators believe in the kind of learning described by the task force, why don't they (we) practice it? Why indeed.

The purpose of this illustration is to show how theory can and should be linked to practice. What teachers believe about how adults learn should be so much a part of an integrated philosophy that any behavior to the contrary would be immediately obvious. The incongruence of the situation would be intolerable to them.

As adult educators begin an investigation of congruence between their values, attitudes, beliefs, and behavior, they may want to begin their own list of principles of learning. Principles gleaned from personal experience are as important for teachers to include as those taken from empirical research studies and experts' writings.

What Is the Teaching-Learning Exchange?

Many phrases have been used to represent the point at which teaching and learning come together. The term "teaching-learning exchange" has been selected as a good descriptor because both the learner and the teacher give and receive in an exchange. An important distinction should be made, however, between the teaching-learning exchange and the separate processes of teaching and learning. "Teaching and learning are really two different functions. . . . If teaching-learning processes are to work effectively, a unique kind of relationship must exist between these two separate organisms— some kind of a 'connection,' link, or bridge between the teacher and the learner" (Gordon, 1974, p. 3). That "connection" takes place during the teaching-learning exchange. Teaching and learning are occurring simultaneously during the exchange, and the roles of teacher and learner change. If not, then there is no exchange. The authors have assumed the context of a teaching-learning *exchange* for their discussion of teaching style.

Another term used frequently to describe the exchange is *education*. The word *education*, from the Latin *educere*, "to draw out or call forth," has been used to describe a "conscious, purposive, informed activity" (Archambault, 1964, p. xxii) promoting what Dewey called "the process of forming fundamental dispositions, intellectual and emotional, toward nature and fellow human beings" (Archambault, 1964, p. xxix). This definition illustrates an important characteristic of the teaching-learning exchange: that of purpose.

All exchanges take place with at least one preidentified purpose in mind. Most likely, multiple purposes articulated from a variety of perspectives (teacher, learner, learners, society, and so forth) are behind any one exchange. As mentioned previously, learner outcomes are an initial focus of teaching, but the word *exchange* implies a giving and receiving on the part of both the learner and the teacher. Therefore an important assumption implicit in the term *teaching-learning exchange* is that the exchange is learning focused (two-way) as opposed to learner focused (one-way).

To summarize, the teaching-learning exchange includes the activities of both teaching and learning but is focused on the learning of all participants. There is at least one preconceived purpose, and the exchange occurs in the social context of the learner and the teacher. This social context encompasses both past and present characteristics of the teacher and each learner and is framed in the movement toward a defined outcome.

What Are Beliefs, Values, and Attitudes?

Combined beliefs, values, and attitudes about the teaching-learning exchange form the basis of one's teaching philosophy. To understand the difference between these three affective dimensions is to also see how they meld together to become a working philosophy.

Beliefs

One perceives beliefs as factual information about a person or thing. Not necessarily true, beliefs can fall into three categories: private beliefs, declared beliefs, and public beliefs (Goodenough, 1971). Private beliefs are unaffected by peer pressure and may not necessarily be shared with others. Declared beliefs are shared and tend to be affected by others' opinions or a norm. Public beliefs are beliefs one holds because one is a member of a certain group proclaiming those beliefs. All three types of beliefs are a part of a teacher's philosophy. Changing a belief to make it more congruent with behavior may be difficult or almost impossible because of the kind of belief it is (private, declared, or public).

Because beliefs are not always based on factual information and thus may be incorrect, inappropriate, or inaccurate, it is thought that external forces, as opposed to internal factual knowledge, may be a major contributing factor to them. One implication for personal teaching philosophy (and ultimately teaching style) is that who we are and what we do as teachers is partially dependent on external forces painting a picture that may or may not be accurate. One of the greatest external forces for any individual is the culture in which that individual grew up, experienced learning, and may still continue to view life. This idea suggests that "the study of beliefs within the context of culture is essential to understanding teachers' actions and choices in the classroom" (Hamilton, 1993, p. 87).

As in other areas of our lives that have strong normative components, such as religion or moral behavior (Sudman & Bradburn, 1982), the way we teach emanates from a set of beliefs that is held with mindful regard. What we know to be "true" about teaching and learning is not necessarily based on fact, does not necessarily come totally from within, and possesses a strong normative and judgmental component. And the cultural context from which we came and from which we still interpret the world is extremely important in the quest to explore, reflect upon, and congruently apply beliefs about teaching and learning. What are some of the common beliefs educators profess about teaching and learning? What are your own beliefs?

Teachers can investigate their beliefs using a variety of approaches. Begin by selecting a framework within which to organize beliefs. For the purpose of remaining consistent throughout this book, the authors have selected as a framework the elements of the teaching-learning exchange: content, environment, teacher, learning community, and learner. Then conduct what Apps (1989a) called a "belief analysis" by examining the listed beliefs for contradictions, reflecting upon the source(s) of each belief, and finally placing a judgment upon the source of the belief. The result will be a list of organized, consistent, and accepted beliefs about teaching and learning that can become the foundation of a personal teaching philosophy.

When exploring beliefs, teachers may want to focus on a particular area, such as beliefs related to the learning community. The Van Tilburg/Heimlich Teaching Beliefs Scale (Norland & Heimlich, 1990) (Resource A) measures two particular dimensions, both of which are related to the teacher's belief about the learning community. The first dimension, *sensitivity*, represents beliefs about the importance of knowing about the learners for the purpose of interaction with the learning community. The second dimension, *inclusion*, refers to the beliefs of the educator about the importance of including the learning community in all phases of the learning experience. Chapter Seven expands upon sensitivity and inclusion. Even though this instrument was designed to measure just two of a multitude of beliefs about teaching and learning, completing it can stimulate an educator to investigate these and other beliefs in a quest to know more about him- or herself.

Values

The "right/wrong" nature of beliefs illustrates why beliefs are closely related to values. Values are qualities, standards, or principles assessed as desirable by a particular group. This description suggests that values belong to an individual within a particular culture as opposed to an individual in isolation. In this respect, they are similar to the public beliefs described above. Noteworthy in this definition is the location of the educator in a context that to a certain extent gives him or her a rationale for possessing specific values related to education.

Another definition, this one from a textbook detailing the process of designing instruments to measure in the affective domain, adds some additional information: according to Klukhohn, a value is " 'a conception, explicit or implicit, distinctive of an individual or characteristic of a group, of the desirable, which influences the selection of available modes, means, and ends of action' " (Mueller, 1986, p. 5). This definition adds the notion that the purpose of values is to guide action.

Values can be hidden or quite obvious. Values are clearly linked to behavior. Putting these two concepts together suggests that values contribute to behavior but may or may not be obvious in their contributions. What questions about congruence arise from the mix of explicit versus implicit values and related overt behavior?

Mueller also compares values with attitudes: "Like attitudes, values involve evaluating. But it is generally agreed among social theorists that values are more abstract, higher-order constructs than are attitudes. They are thus more permanent and resistant to change, and they have a direct or indirect causal influence on both attitudes and behaviors" (Mueller, 1986, p. 5).

What we learn about values here is that they are complex, are resistant to change, and may have a direct influence not only on behavior but on other affective dimensions such as attitude. This idea reinforces our understanding of the powerful effect values can have on our feelings toward situations, things, and people, and ultimately upon our behavior.

Values are so much a part of an individual that even placing names on them may be difficult. An approach that has proven useful in values identification is that of forced choice. One instructor we know likes to distribute a list of twenty-five values (justice, peace, honesty, and so on) and a plastic bag with one hundred tiny cinnamon candies to each participant in a values clarification session. The directions are to "place your candies on the values that are most important to you, being sure that the number of candies on each value is representative of relative importance." Next, participants are asked to move the candies to the values that are most important to "you as a student." Finally, the candies are to be placed on the values that are most important to "you as a teacher." By the end of the exercise, there are red fingers, candies rolling everywhere, and some puzzled teachers questioning why they valued different things as a student than they did as a teacher.

Another, somewhat more formal approach to discovering teaching values is the use of a teaching values inventory like the one appearing in Resource B. This inventory has been used with university faculty to help identify the extent to which they value each of five elements associated with the teaching-learning exchange: content/curriculum, physical environment/resources, teacher/method, learner community, and individual learner. Findings from one study that used this instrument suggested that university faculty tend to value content and curriculum far more than any of the other four elements (Norland, Budak, & Heimlich, 1993). Alternate forms of the instrument for adult basic education teachers and for extension educators also appear along with a scoring sheet.

Attitudes

Attitude, the most familiar of the affective dimensions, has been described as "affect for or against, evaluation of, like or dislike of, or positiveness or negativeness toward a psychological object" (Mueller, 1986, p. 3). The link between attitude and value and belief is that an attitude is the feeling applied toward a person or thing based on a set of beliefs and guided by underlying values. For example, a teacher *believes* that students who are late for a class session "have no excuse" (because she *values* promptness) and so holds a fairly negative *attitude* toward those individuals who are chronically late.

Teacher attitudes have been studied by many. Of particular interest have been the attitudes toward teaching as a profession. Job satisfaction, teacher commitment, and teacher efficacy are three attitudes that have been found to be linked to teacher behavior and student outcomes (Kottkamp, 1990).

In a discussion of attitude as a part of teaching philosophy, however, the "objects" of the attitude will more likely include the elements of the teaching-learning exchange. For our purposes, those are content, environment, teacher, learning community, and individual learner. In fact, the pattern of exploring, reflecting upon, and applying ideas concerning beliefs, values, attitudes, and behavior related to content, environment, teacher, learning community, and individual learner will reappear throughout this book. By the end of the book, readers will have *explored* and *reflected* upon the congruence of philosophy and behavior using the framework of the elements of the teaching-learning exchange and have made some plans to *apply* new ideas (philosophical or behavioral) in their respective adult education settings.

The complex web of interrelationships of beliefs, values, and attitudes, when viewed as a whole, creates a teacher's philosophy. Superimposed upon this web is the teacher's own culture and unique context related to and apart from the teaching-learning exchange. The next section of this chapter addresses this combination of human characteristics and how they interact to help form one's teaching philosophy.

What Is Teaching Philosophy?

Teaching philosophy has been called a personal vision (Brookfield, 1990), a critical rationale (Smythe, 1986), a paradigm/approach, and an orientation or guide (Zinn, 1990). Regardless of the name, your personal philosophy of teaching and learning will serve as the organizing structure for your beliefs, values, and attitudes related to the teaching-learning exchange.

In language borrowed from the research paradigm, teaching philosophy can be likened to the constitutive definition of a variable or construct. The constitutive definition is the formal definition the researcher adopts to express to others just exactly what is being studied (Ary, Jacobs, & Razavieh, 1985). This formal definition provides a "road map" for the researcher to use to design instruments and data collection procedures to "capture" or operationalize that elusive construct. If philosophy represents the constitutive definition, then teaching behavior is what captures that philosophy. The two together represent teaching style, just as the constitutive and operational definitions of variables work together to represent the construct in question (Norland, 1992).

A philosophy is a compilation of one's beliefs, values, and attitudes. It is the system used to guide decision making in the practical world. Philosophy frequently is viewed as theoretical, abstract, and impractical, something studied in college but having little relevance to everyday problems of education (Hitt, 1973, p. 17). However, knowing and articulating a philosophy of teaching and learning can be helpful for teachers in a variety of ways. A philosophy "forces us to state the values and assumptions underlying any educational endeavor" (p. 18). Additionally, it "provides guidance for distinguishing between value judgment and empirical knowledge" (p. 18). Possessing a philosophy assists in identifying "the importance of goals and objectives" and "emphasizes consistency between means and ends" (p. 18). Espousing one's own philosophy "can help provide a holistic view of education" as well as force "us to pull ourselves back from the particulars of the educational enterprise and to consider education in its entirety" (p. 18). Philosophy directs behavior either overtly or covertly, so teachers who identify, examine, alter, and adopt a philosophy assert control over their behavior. Indeed, an awareness of one's own philosophy is what separates the professional from the practitioner (Elias & Merriam, 1980). If no educational philosophy is articulated, decisions are likely to be based on habit or trend—resulting in incongruence and inconsistency in word and deed.

In addition to helping teachers become better educators, clarifying teaching philosophy can contribute to other areas of teachers' lives, specifically the political and professional realms (Brookfield, 1990). Knowing and being able to articulate a cohesive philosophy of why one does what one does will help when dealing in the inevitable politics of teaching. "You may or may not win your case or make your point. You will, however, be much more likely to communicate a sense of confident clearheadedness, a sense that your position is grounded in a well-developed and carefully conceived philosophy of practice" (Brookfield, 1990, p. 17). In a professional sense, articulating a personal philosophy and then sharing it with other teachers within similar professional contexts will help develop a "collective professional identity" (p. 17) based upon shared philosophical tenets. In short, "Philosophizing about adult education will probably not make a philosopher out of you, but it might help you to be a better adult educator" (Zinn, 1990, p. 56).

Many approaches can assist in the identification of a personal teaching philosophy. Choosing a philosophy already identified and adopting it as your own (or realizing that you already have) and selecting a philosophy as a framework for building your own within its general tenets are two logical approaches (Elias & Merriam, 1980). Educators wanting to investigate existing philosophies of adult education have a very good source of assistance in the "Philosophy of Adult Education Inventory" (PAEI) (Zinn, 1983). The instrument is "self-administered, self-scored, and self-interpreted" and places the educator into one of five philosophical orientations: liberal, behaviorist, progressive, humanistic, and radical (Zinn, 1990, p. 59). The categories of information used to interpret PAEI scores include purpose of adult education, learner, teacher, key words, methods, and people and practices (Zinn, 1990).

Another way to formulate a personal philosophy is to explore and reflect upon beliefs, values, and attitudes related to teaching and learning and combine them using a more eclectic approach (Elias & Merriam, 1980). We subscribe to this more "inductive" approach of arriving at a philosophy of teaching and learning. In fact, the structure of this book assumes this inductive, eclectic process of exploration, reflection, and application of both philosophy and behavior in the quest for congruence.

What Is Teaching Style?

Philosophy is formulated by a thorough examination of values, beliefs, and attitudes related to the teaching-learning exchange. The addition of behavior completes the picture and represents teaching style.

Style is a mode of expression. It is achieving "the balance between developing a guiding vision [philosophy] that informs our teaching and responding flexibly to different contexts" (Brookfield, 1990, p. 4). It has distinctive qualities that suggest appropriate behavior for the individual. Style has to do with form rather than content, process rather than product. It includes the implementation of philosophy; it contains evidence of beliefs about, values related to, and attitudes toward all the elements of the teaching-learning exchange.

How you teach is the product of many facets of your life—indeed, all facets of your life. Your experiences as a teacher, your experiences as a learner, your formal education, your likes and dislikes, the groups with which you associate, your health, your home life—all these and more make you who you are. Teaching style is the way in which you use all these things to consciously conduct a teaching-learning exchange.

Most educators agree that learners learn in different ways; likewise, there is an old debate on how individuals teach: do we teach as we were taught, or do we teach as we prefer to learn (Dunn & Dunn, 1979)? The educator is somehow expected to serve all learners equally by adapting methods, techniques, situations, activities to the individual learner. Our premise, however, is that we should accept and encourage diversity among educators regarding teaching style as we accept diversity of learners. Our foundation is an argument for clarity, consistency, and cohesiveness in the use of a philosophy of teaching.

Many prescriptions have been offered to improve instruction. One is that when educators better know their own abilities and limitations, they are positioned to improve their teaching performance (Myers & Myers, 1980). Models of teaching share the central assumption that all significant variations in teaching are a function of variance along one dimension of the individual teacher; the dimension varies from model to model (Nuthall & Snook, 1973). (See Chapter Three for additional information on dimensions.)

A limited amount of research has been done to identify teaching styles, the teacher's preferred patterns of providing learning opportunities for students of any age. Behavior related to teaching style includes presenting information, facilitating discussion, structuring learning opportunities, planning subject matter, and conducting learning activities. Perhaps one explanation for relatively little research on this subject is that the larger society holds such a narrow view of teaching, seeing it as an occupational technique or work process (Bidwell, 1973) instead of viewing teachers as individual performers.

Dunn and Dunn (1979, p. 241) identified teaching style as "the attitudes teachers hold toward various instructional programs, methods, and resources as well as [the students] they prefer working with." Fischer and Fischer (1979) used style to refer to a pervasive quality in the educational activities of a teacher that persists even when content changes. This concept was echoed by Gauld (1982, p. 13) in his definition of teaching style as "the consistent way a teacher organizes and delivers a body of knowledge." Solomon and Miller (1961, p. 12) suggested that style is "a pattern composed of class-room behaviors . . . which are consistent over time and which distinguish [the teacher] from other teachers." Huelsman (1983, p. 15) operationally defined teaching styles as consisting of "a complex of personal attitudes, traits, and behaviors, and the media used to transmit to or to receive data from the learners." Draves (1984) identified what he believed were the emotional, physical, mental, and social characteristics that define the style of a teacher.

In describing teaching styles, many researchers and theorists have developed classification systems. These categorical structures are often similar in appearance. Lenz (1982), for example, believed there were two broad teaching styles: proactive and reactive. She suggested that these stemmed from very different psychological bases, learner centered and teacher centered. Robinson (1979) defined teaching style as a placement within one of five categories on a continuum ranging from "highly content centered" to "highly people centered."

Axelrod (1970) identified five teaching styles based on studies at the University of California: (1) drillmaster or recitation class, (2) content centered, (3) instructor centered, (4) intellect centered, and (5) person centered. These five types are variants and blends of subject-, teacher-, and student-centered instructors. The contrast of instructor-centered versus student-centered teaching is also a common theme in the writings of Knowles (1980) on the self-directed learner, Rogers (1969) on client-centered therapy, and Crouch's (1983) construct of "farmer-centered problem identification." Likewise, restrictions on the learning environment, the specific situation, and institutional guidelines can have an impact on the teaching style (Beder & Darkenwald, 1982).

Nuthall and Snook (1973) defined three teacher-oriented models of teaching based upon other models and writings: the behavior-control model, the discovery-learning model, and the rational model.

Three relationship models were offered by Lenz (1982): the host-guest; the client-consultant; and the partnership. These three models are driven by outcomes. The host expects the guests to return in the future; when expectations are met, clients are satisfied with the consultant services; the partnership is considered successful when both sides live up to responsibilities.

In a study of shared aspects of teaching styles, Solomon and Miller (1961) identified seven approaches used by educators: (1) businesslike, objective, impersonal approach; (2) emphasis on communication; (3) personal approach; (4) self-involvement; (5) sensitivity toward students/interest in students; (6) protective behavior; and (7) stimulating the student. These clusters are structured by the researchers to relate the educator to the student, the subject matter, and the world of the learner. Further, the clusters are defined by student-student, teacher-student, or teacher-subject interaction. These relationships refer to whether the educator receives "gratification" in the subject or the act of teaching and, as we like to refer to it, whether the teacher is a "director," "actor," or "stage manager" in the theater of the classroom.

Continuing the metaphor of the theater to examine teaching style, the following are three roles that the teacher might play. With which do you feel most comfortable?

1. The creative role of originating the work (authors, script-writers; in the classroom, course work planners)
2. The artistic role of interpreting the work (directors, choreographers, designers, conductors; in the classroom, teachers who use textbooks or works not written by themselves)
3. The technical role of carrying out the interpretation (actors, singers, dancers, craftspersons, artisans, musicians; in the classroom, the teacher in front of the class)

The teacher also plays the role of the producer, who brings these three together. When the production works, we have a hit; but the theater of the classroom only works when we use our beliefs as the foundation for our teaching style.

So how can teachers pin down their individual styles? Your style is not necessarily defined by what you do most frequently or what you revert to in a crisis. Rather, it is the comprehensive style that represents the total of your values, beliefs, attitudes (philosophy), and behaviors. Teaching style is how you philosophically approach and then conduct moments of instruction.

The following discussion presents a brief synopsis of various authors' approaches to classifying teaching style. In the quest to solidify your definition of teaching style, review what others have suggested, keep what makes sense, and leave the remainder for the next reader.

Style Based on the Teacher's Characteristics

Many scholars classify teaching style on the personal characteristics of the teacher. For example, Conti (1985, p. 7) believed that the traits of the educator matter most and that these collectively form a "synergistic whole which is referred to as a philosophy" to guide the behaviors of a teacher. Boone (1985) believed that a teacher's philosophy becomes the guiding framework that defines the individual's style. The philosophy is based upon the characteristics of personal values and goals, mastery of concepts and principles, and skill, all combined with professional values and goals.

A similar concept proposed by Ryans (1970) is that the environment in which the educator matured will contribute to the formation of teaching styles. From his study, for example, teachers reared in a home that was above average both financially and intellectually/culturally tended to score higher on originality and imagination, verbal/semantic facility, and judgment scales than teachers from other backgrounds. However, substantial overlapping occurred among groups.

Some scholars, such as Conti and Welborn (1986), believe that the educator creates a learning environment that fits the characteristics (or the style) of the educator. This purposeful use of teaching style makes a difference in student achievement. An educator with a well-defined style of any sort creates the best environment for learning (Conti & Fellenz, 1988). This idea is in line with the commonly accepted concept that an individual's preferred teaching style is reflective of that individual's preferred learning style (Huelsman, 1983).

Personal factors may also affect the teachers' roles. Robinson (1979) identified four such factors: (1) education, previous experience, professional identification; (2) needs for dominance, acceptance, and achievement; (3) other social roles of the educator, such as spouse or group member; and (4) personal goals.

Ryans (1960) identified assumptions about teachers and then offered postulates growing out of the assumptions. From the basic assumption that teacher behavior is a function of the conditions of the environment in which it occurs, he offered six postulates on teacher behavior: (1) there is some degree of consistency, (2) there are a limited number of responses, (3) it is probable rather than certain, (4) it is a function of personal characteristics, (5) it is a function of the general features of the situation, and (6) it is a function of the specific situation.

Jarvis (1985) proposed three different approaches (or styles) that a teacher might adopt, which vary in the dimension of instructor to student responsibility to the learning process. The *didactic* approach represents the teacher-controlled end of the continuum, evident in classes in which a teacher lectures and students take notes. Moving toward more student responsibility for learning, the *Socratic* approach is teacher directed and student responsive; teachers use the classroom as the site for a Socratic dialogue. The *facilitative* approach has the instructor responsible only for creating an inviting environment; the student is responsible for content selection and subsequent learning.

Some scholars, such as Hiemstra and Sisco (1990), believe the teacher is responsible for creating an environment in which the learner can assume responsibility for learning. Their approach is an answer to the ever-increasing demand to address the wide variety of learners possessing diverse needs, and is based on the facilitative model that Jarvis proposed. Hiemstra and Sisco say this personalized approach is the best model for teaching adults.

Similar to Jarvis's Socratic model is the "inquiry teaching" or inductive/discovery teaching model (Bateman, 1990, p. 32). Here the pressure is placed on the learner to become an active (as opposed to passive) participant in the process. The teacher, however, is clearly in charge of the process.

Style Based on Learner Characteristics

It is often asserted that educators should adapt their teaching style to the learning styles of the students (Dunn & Dunn, 1979; Ellis, 1979). This advice appears to be a contradiction of the basic meaning of style, which is a function of an individual's personality, experience, ethnicity, education, and other individual traits. An educator cannot and should not "change" personality to satisfy each and every learner. Instead, the teacher can adopt—and adapt—classroom methods, strategies, techniques, and processes to be more consistent with his or her individual style.

This was very evident to us once not too long ago when we were asked to conduct a workshop on learning styles for a group of teachers. We decided to ask the participants to complete five "learning style inventories" before the workshop, including the Myers-Briggs Personality Type Indicator (Myers & Myers, 1980). At the workshop, we divided into groups based on the outcomes of one inventory. After an activity designed to accentuate differences between the groups, we divided into other groups based on the outcome of another inventory. We held another activity, then divided again based on the third inventory, and repeated the process for the two last inventories. The end result? Nearly every teacher had been in a learning group with nearly every other teacher. No one had been in all groups with anyone else. What we learned most about learning styles that day is that each learner is unique! And if each learner is unique, how do we ever satisfy every learner? That is when we shifted the focus of the workshop to *teaching* style, the only variable in the classroom that can maximize learning for all learners. Teachers' development of their own style provides far more learning opportunities for more learners than anything else they can do.

Knowing our teaching styles can be useful in defining what are appropriate methods for us, adapting methods to our styles, and knowing our own classroom limitations. These ideas are examined further in Chapter Nine.

No Single Definition

We can certainly agree from this discussion on teaching style that no consistent definition of teaching style emerges from the literature. There is, however, a shared concept: educators will, for whatever reasons, tend over time to perform to their strengths. The means of identifying those strengths include clustering, contrasting, and trait identification. We strongly believe that no one style should ever be described as better or worse than any other for all situations. It is likely that within every style there are both excellent and poor educators (Axelrod, 1970). Style is the predilection toward performance, not the methods or the quality of the instructional activity. Style means consistent, overall traits and qualities (Conti, 1985).

To investigate the concept of style more fully, select two people whom you can watch in teaching settings. One person should be someone you know fairly well, and the other a stranger. As you watch them teaching, try to determine why they do the things they do. What are their beliefs, values, attitudes, the whole of their philosophy regarding teaching? Review your notes. Do you find yourself more able to explain the teaching behaviors of the person you know well? If so, the explanation might be that the extra information you have about your friend's personal characteristics helps to link teaching philosophy to behavior.

Now try this activity with *you* as the teacher. Reflect on the last several times you taught. Make a chart that lists your behaviors in each teaching setting. What behaviors were consistent for all settings? Circle them. What behaviors were inconsistent? Make an X through them. Do the consistent behaviors accurately reflect what you think are your beliefs about what teaching should be? Are the inconsistent behaviors representative of beliefs you hold about teaching and learning? How can you develop a consistency in behavior that is related to your beliefs?

Conclusion

Educators who try to adapt to all learning styles instead of focusing on their own teaching style can get "stuck" without a clearly defined teaching style. To move from one style to another requires learning a whole new set of behaviors—a process that takes a long time. It cannot be done instantly as occasion suggests.

How educators relate to groups is a result of both experiences with and beliefs about groups. These beliefs and experiences should be evident in teaching. Many teachers have beliefs about teaching and learning that do not correlate with their behaviors in the teaching setting. This discrepancy between behavior and belief can ultimately result in conflict in the teaching-learning exchange. For example, a teacher frustrated with a class's progress might act upon the advice of a colleague and suddenly change tactics for a session, insisting that class members sit quietly and review worksheets instead of openly discussing them as usual. Such an attempt is doomed to failure if the teacher does not believe that it is the best way to teach. At the same time, the technique might be a smashing success for the colleague who suggested it in the first place.

Explore your teaching style by identifying some adjectives that clearly describe you as a teacher. For each of the words, write down three behaviors you do in *all* teaching settings that support these descriptors. Now write some of your teaching behaviors that *do not* support them. Are there trends in the behaviors that "fit" or do not "fit"? What do you think are the underlying issues for these discrepancies—habit, lack of skill, confusion, comfort? To help in this reflection, record thoughts and ideas that occur to you after teaching. Record the place, time, content, and audience. Use the journal as a forum for reflecting on how your values, beliefs, and attitudes were or were not fulfilled by your teaching strategies in each situation. Include plans for applying what you have discovered.

Understanding your beliefs about teaching and learning and discovering how to operationalize those beliefs in the exchange will improve both your instruction and the effectiveness of your instructional activities. Having a well-defined sense of who you are as a teacher and having a consistency between what you believe and what you do will enhance your instructional behaviors. There is no right or wrong, good or bad, better or worse teaching style. There are simply differences. What is good or bad, right or wrong, better or worse is how the beliefs that contribute to the style are acted on in the instructional setting.

One benefit in understanding your own teaching style preferences is the empowerment that this understanding offers in helping you meet the diverse needs of learners. All learners have different preferences for learning that are often satisfied by the utilization of multiple methods and strategies for instruction. When you understand your own beliefs about instruction, you are more able to adapt methods to your belief system that will satisfy divergent learning strategies. Because you adapt methods to your style, the methods do not conflict with your approach. Rather, the methods can be adapted by learners to their own learning preferences without compromising your beliefs about teaching and learning.

As all of us continually seek to improve our instruction, we can free ourselves from the restrictions of methods *if* we understand our values about teaching, and *if* we understand our beliefs about teaching and learning. Instead of defining instruction by methods, we can define outcomes based on our individual belief systems and adapt methods and strategies for instruction to accomplish these outcomes.

In the ongoing efforts to improve teaching, educators begin to realize that there is no ideal teacher. An understanding of differences in teaching style allows the valuation of diversity in instructional practice.

Chapter Three

Analyzing the Instructional Process

Improving as a teacher involves an introspective growth process that combines exploration and reflection of one's philosophy (the paradigm formed from beliefs, values, and attitudes) and behavior related to teaching and learning. The goal of this chapter is to provide an organized structure within which adult educators can seek information about their philosophy and behaviors in an effort to make changes toward congruence.

This structure encompasses the entire teaching-learning exchange, including planning, implementation, and evaluation of the actual exchange. Elements of the teaching-learning exchange include content, environment, teacher, organization (educational provider), learning community, individual student, and culture (the greater culture within which the teaching-learning exchange takes place). This chapter introduces these elements in preparation for Chapters Four through Eight, which address the five primary elements (content, environment, teacher, learning community, and individual learner) in depth.

49

Elements of the Teaching-Learning Exchange

In any given situation, elements intrinsic to the teaching-learning exchange interact to create a dynamic interchange. These elements have been identified and clustered in various ways: the purpose of education, the content, the student, the principles of teaching and learning, and the knowledge and skill of the teacher (Newcomb et al., 1986); the learner, the overall purpose of education, the content, the learning process, and the teacher (Apps, 1989a); and the learner, the teacher, the organization, and the content (Seaman & Fellenz, 1989). What are the elements of the teaching-learning exchange as you have them conceptualized? Sometimes a new look at an old question provides insight, so before reading on, schedule a visit to an educational setting with which you are not familiar. Allow yourself a different perspective on adult education. If adult basic education is your field, then visit a training program at a local business. If you teach in a community college, view an informal extension education program. Prepare to observe the teaching-learning exchange taking place. Write or sketch what you see as the major elements. Are these the same as you would have named in your own classroom or educational setting?

For us, the seven elements specified above define the structure of the teaching-learning exchange. All that happens before, during, and after the exchange is represented within these seven elements (Norland, 1993; Norland & Heimlich, 1990, 1991).

The way in which a teacher approaches each element and the manner in which he or she encourages or hinders the interaction of the elements reflects that teacher's style. Furthermore, the process the teacher uses to facilitate (or inhibit) interaction among elements is directly related to the teacher's formal and informal educational experiences as well as to other life experiences not directly related to the educational process. Throughout the exploration of the elements of the teaching-learning exchange, readers will want to reflect upon their own past experiences with education in an effort to determine the "whys" of their philosophies and behaviors. This information will be of great value as they begin to align philosophy with behavior or vice versa.

Content

The first element is content. Content is the specific domain of knowledge, skills, abilities, processes, and affect addressed during the teaching-learning exchange. It is often referred to as *curriculum,* *subject matter,* or *program,* indicating a very specific focus. However, it may also include the more generic cognitive, affective, or psychomotor processes. Content can be identified by the specified objectives of the teaching-learning exchange. For example, objectives for a career exploration course might be the following: the student will be able to correctly complete a job application form; the student will illustrate the necessary skills needed to operate required equipment through a series of manual operations; the student will report, through personal journal entries, a more positive attitude toward specific career opportunities. In this case, the content includes knowledge of job applications, skills to operate equipment, and attitude toward career exploration.

Method of instruction (lecture, demonstration, games, for example) is not included in our definition of content. Method belongs to the teacher and is referred to as a kind of teacher behavior. Chapter Nine addresses method in depth.

The medium for the content, however, is an important concept directly related to content. Media are the sensory presentations—visual, audible, and so on—that are used to deliver content. Content presented visually might be contained in a workbook or instruction manual or presented on an overhead transparency or on the chalkboard. Audible content might be what was said during a lecture or group discussion. Content can also be presented using touch (tree identification by feeling the bark), smell (learning to distinguish among chemical compounds for use as cleaning solvents), and taste (selection of appropriate herbs for culinary practice), although perhaps not with the same frequency as it is presented for sight and hearing.

The combination, then, of what is to be learned and what senses are stimulated to help in that learning (the medium) represents the first element, content. To what extent do you focus upon the nature of the content when planning, implementing, and evaluating the teaching-learning exchange? What rank would content hold for you among the seven elements? Does it matter more to you *what* you teach or *who* you teach? Chapter Four will expand this discussion.

Environment

The second element, environment, encompasses both the physical surroundings (apparent and transparent) of the teaching-learning exchange and the psychological environment. Examples of the physical environment would be the building, room, temperature, and furniture. The psychological environment suggests a "climate" perceived by the participants that is created by the manipulation of the physical surroundings (Knowles, 1980).

Skillful teachers can manipulate student behavior by "confronting the physical and psychological characteristics of the classroom, rather than the student" (Gordon, 1974, p. 156). For example, in an adult discussion group, forming the chairs in a circle or U-shape to ease eye contact between members could very well enhance discussion. In a lecture format, the same configuration could distract class members' attention from the main points.

"For teachers to be effective in modifying the classroom environment they need the ability to think creatively about possible changes, using a systematic model for classifying various types of environmental modification" (Gordon, 1974, p. 158). Gordon provided eight examples to illustrate how teachers can use the environment to achieve their goals. *Enriching* the environment can deter unwanted behavior, whereas *impoverishing* the environment can help address too much stimulation. By *restricting* an environment, teachers can help to correct "wrong place, wrong time" behavior. For environments that seem like prison cells, *enlargement* can help. A *rearrangement* can assist with traffic pattern problems. Gordon suggests that teachers *simplify* environments that are too distracting, *systematize* confusing arrangements, and *plan* ahead to prevent unwanted situations (1974, p. 160). Preece adds, "Although teachers have no control over the construction of classrooms, they can make the best of what they have" (1987, p. 11).

The combination of physical attributes of the teaching-learning exchange context and the potential influences of those physical attributes upon the other elements represents the second element, environment. How important is the physical environment for you in setting the stage—in creating the appropriate climate for learning? Does it matter *where* you teach? Chapter Five expands the discussion of environment.

Teacher

The next element, the teacher, refers to the individual officially responsible for directing the exchange. Whether that individual accepts that responsibility totally is not an issue within the definition of teacher. A begrudging yet effective jury foreman could well act as a teacher under this definition. "Leadership, setting the tone, and being a role model are recognized qualities necessary for good teachers. Yet none of these can be taught to a good teacher" (Preece, 1987, p. 25).

Of the seven elements interacting within the teaching-learning exchange, the teacher is the one that has the greatest potential to affect the majority of the others. The teacher is traditionally the one who selects the *content,* arranges the physical *environment,* and initiates and directs interaction with the *learning community* and the *individual student.* The teacher is also the one who represents the *organization* within that exchange. And the teacher is the one who helps to interpret any cultural influences from the *greater culture.*

Adult educators will vary the extent to which they manipulate each of the elements, but they all have the *potential* to play the major role in orchestrating the teaching-learning exchange. Picture a musical conductor simultaneously directing the entire orchestra and also playing a primary instrument in the orchestra. Sound difficult? We can only imagine—until the next time we step into the classroom ready to teach (with our batons in one hand and our tubas in the other).

To know where the element *teacher* fits into the teaching-learning exchange, we need to know how much the teacher's needs are the focus of the planning, implementing, and evaluating of the exchange. As difficult as it is to imagine a musician both directing and playing in the orchestra, this is the analogy of the teacher both facilitating and being an element in the teaching-learning exchange. Chapter Six will explore this complicated relationship further.

Organization

A secondary element in the teaching-learning exchange is the organization—the formal provider and most often the financial backer of the educational endeavor. Organizations can fall into three taxonomies based on the nature of funding: (1) tax supported, (2) nonprofit, and (3) for-profit (Apps, 1989b). The characteristics of the organization and thus the kind of adult education offered is very much influenced by the taxonomy in which it fits.

Take the example of an educational program designed to teach farmers new techniques in use of pesticides. A tax-supported organization would need to consider and be accountable to the local citizens when selecting the specific information given. In this example, the tax-supported organization might want to place heavy emphasis on environmental considerations. However, a nonprofit organization conducting the same educational program might very well base its content on the beliefs and values of the organization, regardless of and perhaps in direct conflict with the opinions of the community. And a for-profit organization might arrange its educational program around the promotion of some new pesticide-related products it was marketing.

The organization typically does not play a direct role in the teaching-learning exchange (thus the term *secondary element*) but is represented by the teacher, who is most often a formal employee of the organization but is sometimes a volunteer or contract agent. The organization does not have a direct impact upon the teaching-learning exchange but has an indirect effect through the teacher. The nature of the effect is guided by the match or mismatch of the teacher's philosophy and the organization's policies, mission, and philosophy of adult education. A teacher who matches his or her organization's philosophy will most likely communicate that philosophy clearly in word and action. If there is a mismatch, the teacher will most likely communicate his or her philosophy regardless of that of the organization. In this case, the organization may not have any impact on the exchange or may have a negative impact based on the teacher's interpretations and actions regarding the organization.

Important organizational characteristics that can affect the adult education provided by that organization include factors internal to the organization such as "(1) the history and traditions of the organization, (2) the current structures that govern the flow of communication and authority, (3) the mission of the organization, (4) the resource limits, (5) the standard operating procedures, and (6) any philosophical constraints that limit who can be served or what types of needs can be addressed" (Sork & Caffarella, 1989, p. 235). Perhaps most important to the teacher is an organization's culture: shared values, beliefs, assumptions, perceptions, norms, and artifacts (Ott, 1989) that constitute something analogous to an individual's personality, hidden yet unifying (Kilmann, Saxton, Serpa, & Associates, 1985).

Important factors external to the organization include "(1) the relationships (competitive or cooperative) between the organization and others that serve the same client groups, (2) any comparative advantage enjoyed by the organization that makes it easier to respond to needs, and (3) the attitudes toward the organization held by influentials in the community" (Sork & Caffarella, 1989, p.235).

Think about the organization for which you currently work or have worked previously in an adult education context. Was it tax supported, nonprofit, or for-profit? How did its funding status affect its educational component? Was its primary mission adult education? What was the organizational culture like? How did your values and beliefs about education match with your organization's? How much of the organization's personality did you bring into the teaching-learning exchange with you? Was the personality of your organization a help or a hindrance in your teaching? What internal factors affected your teaching the most? How did the external factors affect your teaching? Can you picture an organization that would be a perfect match for you? What would it be like?

For yet another perspective on organizational match, select an adult education organization with which you are not very familiar. Make appointments to interview administrators, teachers, and students. Ask the following questions: (1) What is the mission of this organization as it specifically relates to adult education? (2) To what extent do the educational programs reflect that mission? (3) What is your own mission, related to the educational programs of this organization? To what extent does your mission reflect the organization's? (4) How would you describe the culture in which this organization exists? (5) What are the external cultural influences that constrain or empower teachers and learners to fully participate in this organization's educational programs?

Now compare the answers of the administrators to those of the teachers and the students. What does this comparison say about the success of the organization, teachers, and students to utilize organizational characteristics and culture to positively influence educational programs and experiences?

Learning Community

The fourth primary element is the learning community. The group of learners coming together can be considered a community formed for the purpose of learning. A sense of community develops as the group recognizes characteristics they share that bond them (Brookfield, 1990). Community membership is defined by shared characteristics but illustrated by symbols and artifacts.

For example, reflecting upon our experiences as adults returning to graduate school, the authors both remember a true feeling of community forming every time they enrolled in another graduate-level statistics course. And the symbol of membership recognized by all members was the stack of computer printouts carried religiously to class (and all over campus). Class members greeted each other with nods and smiles of recognition when they saw each other with the familiar printouts. The kind of learning community formed in this example might be called artificial because the community did not exist until the educational experience happened.

Another type of learning community can be illustrated by the civic club to which one of the authors belongs. The club's primary mission is not adult education for its members but social action for the betterment of the community. However, almost monthly, the members participate in formal educational programming aimed at improving members' knowledge and skills in community development. This "learning community" is a preexisting learning community whose common bonds are those related to the preexisting organization but whose activities from time to time include adult education.

A third type of learning community is one in which members are linked because of some outside phenomenon they have in common. Any adult educator who has worked in Holmes County, Ohio, has probably experienced this type of learning community because most of Holmes County is populated by Amish families. The common bonds for almost any adult learning community formed in that geographic location would include those associated with the Amish culture and religion.

Thus learning communities are formed when adults come together for the purpose of learning but can vary greatly in their makeup and common bonds. Educators must recognize the existence of learning communities regardless of the emphasis they actually place upon them. And teachers certainly vary in their beliefs about, values related to, and attitudes toward the existence and utilization of learning communities.

The Highlander Education and Research Center, located in the mountains of eastern Tennessee, takes the idea of a learning community seriously. In its mission statement, the center states: "We bring people together to learn from each other. By sharing experience, we realize that we are not alone" (Highlander Education and Research Center, 1989, p. i). Shared experiences create characteristics that support a unique culture and form a community, whether those experiences are incurred before or during the teaching-learning exchange.

What kind of learning community is your typical class or group of learners? What are some of the characteristics they typically share? How do those common bonds affect your teaching and their learning? Chapter Seven investigates these questions and more.

Individual Learner

The fifth and final primary element in the exchange is the individual learner. Every teaching-learning exchange has one or more individual learners. Even though shared characteristics of these individuals create a group or community, unshared characteristics allow the members of the group to remain individuals. Successful teachers are those who realize that the group of students not only represents a culture with a shared voice but also consists of individuals with unique voices (Hamachek, 1975). The individual student represents the ultimate recipient in the teaching-learning exchange.

The individual student also represents a major dilemma for many adult educators. How many times have teachers asked themselves, "Do I sacrifice the needs of the many to satisfy the needs of the one?" or, in simpler terms, "How much class time can I take to deal with individual student needs?" Teachers wrestle with individual needs versus group needs daily. They also are in conflict with the decision about how much they should tailor their behavior to individual student learning style (Even, 1987).

Have you found yourself in the situation described above, where there is an obvious need of an individual but the learning community does not share the same need? What have you done in the past? Why? How did it work out? What beliefs, values, and attitudes did your behavior suggest? Does this fit with how you see individual versus group needs? Chapter Eight will help clarify these and other specific issues related to the individual student.

Culture

Completing the set of seven elements is a secondary element in the teaching-learning exchange, the greater culture in which the exchange takes place. *Culture* is simply defined as behavior patterns that are socially acquired and communicated. The mode of communication is through the use of symbols such as "customs, techniques, beliefs, institutions, and material objects" (Fairchild, 1970, p. 80). Every society has a dominant culture that projects norms of behavior, and this dominant culture necessarily infiltrates the teaching-learning exchange.

The dominant culture of the society of the United States during the twentieth century has been characterized by the valuing of evidence of achievement, activity/work, efficiency, progress, material comfort, equality, individual personality, and freedom; humanitarian mores and a moral orientation; external conformity; science/secular rationality; nationalism; democracy; and racism (Locke, 1992, pp. 1–14). These characteristics of the dominant culture continually exert influence on any adult education taking place within the society. The implication for this statement is that the mainstream or dominant culture will always have an impact on the interaction of the elements of the teaching-learning exchange. The impact will vary, however, depending upon the willingness and ability of the teacher and students to become immune to its influence.

Because culture is tied to society, culture must enter the teaching-learning exchange through human involvement. This cultural impact happens through the teacher and students and to a lesser extent through human products such as curriculum. Can you describe how the curriculum used in your teaching has a flavor of the dominant culture present? To what extent do you, as the teacher, bring evidence of the dominant culture into the teaching-learning exchange? Do the learners represent the dominant culture? For many adult educators, the answer to that question is no, in that learners really represent a distinctly different group or groups. They do, however, bring much evidence of the dominant culture into the classroom.

Societal norms and values seep in no matter how hard the educator tries to patch the cracks. Maybe what is needed is an approach to facing the culture and its impacts head on. Just what does the dominant culture say about adult education, and how does this information affect your experiences in the teaching-learning exchange?

Educators may want to explore this question in depth, and the print media are a good place to begin. Secure articles from the popular press—from local and regional as well as national and international newspapers and magazines. Tape them to a poster board. Scan this group of articles for trends, underlining words and phrases that are repeated throughout. Most likely what you see are the same messages your learners are being sent. Once recognized, these issues can be addressed. Once identified, cultural influences can be lessened or enhanced as desired. Try the same activity with your television watching. What are the messages in the news and in the situation comedies?

Locke (1992) has provided a good introduction to the characteristics of a dominant culture that inevitably influence our teaching and learning experiences. Are there additional, situation-specific characteristics of the culture in which you teach? If Locke's dominant culture represents America in the 1990s, what additional cultural impacts are there for you in a specific geographic location with specific political, social, environmental, and other characteristics? In your quest to grow as an adult educator, be sure to include an investigation of your beliefs, values, attitudes, and behavior related to the greater culture.

Assumptions About the Five Elements

A teacher's philosophy of the teaching-learning exchange is based on his or her beliefs, attitudes, and values related to each of the elements individually as well as on how the teacher sees the elements relating to one another. In later chapters, each of the primary elements will be explored in depth. For the time being, we will focus on three assumptions that relate to the five elements:

1. Each element is present and active in any teaching-learning exchange.
2. All the elements are interrelated.
3. The elements all function within the context of larger external systems and related culture.

Each Element Is Always Present

Even if the exchange involves a teacher-absent situation (such as distance education), single-learner situation (such as one-on-one tutoring), or a physical environment that is essentially nonexistent (as in a correspondence course), all the elements are still very much a part of and play an important role in the exchange.

How can this be? A closer examination of the examples above with elements that, on the surface, appear to be absent from the teaching-learning exchange can illustrate that each element is always present.

Teacher Apparently Absent. In distance education, even though the teacher is not physically present, the essence of the educator is portrayed within the delivery of the information and the curriculum design. The personal characteristics and educational philosophy of the teacher are illustrated through the planning and delivery of material.

Learning Community Apparently Absent. When a single student forms the "learning" portion of the exchange, the "culture of that particular student" (the characteristics shared by the potential group of students) still has considerable influence on the teacher and the individual student. An experience one of the authors had repeatedly can clearly (and painfully) illustrate this point.

Responsibility for teaching program evaluation techniques to extension educators in Ohio included small group, large group, and one-on-one educational experiences. But because all learners, regardless of the learning configuration, were members of a unique learning community—extension educators who basically disliked program evaluation—the shared characteristics of this learning group were always present. The frustration related to program evaluation that those adult learners had was shared throughout time and space.

Physical Environment Apparently Absent. When the physical environment is essentially invisible or unidimensional (as in the case of a teaching-learning exchange occurring through correspondence), characteristics of the exchange still contribute to the psychological environment or climate just as the physical room arrangement influences the psychological environment of a classroom. When teachers prepare materials to be used in a correspondence course, the physical attributes of the paper, printing, graphics, wording, and so forth all contribute to the "learning environment" for the learners. They are the physical attributes that can help to create a psychological climate for learning. Whether or not the elements are actually visible or apparent to the observer, they are present and applying unique influences to the teaching-learning exchange.

All the Elements Are Interrelated

When educators make decisions about any one of the elements, they must consider all elements. Planning the environment without considering content, reacting to the group without knowledge of each individual, selecting content without information on the group or the individuals, or making decisions on any of the four elements without considering the teacher just does not make sense. All the elements are interconnected. They exert forces on each other.

Part of a teacher's philosophy about the teaching-learning exchange is formed by how he or she chooses to address the elements and their relationships. Taking the correspondence example from above, the relationship of the teacher with the learning environment and the perceivable relationships of the individual with the group and the environment may at first appear not relevant. Yet suggestions that the educator makes to help structure the course when addressing the collective group of individual learners in disparate settings reflect the beliefs the educator holds about each of these elements working together. The educator who believes that these elements are irrelevant misses an opportunity to reach students on a very important level. On the other hand, the educator who consciously addresses all the elements in every teaching-learning exchange is acknowledging the very real world of the learner wherever the learner may be. In doing so, the educator is acting upon and enhancing personal beliefs about each of the elements.

Elements Function Within a Larger Context

The internal elements of the teaching-learning exchange occur in the context of a larger external "climate" that is typically not under the teacher's control. As has been suggested above, two specific entities contribute to this climate, the provider organization and the larger culture in which the teaching-learning exchange takes place. Societies—global, national, local—all influence the interaction of the elements. Within the context of the specific teaching-learning exchange, the organizations with their administrative policies, the formal and informal structures in which the exchange itself is linked, and the current systems in which we work perpetuate or actually "reproduce the existing class structure of the society" in which the education takes place (Weiler, 1988, p. 9).

The larger context in which learning occurs comes replete

with rules and expectations for behavior, for learning, and for social exchange and interaction. The cultural set of behaviors that is dominant will be that of the larger, external culture. The way an educator uses the primary elements will be constrained by the organization and the larger culture.

An educator can be constrained or empowered by these external influences. An important point here is that the organization and the greater culture can and will affect the teaching-learning exchange. It is up to the teacher to (1) be aware of the potential influences, (2) collect data on them, and (3) make purposeful decisions about how to utilize them for the best outcomes possible.

Any teacher connected to or working for an educational organization is responsible for knowing the organizational mission, its stated and unstated implications, and specific outcomes sought by that organization. This information comes from written material, interviews with members of the organization, and other sources. Whether teachers agree or disagree with the organizational philosophy, they should know their obligations in specific teaching-learning exchanges funded by, directed by, supported by, or conducted in the name of a particular institution.

Additionally, it is the educator's responsibility to know the characteristics of the greater culture in which the teaching-learning exchange is taking place. If we accept Niebuhr's (1951) view of culture as artificially created by humans—a secondary environment placed within the primary natural environment—then culture can really only affect the teaching-learning exchange through its human participants: the teacher, the student, and the group (through the individuals). Knowing the greater culture and managing its effects as best one can is vital to the teacher's ability to maneuver the treacherous waters of emotion-laden learning environments (Brookfield, 1990, p. 2).

Adult education is different in rural as opposed to urban settings because of differences between rural and urban cultures. Even within the larger culture of, for example, a specific rural community, there are tremendous influences that arise from smaller but more definable cultures. An excellent illustration comes from the work of Stephen Harris (1981) with Australian Aboriginal learning styles. He identified specific characteristics of the Aboriginal culture that would directly affect the way teaching and learning take place. Knowing this culture's characteristics of present-time orientation, authority, conservatism, personal independence, and several other traits helped educators structure successful learning experiences for Aboriginal people.

Specific suggestions for teaching within the cultural context of a specific learning community are offered in Chapter Seven. Even though these are focused on the culture of the learning community, the suggestions are transferable to the greater culture as well.

Interrelationship of Elements

The relationship of the five primary elements to two more secondary elements, organization and culture, suggests a much bigger picture of how teaching and learning can take place. If we were to draw an illustration representing how the elements were interconnected, but limited the connections to those elements that could control or affect the others, the picture would be rather telling, if somewhat simplistic (Figure 3.1).

Culture would enter the teaching-learning exchange through the teacher and the student. The organization would enter the exchange through the teacher and his or her interpretation of mission and policy. Content and environment would be controlled only by the teacher and would influence the exchange at the will of the teacher. The individual would affect the exchange through his or her own behavior and effect upon the group's behavior.

View Figure 3.1 and establish your own lines of "control." Even though all the elements are interrelated, only some of the relationships are control relationships. Where do you, as a teacher, want your lines of control to be? Where are they currently?

Control can be exerted at only certain entry points to the teaching-learning exchange. However, we have discovered that because of the exchange's dynamic nature, the elements constantly interact in relationship to one another. One element's relationship to another element forms a dimension that can be conceptually and visually represented as a continuum. In fact, some of the dimensions formed by the relationships of the elements are quite familiar to adult educators.

**Figure 3.1. Elements and Their Impact
Upon the Teaching-Learning Exchange.**

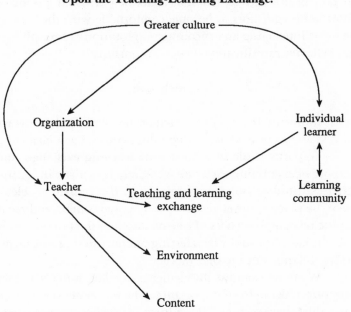

Perhaps the most familiar dimension in teaching style literature is Conti's relationship between the teacher element and the individual student element. Conti's teaching style inventory, Principles
of Adult Learning Scale (PALS), measures teaching style on a continuum of teacher behaviors, from teacher centered to individual
student centered (Conti, 1983). Further investigation of that dimension suggests that the way in which the teacher conceives, plans,
and executes his or her portion of the teaching-learning exchange
is influenced by where the teacher falls on that dimension.

Certainly other dimensions have been proposed (see Chapter
Two), but all have one thing in common: each dimension is formed
using the interaction of two or more elements in a context possessing seven. To further an understanding of the potential relationships among elements, try combining pairs of elements to see if the
combinations make sense. Is there an intuitive rationale for combining content and culture? What is the dimension that links those two
elements? How about organization and teacher? Pairs that at first

glance look unrelated may indeed have a shared dimension. The purpose of this activity is not to break new research ground but to allow adult educators to become comfortable with the concepts of elements interacting and encourage exploration of how philosophy and behavior can illustrate these relationships.

Conclusion

In the following five chapters, each of the primary elements will be defined and examined as an individual entity. Each element plays a very important role in the teaching-learning exchange, and the purpose of examining each one separately is to assist in identifying beliefs, attitudes, and values related to the individual elements. Then, by placing the elements in a dynamic context and recognizing the relative influences of one on another, the teacher can begin to formulate philosophy by referring not only to single elements but to their relationships to one another.

When we examine the elements in relation to each other, we recognize a hierarchy of importance. The following statement illustrates this phenomenon: "[One form of teacher-training] rests basically on the assumption that the quality of the teacher-learner relationship is crucial if teachers are to be effective in teaching anything—any kind of subject matter, any 'content,' any skills, any values or beliefs" (Gordon, 1974, p. 5). The role of content, in this view, is secondary to the role of the teacher-student relationship. A teacher might believe that this is true all of the time or only in a specific context.

To investigate how you order the elements, take some 3-by-5-inch file cards and write an element on each one. Arrange the cards in the order that represents the importance of each element. Record the results and put them away. Continue to do this each time you conduct an educational program that varies. Do your results vary with the situation or remain pretty much the same? What do your findings tell you about you?

In the following chapters, we will concentrate on the elements, on their ability to influence the teaching-learning exchange, and on the dynamic nature of the elements' interrelationships. In doing so, we will look for trends in philosophy and behavior as well as for unique situational beliefs and behaviors. Through this process, educators can recognize consistency in decisions and actions across different settings and deep within settings. Contextual characteristics that seem to relate to unusual or unique thinking and behavior can be identified. We believe that this method of self-examination can help you to become a better educator.

Part Two

Reflecting on the
Teaching and Learning Exchange

Chapter Four

Content

W hat makes someone a "good" teacher? Is it the subject? Recall the best teachers you have had, either as a child or an adult. What did they teach? Are you now teaching what they taught? Most likely, the subjects are varied; perhaps the excitement that came from one of these teachers was later undermined by another, lesser teacher.

What led you to become a teacher? Freitag (1991) provides us with this story: "At age 12 I had already become enchanted with mathematics and wrote in my diary, 'I want to become a mathematics teacher.' Shortly afterwards, there was an amendment: 'I have changed my mind. I don't want to become a mathematics teacher, I want to become a *good* mathematics teacher'" (p. 167). In this story, the writer not only hopes to become a good teacher but identifies specifically what will be taught.

Content is inherent in any teaching-learning exchange. This chapter explores what content is, how it is shaped, and how it is related to the exchange in the context of teaching adults. Ultimately, the goal is to achieve that part of "good" in teaching related to the content, whatever it may be.

However, we do not want to place too much emphasis on content, something that is often done in learning settings regardless of age and subject. A danger lurks that content by design can overwhelm teaching and relegate learning to accepting content. Taking our own advice, we share openly our bias about the place we think content should take in the teaching-learning exchange. With that, we can move forward.

Exploring Teaching and Content

The end-product of education is an educated person, not the lesson, the plan, the workshop, the subject, the lecture, the activity, or even the learning (Skilling, 1969). Yet in our teaching settings, teachers are often constrained by the definition of teaching related to content. In formal schooling, the curriculum often defines what outcomes of teaching are desired. In workshops, seminars, or programs, the "learning objectives" of the sponsoring agency often restrict what is to be taught. Even the manner in which student success is measured is often content rather than learning oriented (Queior, 1986). As Hedges (1989) suggests, what teachers really do is teach students a subject, rather than teaching a subject to students.

Content related to teaching and learning can be examined from two divergent perspectives: (1) the requirements of the content on the teaching-learning exchange, and (2) the application of content to a teaching-learning setting. Historically, much of the focus in education and curriculum development has been on the content to be shared. Yet in a taxonomy of forty-eight teacher competencies, only two directly relate to content or the teacher's mastery of the subject (Hedges, 1989). Content is, however, one piece of the teaching-learning exchange, and must be critically considered as one of many pieces.

The Requirements of Content

Most adult educators, trainers, or instructors are involved with a subject that has special meaning to them. At some point in career preparation, each person identifies some subject or content that has personal appeal. Or, perhaps because of proficiency in a certain work area, an individual begins conducting training programs in that area. Whatever the reason, most adult educators enter the profession from a "content" orientation. To use content in the development of individual teaching style, we can isolate it as an element and explore its meaning and the requirements that it brings to the teaching-learning exchange.

The content of the instructional event provides one means by which we can examine the teaching-learning exchange. As will be discussed later, content is not always the purpose of instruction, but it is the basis for the instructional event. Information, or content, is but one of the three reasons Cross (1983) gives for adult learners attending a program, class, training, or workshop.

A teacher is expected, is required, or desires to present certain knowledge, skills, or attitudes to the learner(s). These outcomes comprise the body of "content" that is to be shared, and the content itself shapes much of the learning setting. Content, or what is being taught on the intentional level, may dictate the order of presentation, competencies on the part of the teacher, specific evaluation efforts, practice, equipment, facility arrangement, time required, and other tangible outcomes (Seaman & Fellenz, 1989). In addition, content may sometimes dictate the teaching strategy to be used. To effectively communicate the content to the learner, the teacher considers the type of content and the level of content desired and employs feedback from the learners regarding the mix of content and strategy. This is true whatever method, technique, or strategy is used. Simply changing the method or the strategy of instruction can significantly shift the emphasis of importance related to the content and the learning outcomes.

In the teaching-learning exchange, several types of content operate together. All must be considered by the teacher in planning. There is the scheduled subject matter: the activities and dialogue or communication directly relating to the lesson. But scheduled subject matter is a small part of what is really shared in the teaching-learning exchange. There is also nonscheduled subject matter, the discussion of other subjects or ideas. A third type of "content" is the "sociation" of the exchange—that is, the content of being sociable and following conventions. Finally, there is the content of organization, which relates to administration, organization, or functioning of the group itself (Harmin & Gregory, 1974). Content in the teaching-learning exchange relates to all types and all levels of content that are part of any exchange.

Bloom (1956) suggests that there are various levels of content and that the astute teacher is aware of these levels. The primary level involves the learner's desire to learn and ability to function. The teacher should be able to select and effectively use various strategies based on the student's desired level of learning. Strategies of instruction related to the content can lead to learning at higher levels of cognition or can shift the focus from cognitive learning to affective, psychomotor, or integrated learning.

Several factors influence a teacher's decisions about content. How a teacher decides what will be taught in a course reveals these factors. The educational philosophy of the teacher, the educational philosophy of the organization/institution, the program objectives, the teacher's expertise, available educational facilities and equipment, the community's resources, and the articulation of this course/workshop/program into other learning events are some of these influencers (Newcomb et al., 1986).

Teachers can gather information to help decide content-related matters; some possible sources are "community" surveys, competencies needed (job analysis), input from advisory committees or groups, and curriculum guides containing recommendations by experts. Most of us, however, use the popular technique of intuition and seat-of-the-pants brainstorming. However we make the decision, the content selected will require certain conditions, standards, or approaches to be met.

The Application of Content

A second way of viewing content is through its application. Who are the recipients of the content, and what will they be able to do with the information when they get it? This approach is an attempt to satisfy the two basic conditions Freitag (1991) sets out as prerequisites for teachers: a grasp of the subject matter, and a deep and abiding love of people and of one's discipline.

In this context, content becomes that which is needed by, wanted by, and used by the learner. The arena of meaning-making in education reflects the importance of merging required content with an application of content by the learner. Further, the performance requirements placed upon learners are often arbitrary and unrelated to natural, human learning situations. Outcome measures of learners are often what the teacher wants the learner to have, rather than what the learner needs to be and do in order to learn (Postman & Weingartner, 1969). Rogers (1983) strongly supported the concept of application of content when he suggested that anything that can be taught to another is relatively inconsequential and has little or no significant influence on ultimate behavior. He believes that the only learning that significantly influences behavior is self-discovered, self-appropriated learning. Much of the time of learning is spent on giving learners answers rather than exploring how the questions came to be.

The application of content considers the needs of the teacher, the needs of the subject, the needs of the organization/institution, and the needs of the learner as interrelated concerns that grow from the subject matter. What we teach is the content. However, content does not make a "good" teacher. Suffice it to say that what we teach is not necessarily why we teach it.

At this point in the discussion, what is your definition of *content*? A teacher we know uses the following process for helping adults in her programs "get to the bottom" of their definitions regarding her topics by using right-brain and childhood/recall activities. We've adapted the steps to content. Write down your definition of content. Beneath it, using your nondominant hand, write a paragraph reacting to your own definition of content. After you have finished this, use a *crayon* and print in block letters a list of beliefs you hold about content as a learner. Then, in ink and cursive, write a list of beliefs you hold about content as a teacher. Reflect on this page. What messages are there for you, if any? What is content for you?

Content Versus Purpose

Most teachers agree that content is the body of information being addressed in the teaching-learning exchange. Content is the focus of the exchange upon which objectives are based and learners are assessed. Synonyms abound for *content* and include *body of knowledge, curriculum, subject, subject matter, theme, course of study, facts,* and *data,* to name a few. In teaching, the content is usually well defined, using standardized parameters. It is assumed to be the major, necessary, *and* sufficient reason for the teaching-learning exchange.

So why do we teach? What is the purpose of instruction if not to impart content to the learners? Various purposes of adult education have been suggested. Jersild (1955) thought that perhaps the purpose was to assist the individual in growth and to aid each learner in knowing self and in accepting self. Others have suggested that the purpose of adult education is to impart knowledge, help students meet new situations as they arise, prepare students to make long-term decisions (maturity, independence, creativity, judgment), foster critical thinking, provide training/education to foster vocational success, help the student to discover a personal value system, improve the student's standard of living, or produce motivation to change and continue education (see, for example, Skilling, 1969; Mueller, 1940; Sizer, 1973). Of course, the recognition of individuality and the nurturance of empowerment of the individual are guiding principles for many adult educators and speak to the purpose of education versus the content (Hitt, 1973; Queior, 1986).

Whatever personal reasons held, the purpose of instruction is not always part and parcel of the content of the instructional exchange. The content is a necessary and ofttimes driving factor of the purpose, but the purpose goes far beyond what is taught into why it is taught. Why teach this? Why teach at all? What do I believe is the relationship of content to teaching, learning, and the whole exchange? One way of getting at your own beliefs regarding the purpose of instruction would be to answer these questions:

- If I could only accomplish one goal with my (typical learners), it would be . . . .
- The only goals(s) for which I would sacrifice content would be . . . .
- The way I see content fitting into the purpose of education is . . . .

- If I were to rank content and (the task of addressing it) as a goal of education, it would be . . . .
- The educational organization for which I work (used to work, will work for someday) would say that content is . . . in terms of importance.
- (Un)fortunately, I agree/disagree with this organizational philosophy because . . . .

How adult educators answer these questions reveals how they view content in relation to the purpose of instruction.

Considering Content in the Teaching-Learning Exchange

Given that most of us came through formal educational systems in which content was the centerpiece of education, it is somewhat difficult to consider that content is in constant interaction with the other elements of the instructional exchange and not the requisite centerpiece of a teacher's belief system on teaching. This orientation is heightened by the current movement in pedagogical education to focus on content through standardized measures.

As we explore how the other elements interact with content, a concept to keep in mind is that of education as related to function versus education as related to process (Magendzo, 1990). Education *as a function* centers on technical efficiency with measurable outcomes. The meeting of outcomes expected of learners is held as more important than other real effects of teaching-learning. Education as a function, then, refers to the inculturation aspects of teaching-learning as well as the structure of educational events around "learning objectives" established by the teacher, the institution, or another body.

In contrast, education *as a process* looks toward the wider, further-reaching possibilities of learning and the ultimate effect of teaching on the individual and the community. Education as a process is participatory throughout the development of the exchange. In education as a process, learning is the purpose of instruction: learning to learn, learning to solve problems, learning to analyze critically, learning to think. Even though many teachers will subscribe to the value of education as a process, they rely on content-centered instructional activities because of a lack of experiential models. We must stress, however, that teaching as a process includes content and relies on content as a means in the process.

Content is more than what is imposed upon the learner. Content relates to the individual learner in many ways. For learning to be maximized, it is critical that the teacher respect the relative value of content to each learner. This relates directly to the assumption Knowles (1970) presents regarding adult learners as seeking knowledge, information, or experiences that will fulfill societal expectations. The content must be relevant to the learner not only in substance but also in presentation format. How information is presented directly relates to the ability of various learners to transfer "knowledge" from one situation to another; transfer skills are widely inconsistent among learners. The needs of the individual learner coupled with the expectations of that learner constrain the depth and level of content the learner desires and is able to assimilate. This concept is illustrated nicely in a Far Side cartoon by Gary Larson in which a student says, "May I be excused? My brain is full." The learner is not always where we expect the learner to be, in relation to content.

The teacher-learner dyad related to content is further complicated by the introduction of the group. The complexity of the individuals' varying relationships to the content is striking. How many groups has any educator led in which a learner who is excited and committed is sitting directly in front of a learner who is there for who knows what reason? Adding to this complexity is the relationship of the group to the history of its involvement with the topic. Attitudes of the group toward content are formed in three ways: through past involvement with the content; from past history with a similar content; or from what others say about the content or similar content (Van Tilburg [Norland] & Heimlich, 1987). In adult education settings, it is often the content that initially draws individuals into a program, but the group created by these individuals will have a different relationship to the content than will any of the individuals who comprise the group.

Content and the environment have a symbiotic relationship.

The physical and affective environments can enhance the content, work against the content, or be neutral in relationship to the content being presented. In many disciplines, the environment and the content are often considered to be so related as to be inseparable. For example, imagine technical skill-building training not conducted by a simulation or field experience, or a piano lesson conducted outdoors without a piano, or a fine arts program such as pottery throwing taught in a theater lecture hall. Of course, any of these classes could be conducted in these unlikely places—and perhaps be more effective for some learners than in the more traditional settings—but these examples highlight the relationship that occurs between content and environment.

Further, content can be made more or less significant by its relationship to the environment. The affective quality of the physical space can heighten or diminish the emotive reactions of the learners to the content. If a group of adults is returning to school for a business math literacy course, math anxiety can be heightened by the appearance of a "classroom" reminiscent of the past. Anxiety might be lowered if the same content were presented in a lounge area with a chalkboard on rollers or in the company's boardroom. Content has a fascinating relationship with the environment on a psychological level.

Content can also dictate some aspects of the adaptable physical environment. Equipment, tools, space, activities, and other resources may be necessary to communicate the content most effectively. These demands of content are placed upon the environment and acted upon by the educator who adapts the physical space.

The educator's relationship to content is polarized by the age-old conflict found in many adult education organizations: does the organization want generalists who are expert teachers, or experts who will teach? One does not necessarily exclude the other. When faced with a challenge of unfamiliar content, teachers often seek immersion in the content in order to feel "prepared." In this manner, we have all been inculturated into the orientation of content without the benefit of applying personal beliefs to the relationship of content and other elements.

This does not have to be the case. Take the example of a consultant who is asked to conduct a daylong workshop on a topic with which she is unfamiliar. For some reason—the payment of a favor or the need for a day's work—the consultant accepts. As the day of workshop approaches, the consultant begins to realize there is no way to gain even a basic understanding of the content before the day arrives. What to do?

This is a perfect example of when a solidly thought-out process can overcome weak content. Why not structure a day full of brainstorming, discussions, prioritizing, and decision making around the topic? The group pools its knowledge. Experts within the group gain a chance to share their successes. Novices have a chance to ask basic questions. In one case where this technique was used in a not-for-profit board retreat, participants tried complimenting the facilitator at the end of the day on his expertise, and more than one doubted his protestations that everything he knew about the subject he had learned from them that day. The moral? We cannot always facilitate learning when we don't know the content, but there are many times we could—if we would concentrate on process content rather than task or functional content.

The relationship of the teacher to the content is, like all other elements of the teaching-learning exchange, on a dimension. Just as all other elements are vital, so too is content; not all educators consider content equally in initial considerations for teaching preparation, nor should they. The comfort of the teacher given the degree of content familiarity is one part of the relationship between content and teacher. A second piece of the picture relates to how the teacher uses the content: is the teaching exchange driven by the content, molded by the content, or structured with content "inserted" as appropriate? These varied views of content represent degrees of individual beliefs and behaviors, with everything ranging between. We use an activity with adult educators in extended workshops to help visualize the way they view content and its relationship to the other elements: we build models. Using any medium (we usually use found junk), the participants create two models visually relating content to the other elements of instruction. On the first model, they place content in the center. In the second model, content is placed in a spatial relationship to the other elements as the individual believes it to be. We ask participants to be cognizant of colors, materials, shapes, textures, and mass of the elements of the models. The elements of instruction are minimally labeled on each model. The individuals then show the models to three other people, one at a time. These people explain to the participant what the models mean to them. The participant reflects on how similar or different the three responses were. Just as in creating the models, people interpret models from their own bias regarding personal beliefs about content and the other elements.

This process of visually exposing how each participant places content in relationship to the other elements and then seeing other models and receiving feedback on one's own is a powerful process of exposing beliefs about teaching-learning and content. Knowing deeply held beliefs is necessary; when we can challenge our beliefs about content, we can begin to act accordingly rather than react with others' models of instruction.

Congruence Between Content and Teacher Behavior

Even educators who strongly believe in process education teach with a content base. In some cases, the process itself is their content. Education and psychology are inextricably linked: process as content is the psychology of learning, group dynamics, group process, decision making, problem solving, and therapeutic processes. Given this assumption, we can make a gross generalization that all teachers teach with content by viewing *process* and *task* as behaviors related to "giving content."

However, not all teachers use content in the same manner. Beyond methods of instruction, this difference is indicative of individual beliefs held by each teacher related to content and its role in the teaching-learning setting. How this plays out is related to educators' personal awareness of their own beliefs and use of content. Socially, the educational system is being driven toward increasing emphasis on both content and life skills such as problem solving, decision making, and critical thinking. Even teacher education programs in universities tend to be in a reformist mode, with preference given to content competencies in increasingly varied and alternative ways (for example, fifth-year education degrees and professional education certification programs). This trend does not mean that teachers must all perform with the same level of content expertise but does suggest that all teachers must be cognizant of the role of content in the exchange.

Many of the taxonomies of teaching style discussed earlier place content on a continuum of "subject centered" to "people centered." Content is usually relegated to the lower score, the left column or some other position that suggests that a teacher moves from content to human orientation. The question that arises is, why can they not exist concurrently within each educator? As with each of the elements, they do exist within each educator; but there is an orientation or starting point from which the approach to the teaching-learning exchange will be developed. We can consider the elements of instruction to be a single dimension in which "content" anchors the nonhuman side of the dimension and "individual" anchors the human side of the line. All teachers will fall somewhere on this line in both initial orientation and behavior. Content is what is shifted in the learning process. Whether an educator believes that all knowledge is contained in the learners already or that learners are empty vessels, content is the "stuff" around which outcomes are constructed. Content is in essence what is transported in the teaching-learning exchange, either from subconsciousness to consciousness or from the unknown to the known. The information transfer is measured by content: skills, attitudes, aspirations, knowledge.

Educators with a content orientation will initially ask questions that begin with "what." What am I to teach? What learning will occur? What is the subject that draws these participants together? What are the learning objectives of the participants? These "what" questions indicate an orientation that initially begins with a focus on the nonhuman piece of the information transfer. This is not better or worse than an initial orientation on the human side of the process. It simply is.

All educators must, at some early point in the preparation/planning process, identify content. How much to share, as well as the basic what to share, is a question we all ask. If content orientation is not a value-laden position, then we can fully explore our own beliefs around content and its role in our teaching-learning exchanges.

There was a catch in the sentence above—and that was the introduction of the concept that content centeredness may be value laden. Ask educators with whom you work "which is better, to be content centered or to be learner centered?" What types of responses do you get? An unspoken bias against content orientation often surfaces, and any bias can tend to block awareness of individual beliefs. The filter of prejudice is not limited to social issues; it is also a part of how we view ourselves.

How do you consider content in teaching-learning? One way to examine this is to look at your behavior in relationship to how content is used in your teaching sessions. Many educators claim to be constrained by time and therefore resort to content presentation (through directive and/or presentational methods) for many instructional episodes. Yet how often can behavior be content oriented before we suspect that the real belief of the educator is more toward the content than toward the human end of the teaching elements dimension?

In a study conducted to measure adult educators' beliefs about their teaching and give an estimate of "style," there was a continually surprising, singular phenomenon. Many educators, after completing the questionnaire, commented on how difficult it was to answer certain questions. The questions that troubled them were all addressed to the researchers as "I really believe this and I try to do it this way, but most of the time I can't" or "Do you want what I do or what I believe?"

Our theory? These are educators who have behaviors that don't match their beliefs. They think they should believe certain things regarding what is more important, content or learner, but they realize they don't believe what they think they *should* believe. That is the ultimate in no-win situations.

It is important for all teachers to reexamine biases regarding content. We all teach content, we are all experts in some content areas, and we all use content as a "draw" for participants in our programs. Only when we have removed the value-based concepts around content from our examination are we able to clearly explore the importance we place on content in the teaching-learning exchange and then begin to integrate content with the other elements.

If possible, find the notes/materials/handouts/texts from a workshop, training program, or course you took several years ago. Thumb through the materials. Are these materials the "content" of the class? All the content? Some of the content? Are there things you believed were important at the time of the program that you have since forgotten or don't care about? Are there specific bits of information that you have held with you over the years? Would the "content" of the program have held meaning for you if you had not been involved in a teaching-learning exchange? What might this suggest about content as an element?

The first step in determining our beliefs regarding content is to critically analyze what questions we ask when first considering a program. Do we focus on who or what? The manner in which the educator frames the first few questions is a tremendous indicator of the relative importance content holds for that teacher. How many of the other elements are considered before asking about the content? Is the initial thought on what is to be taught or learned?

Once the orientation toward content is identified, it is possible to construct the teaching-learning exchange through an exploration of content and its requirements and relationships to each of the four other elements. It is the relationship between content and the learner or group that allows for meaningful learning. The meaning is heightened or lessened through the interplay of content and the environment. It is through the relationship between the teacher and the content that what is to be learned is revealed.

We give importance to content when we view instruction from a need-to-know point of view. We may ask ourselves what the learners need to know regarding this subject, or what we believe they need to know.

These questions arise in all teaching-learning settings; the difference is the sequence in which they occur or how early in consideration of the teaching event these questions arise. We cannot teach without content, and content can be a logical point from which to begin exploring the teaching-learning exchange. Whatever the content we teach, it is in part how we use content that makes us not teachers, but *good* teachers.

A Note from the Authors

This chapter was very therapeutic to write. It was difficult because we have our own biases regarding the relative importance of content in teaching. But what we gained from it is surprising.

Even though we have spent years together discussing, arguing about, laughing about, and challenging the concepts of instruction, we hold many deep-rooted biases. It is extremely difficult to attempt an honest presentation of concepts when there is an inherent dishonesty underlying the premise. In fact some people might call us "anti-content-orientation" snobs—even though we are both content experts in different fields and are called upon continually to present content. Writing this chapter has given us a valuable new perspective. Although neither of us is content centered, we both work with colleagues who are. It is easier to respect their teaching-learning decisions now than it has been in the past.

Chapter Five

Environment

What surrounds us is what we call our environment. But how we respond to and act within our environment is not limited to an aesthetic appreciation of our surroundings. Remember Charles Dickens's *A Christmas Carol*? Here's one description of the Cratchit family: "They were not a handsome family; they were not well dressed; their shoes were far from being water-proof; their clothes were scanty. . . . But, they were happy, grateful, pleased with one another, and contented with the time; and . . . Scrooge had his eye upon them, and especially on Tiny Tim, until the last."

How would you describe the Cratchits' environment in Charles Dickens's classic tale of Scrooge? Does your description consist of just the physical environment? It would be easy to describe the environment as poverty-stricken, and that description would be partially correct. This passage, however, gives us a clue to another component of the Cratchits' environment, how they feel about it, or put another way, their affective environment. If the Cratchits' shoes cannot keep their feet warm and dry and their clothing is "scanty" in the middle of a cold, damp London winter, why do they feel "happy, grateful, pleased with one another, and contented with the time" emotionally?

An individual's affective environment can be and usually is closely related to the physical environment, but as Tiny Tim and the rest of the Cratchit family experienced, the introduction of an additional stimulus (in this case, the close family) can intervene in that relationship. Awareness of the family's love and support gives family members additional cognitive information with which to interpret the physical environment. Even though the larger physical environment was negative, the Cratchits' affective environment (based on their cognitive interpretation of it) was just the opposite because the family was there to help them interpret that physical environment.

In the teaching-learning exchange, the purpose of the physical environment is to assist in the creation of a positive affective environment (Long, 1983), thus enhancing the quality of the total learning experience. This affective environment or psychological atmosphere in which the group works (Bany & Johnson, 1964) can be manipulated not only by rearranging the physical elements but by introducing additional stimuli to help with an individual's interpretation of the elements. Often that additional stimulus is another human being.

Teacher behavior is probably one of the most effective environmental interpreters, having the potential to enhance or destroy the environment for learning at the drop of a hat. "The learning environment can be a powerful teaching instrument at the disposal [for interpretation] of the teacher, or it can be an undirected and unrecognized influence on the behaviors of both teachers and [learners]" (Fraser, Anderson, & Walberg, 1982, p. 5). This is nothing new. For decades, research has correlated the "classroom climate" with student behavior, teacher behavior, and accomplishment (as in Lewin, Lippitt, & White, 1939; deGroat & Thompson, 1949; Flanders, 1951; Malehorn, 1984).

For many years, environment has been thought to be one of the fundamental pieces to the puzzle of understanding human behavior and, more specifically for this discussion, learning setting behavior (Haertel & Walberg, 1988). Learner interest, willingness to participate, and performance, all behaviors that point to "learning," are related to environment. The physical and affective constructs of environment have, as a base, the physiological grounding of physical reactions of the nervous system reacting to the stimuli called the environment (Strecker & Appel, 1962). The logical sequence, with learning as the end-product, goes something like this: the teacher acts out of an integrated vision (of the role of environment and the other four elements in the teaching-learning exchange) to help learners interpret their physical environment, so as to help create a positive affective environment in each learner, which should lead to a higher probability of learning for each learner.

Our goal as teachers is to use all elements of the teaching-learning exchange in a congruent way to maximize the opportunity for learning. The best way for a teacher to approach the elements is by matching behavior to philosophy (or vice versa). Thoughts about and behaviors related to environment are a critical point of congruence for a teacher.

Much as the Cratchits were "happy, grateful . . . and contented with the time" in their environment because of their close family ties, students can cognitively interpret their physical environments to create a more positive affective environment, and the teacher can play an extremely important role in helping them do it. We can be most successful in assisting in that interpretation if we know what we believe and value about environment and if we align our behavior with those beliefs and values. This chapter can be helpful in working toward such alignment through the understanding and answering of four questions related to environment:

1. How do I define environment and understand its relationship and interaction with the teacher, the student, the group, and the content?
2. What do I believe, value, and feel about environment—what is my philosophy?
3. How does my behavior support or refute that philosophy?
4. Finally, what can I do to make my behavior and my philosophy more congruent?

Defining Environment

When you think of a *pleasant* environment, what comes to mind? Here's one description: "There would be comfortable, overstuffed chairs, the smell of baking bread, the warmth of a wood fire, soft flowing music, and perhaps quiet laughter." Notice how this description creates a fairly complete picture using information from several senses: sight, sound, smell, and even touch.

We say "fairly complete" because that description attaches a particular affective dimension to the scene—remember, the request was for a *pleasant* environment. Such pleasantness is not overtly stated but is implicit, assumed. Someone else's affective environment may be entirely different from the one implicitly attached to the above description.

- "Overstuffed chairs aggravate my allergies!" (discomfort)
- "I'm on a diet—the smell of baking bread makes me hungry!" (frustration)
- "My house burned three months ago—fires scare me to death!" (fear)
- "Soft music reminds me of a funeral!" (depression)
- "Quiet laughter always makes me think someone is laughing at me behind my back!" (insecurity)

What happened? The description included only the physical environment. What it lacked was a cognitive interpretation of that physical environment and an emotional reaction to it.

Any complete definition of environment needs to convey physical aspects of the environment *and* an individual's affective reaction to it based on cognitive interpretations of those aspects. In addition, we need to value the interrelationships of the elements with the environment. Consider the "ripple" effect of a harsh, curt, or disciplinary remark directed toward one participant on all the learners (Kounin, 1970). One action on one element can change the balance of all of them.

The leaders of a six-week class for crisis hotline volunteers found this out firsthand. One of the participants told the leaders before the class began that because of a conflict, he would have to leave a few minutes early. No problem. Class went smoothly, with both leaders and group members engrossed in a series of activities. In the midst of processing one activity as a lead-in to the final activity, three group members prepared to leave. It was thirty minutes before the end of class. Without thinking, one of the leaders asked one of the participants, a friend, "Where are you going?" As soon as it was asked, the leaders knew the answer. All three participants rode in the same car as the one who approached the leaders before class. But the mood in the room significantly changed. When the leaders returned to the activity, the volunteers were much quieter and harder to "draw out." The final activity, though effective, was done with less than full enthusiasm.

What was going on? The leaders and class discussed this in their next session. The discussion took more than an hour. The leaders' points of view were based on two factors: (1) the earliness with which the group members left—half an hour was not a few minutes, and (2) the surprise at seeing three leave when they were prepared for only one to go. On the other hand, group members perceived the leaders' reactions as threatening. The situation reminded them of school. Because group members had attended out of their own free will, they were surprised that the leaders even reacted to someone leaving early. The bottom line? The perceived environment varies from individual to individual, and everything we do as teachers has an impact on this affective environment.

Many educators have offered a holistic concept of environment, though each may have contributed slightly different descriptions of the pieces that make up the whole (Hiemstra and Sisco, 1990). Fraser (1986) lists four distinct aspects to environment: (1) ecology, the physical and material aspects; (2) milieu, the social dimension concerned with the presence of persons or groups; (3) social system, the social dimension concerned with the patterned relationships of persons and groups; and (4) culture, the social dimension concerned with belief systems, values, cognitive structures, and meaning. Regardless of how the various aspects of environment are categorized, the issue is what the environment encompasses and how a teacher perceives its importance.

For the purpose of simplicity and utility in discussion, let us use the following concept of environment: (1) the physical environment, (2) an individual's cognitive interpretation of it, and (3) the affective reactions to those cognitions that create the individual's affective environment.

In this view, *environment* is an individual concept held by each individual learner and teacher. This definition allows room for the teacher to manipulate the learning environment only by assisting with individual cognitive interpretations of the physical environment.

Included in the physical environment are all elements that can be perceived by one of the five senses: sight, hearing, taste, touch, and smell. Examples are furnishings, odor, other people, color, temperature, hardness of chairs, sounds, *and* the teacher.

The affective component includes an individual's feelings and emotions, not toward the physical environment but toward that individual's cognitive interpretations of the physical environment. Remember that cognitive interpretations are perceptions of reality, not reality itself. These cognitions may include accurate perceptions but more likely will include inaccurate ones in addition to, or instead of, reality. These interpretations will focus not only on single elements in the physical environment but on complex interactions as well.

Here is an illustration. Given the physical description of the "pleasant environment" above, one cognitive interpretation could include thoughts like: overstuffed chairs remind me of my den at home; baking bread means there is someone cooking; wood fires smell like the out-of-doors and autumn; soft music is the kind that my parents liked to listen to; quiet laughter means the people who are together must be good friends.

Notice how each cognitive interpretation is value- or emotion-free and relates to only one specific element. We could speculate about the affective environment created by these interpretations. We could also imagine how an individual might combine the individual elements in a complex picture, with elements interacting in a dependent or causal relationship based on previous experiences, emotions, and a wealth of other factors. We would probably be at variance with each other in our speculations and imaginings as well as with the holder of those cognitions.

For simplicity's sake, we can conceptualize environment as

physical elements and individual affect, with cognitions being an important link between the two. Here is a definition of *environment* specific to the teaching-learning exchange. Environment is one of the five elements in the teaching-learning exchange. It comprises two major domains: the physical and affective. The physical domain includes anything that can be perceived by one of the five senses and can be described objectively. The affective domain includes individual reactions to the cognitive interpretation of the elements and their interaction and varies from individual to individual.

The Physical Environment

B. F. Skinner spoke about physical environment in this way: "I spent a lot of time creating the environment where I work. I believe people should design a world where they will be as happy as possible" (Gross, 1991, p. 169). If you are like Skinner, the first questions you might ask when given a teaching assignment might be: "Where is the class going to be?" "What does the room look like?" "Are the chairs movable?" "Is there air conditioning?" "And, oh, yes . . . who are the students?" If this questioning route sounds familiar, be advised that physical environment may be an important component of learning environment for you as a teacher. You may depend on and use the physical environment in your teaching to a great extent. Whether you do or not, each learner will perceive and use the physical aspects of the environment differently. To be able to deal with all the different learner interpretations, perceptions, and reactions most effectively, you can address the physical environment in a manner that best reflects your teaching philosophy.

Hiemstra and Sisco (1990, p. 245) collected phrases for physical environment, including: "the ecology of study areas" (Sommer, 1970); the sum total of "physical comfort, climate setting, and classroom arrangements" (Knowles, 1980); and "arranging facilities, equipment, and materials for adult instruction purposes" (Knox, 1986).

The physical environment also includes what some authors have called the social context: the presence and interaction of human beings as a part of the physical environment. A learning community

(Brookfield, 1990) is a good example of the presence and interaction of human beings as a part of the physical environment.

Two elements of the physical learning environment, as it has been traditionally viewed, are the architectural facility and the arranged environment (Loughlin & Suina, 1982). They interact to strengthen or weaken support for learning. Even when the architectural facility is lacking in desired characteristics, the arranged environment can compensate to a certain extent. The teacher is the one to assess the architectural facility and then make decisions regarding the arranged environment.

The architectural facility establishes the space, organizes access to external space and resources, and determines basic conditions of light, sound, temperature, intrusion, color, texture, and hardness or softness. It is one aspect of physical environment over which most educators have virtually no control. To realize our own preferences and limitations related to this aspect can help us adjust when we do not have control and help us make good decisions when we do. But just because the setting is imposed does not mean teachers are "stuck." Well over half a century ago, Stormzand and McKee (1928) lamented that teachers and administrators accept the structure of public schools as "givens." Further, they bemoaned those who "blindly continued following [the formality imposed by the buildings] at its traditional worst, when much could have been done to mitigate the unnatural, formal ways of school management and instruction" (pp. 4–5).

What we can do is adjust the physical environment by addressing the second aspect, "the arranged environment." The arranged environment is composed of the active and responsive elements arranged by the teacher within the spaces provided by the architectural facility. To be more specific, "A conceptual view of the arranged environment is a much larger and at the same time a more basic concept [than arrangement of furniture and resources]. It rests upon understandings of relationships between physical settings and behavior, between environmental arrangements and learning. Common principles can be derived from this knowledge, and they can be used to establish arranged environments harmonious with program purposes and [teacher] styles in many different settings" (Loughlin & Suina, 1982, p. 4). Hiemstra and Sisco (1990) suggest the following as helps for creating a positive physical learning environment: (1) proper room arrangement—comfortable, appropriate for adults, limits distractions, takes into account special physical needs enhancing participation; (2) monitoring the physical environment—temperature, air flow, lighting, distracting noise; and (3) monitoring personal comfort of individual learners—refreshment breaks, lavatory breaks, smoking areas.

We have all addressed specific weaknesses of an architectural facility by manipulating the arranged environment. This is where all the "how to's" of room arrangement, color theory, lighting design, visual utilization, and the like come into play. Even the simple act of closing a door to a classroom can create intimacy, shut out noise and other interference, warm up or cool down the temperature, help to relax a tense situation, indicate cohesiveness, or indicate the beginning or ending of a situation.

However, both the architectural and the arranged environments are external to the individuals using the space. Whereas some teachers might close a door to produce any of the above affective measures, other teachers may not even realize whether the door is open, closed, or off its hinges. Again, the bottom line here is that you know how important the physical environment is to you, understand how you can use it if you so desire, and make environmental decisions congruent with your other teaching decisions and your teaching philosophy.

Cognitive Interpretations and the Affective Environment

An excellent illustration of cognitive interpretations of the physical environment and the link to the individual affective environment is the work done by Moos (1974, 1975, 1976, 1979). Moos suggested three general categories of dimensions related to environment based on studies of classroom environments and also university residences, hospital wards, community-based treatment settings, juvenile and adult correctional facilities, military companies, families, social and therapeutic groups, and work milieus. He listed the physical environmental characteristics, focusing on human interaction first and then associated affective characteristics and some related behaviors based on cognitive interpretations.

Relationship, the first dimension, is described as "the nature and intensity of personal relationships within the environment, the extent to which people are involved in the environment and support/help each other" (Fraser, 1986, p. 16). The associated affective characteristics and accompanying behaviors include cohesiveness, friction, favoritism, cliquishness, satisfaction, apathy, involvement, affiliation, support, personalization, and participation.

The second dimension, personal development, is described as the conditions in which personal growth and self-enhancement occur. Associated cognitive interpretations and thus affective environmental characteristics include speed, difficulty, competitiveness, task orientation, independence, investigation.

The system maintenance/change dimension, described as "the extent to which the environment is orderly, clear in expectations, maintains control and is responsive to change" (Fraser, 1986, p. 16), is related to such cognitive interpretations and affective environment characteristics as diversity, formality, material environment, goal direction, disorganization, democracy, order, rule clarity, teacher control, innovation, differentiation, and individualization.

A wide variety of instruments are available for assessing the teaching-learning environment. Here is a list compiled by Haertel and Walberg (1988, p. 52):

- LEI (Learning Environment Inventory) (Fraser, Anderson, and Walberg, 1982)
- CES (Classroom Environment Scale) (Moos and Trickett, 1987)
- ICEQ (Individualized Classroom Environment Questionnaire) (Fraser, 1985)
- MCI (My Class Inventory) (Fraser, Anderson, and Walberg, 1982)
- CUCEI (College and University Classroom Environment Inventory) (Fraser, Trengust, and Dennis, 1984)

Because the teacher has the potential to enhance or destroy the environment for learning in many major and minor ways, teacher behavior is one of the most effective environmental interpreters. There are many intrapersonal, interpersonal, and institutional messages that are intended or not intended, extended or not extended, received or not received, acted upon or not acted upon. The understanding or lack thereof contributes to educational environments that are anchored in attitudes of respect, care, and civility, and that promote positive relationships and encourage human potential (Purkey & Novak, 1984). Bany and Johnson (1964) suggest that because of training and background, some teachers believe that learning takes place when the room is quiet and still, some equate good learning behavior with immediate compliance with the teacher's requests and demands, and others equate good behavior with an eagerness to learn, questions and discussion, and concentration on the tasks at hand.

In arranging and rearranging the physical environment, the teacher arranges and rearranges the affective environment as well. Some might even suggest that the teacher *is* the environment. But as Richards (1980) suggests, "One should not mistake the finger pointing for the moon. Teachers are like fingers pointing. The TEACHER is what they are pointing toward. . . . The TEACHER is the wholeness in which we participate" (pp. 170, 178).

Teachers, then, can be the environment or at the very least serve to help interpret it. The environment is created not by what teachers do but by the way in which they do it and by their underlying attitude toward the individual (Bany & Johnson, 1964). We can use the physical environment, to the extent appropriate for our personal teaching style, to establish and interpret the affective environment.

Reflecting on the Environment

Close your eyes for a moment and imagine what you might hear, see, smell, and feel in a setting that reminded you of your early school days. What images come to mind?

Perhaps you see images of your own Mrs. Surenough in a trying first-grade year, or Mrs. Flutehammer and a very difficult fourth-grade year. Or Mrs. Good (really, that was her name) and the wonderful sense of creativity she brought out in each of her overly eager fifth graders. Whatever the memory, the physical environment created, or rather re-created, the psychological environment for each of us. How powerful are sights, sounds, and smells for any student, not only to bring memories to mind but to carry along with them the feelings attached to those memories!

The power of these images became evident during an extended workshop on teaching style. In one session, the group took a field trip to see firsthand different physical environments in which adult education occurred. One site was an old high school that had been closed for a number of years before reopening as an adult education center. The building was a classic: oversized doors, undersized lockers, beautiful architecture inside and out, hallways that echoed with the slightest noise, and wonderful pea-green walls that housed the many glass trophy cases crowded with memorabilia from the early 1900s.

Class members and leaders alike were startled at the strength of their feelings when they entered the strange yet familiar building. Even more amazing were the thoughts and physical reactions they experienced when they gathered in the classroom they were to use for the morning. The room was just as many had remembered from their youth: small tables and chairs, dusty blackboards, bulletin boards with maps of the world, posters of kittens and puppies with cute sayings on them, scuffed 1950 linoleum floors, a large wooden teacher's desk complete with books, pencil holder, and a bouquet of flowers, and various types of plants growing on the window sills in tin cans and milk cartons. Déjà vu! They were all back in school! And it was the physical environment that took them there.

When thinking about the physical environment of the teaching-learning setting, keep in mind these principles:

- The physical environment has the potential to affect the teaching-learning exchange through its effects on the psychological environment. However, those effects come from individual perception, not actual physical layout.
- Environment is individual perception. "Environmental influences affect each person in an individual manner even when the ways of life appear uniform in a standardized environment . . . . Each one of us lives, as it were, in a private world of [our] own" (Dubos, 1968, p. 41). This suggests that even though our phys-

ical environment may be the same, the psychological environment created from the physical is quite individual.

• All teachers choose consciously or subconsciously to use a combination of their own behavior and the elements of the physical
environment to help establish the affective environment.

Toward one end of a continuum, teachers can establish an
affective environment through their own conscious actions (regardless of, and possibly ignoring, the characteristics of the physical
environment). Toward the other end of that continuum, teachers
can pay minimal or no attention to affective environment, allowing
each learner to create and interpret his or her own psychological environment through perception, understanding, and meaning of the
physical elements present.

The extent to which a teacher uses the physical environment
to enhance the teaching-learning exchange indicates the extent to
which a teacher is environment centered. The teacher who is environment centered will intensively utilize the elements of the physical environment by concentrating on such things as the design of
furnishings (anthropometry), design of space (ergonomics), use of
space as culture (proxemics), and stimulation of senses by physical
elements (synaesthetics). A teacher who focuses on the physical environment believes that environmental features such as flexibility,
attractiveness, and comfort are important in optimizing learning
(Hiemstra & Sisco, 1990).

Some of the things that teachers believe about their environment are reflected in their beliefs about the needs of the learners
within the physical space. Health, comfort, interest, roomy working
space, accessibility, and function are all questions that are answered
by beliefs about learner needs (Stormzand & McKee, 1928). Further,
the affective space that teachers create reflects their individual values
of trust, respect, and challenge (Malehorn, 1984) and how they use
these values in the teaching-learning exchange. Even realizing that
the physical environment may not be able to be changed radically,
a teacher can still understand the physical environment and how he
or she individually can affect it in positive ways (Hiemstra & Sisco,
1990).

Philosophy and Behavior

To help discover and enhance your teaching style, pause for a while to reflect upon environment and the behaviors you use related to the environment. To do this, identify the extent to which you focus on the environment, and the way you use the environment in the teaching-learning exchange.

Perhaps the most effective way to apply these ideas to action is by visualizing various physical environments that create specific psychological environments. Picture the most inviting environment you can. What would it look like? Smell like? Sound like? You don't need to picture an environment related to teaching or learning, just any one that fits for you. How about the most comfortable environment? Can you imagine an environment in which you would feel threatened? or nervous? How about confident? What would that environment be like?

Continue creating environments in your mind (or in pictures or writing) that would fit the following words: *bored, creative, stimulated, motivated, involved, empowered, joyful.*

Holding these images in mind, begin to put them together in one picture. What is your relationship to the environment in which you place yourself? Further, how do you behave within the physical space that contains your instructional activity?

How the individual teacher acts within the physical environment helps guide the learner's affective reaction to it. To pretend that learners are not affected by the physical environment to varying degrees and in varied ways is to ignore the element of the environment in the teaching-learning exchange.

Consider: how does the environment interact with each of the other elements? Picture a control room training program with no simulation, or a music theory class with no piano. Content often demands that we arrange the environment to suit its needs. Picture an auditorium with hundreds of seats in fixed theater seating being used by a class of ten, or a room designed for thirty seating more than fifty participants. The group places demands on the environment. Along with the preceding discussions of the teacher and the student, these examples show clearly that each and all of the elements do relate to the physical environment.

As a teacher, how do you act within a given environment? And how do you *react* to the same environment? Your own affective and behavioral responses demonstrate your behavior related to the environment. Do you accept the environment as it is given? Do you ignore it? Adapt it? *Use* it?

Teachers manipulate the environment in the teaching-learning exchange in many ways. Each teacher can critically examine personal behaviors in the setting and ask, "Am I aware of where I am and all that it means?" Recognizing how teaching behavior relates with the environment, a teacher gains more control over both.

Congruence Between Environment and Teacher Behavior

Complete the following sentence: "I absolutely could not teach without. . . ." What are your "must haves" for teaching? Does your list include clocks, markers, chalk, paper, name tags, pencils/pens, paper clips, tape, scissors, flip chart, tape recorder, blank tapes, portable overhead projector, slide projector, poster pads, portable PA system, Post-it notes, whatever you need to function in a teaching situation? What about aesthetic requirements such as a favorite piece of clothing (hat, smock), coffee cup, poetry, personal items to share with the group, music, comfortable shoes, snacks?

Each of us operates by personal rules of thumb about the physical environment needed for a successful teaching-learning exchange. These rules of thumb, when made explicit, are full of value-laden words such as *safe, comfortable,* and *clean.* These rules also include the physical demands we each place on our teaching space: equipment needs, visuals used, movement, lighting, sound—all our expectations of the physical reality. The ultimate question of congruence is, "Do I create, adapt, and use the environment of the teaching-learning exchange so that it supports my values and beliefs?"

As we examine what we each identify as our rules of thumb, an interesting issue arises. Some of the values we hold about the environment may appear to be in conflict. We want the environment to be, say, exciting, but we also value a relaxed atmosphere.

Or we may say we desire a reflective and at the same time directed environment. So are our values incongruous before we start?

Common physical, emotional, and psychological themes underlying our rules of thumb may reveal a deeper unity of our core beliefs about the environment in the teaching-learning exchange. What are the sensory stimuli of each of the rules? What are the psychological values under each assumption? What physical consistencies underlie all the apparent conflicts?

As you examine the underlying elements you identify, ask yourself: To what extent can I achieve this effect: (1) with the help of the physical environment? (2) in spite of the given physical environment? In other words, does the psychological environment really rely on physical elements, or can you create the same psychological environment in spite of the physical environment? Your answer represents the extent to which you focus on environment.

Often we must act in spite of the physical environment. So, given less-than-desirable physical environments, you can still be an effective teacher and be congruent in your teaching style by focusing on and creating the underlying elements you need for effective instruction rather than seeking a physical environment that already provides what you desire.

For example, in the above illustration about the field trip to the old high school, what would you have done as a teacher upon entering this physical environment? What would you have done before and during the teaching-learning exchange to enhance the psychological climate for students?

In the above case, the group leader ignored the physical environment and moved on. Students completed their "mini-lessons" while internally processing their various reactions. Later, the group discussed how members used the space. Reactions ranged from "I hated high school" to "I loved high school" and "This space feels awful" to "This room feels like home." As they processed these different reactions to the same physical environment, all discovered the constraints the place put on some and the freedom it seemed to afford others, as both teachers and learners.

To what extent can you select the architectural facility in which you teach? If you have choices related to the building and rooms in which you teach, be prepared to make them. What do you need? What do you prefer? What can you "live with"? What can't you? Define for yourself what makes an environment "preferred." This preference should include the affective as well as the physical and can give you insights into how you can begin to use the environment in your instruction.

Environment is inherent in every teaching-learning exchange. How both teachers and learners react to the environment affects the success of the exchange, whether the teacher consciously uses the environment or not. By taking charge of those environmental elements that we can control and using them to support our individual styles, we avoid inadvertent obstacles to the exchange and improve chances for success.

Chapter Six

The Teacher

Becoming a teacher is an arduous process at best; becoming a good teacher is even more so. Are good teachers made or born? Or are all people born with the necessary prerequisites for being a "good" teacher, with only some of them developing to their potential? The teacher in the teaching-learning exchange is almost a nebulous concept: who is the teacher? Is it the body in front of the classroom? The secret behind passing a test? A coach? A cheerleader? A motivator? A friend? An ideal? According to Greenberg (1969), "The human, emotional qualities of the teacher are at the very heart of teaching. No matter how much emphasis is placed on such other qualities in teaching as educational technique, technology, equipment, or buildings, 'the humanity of the teacher is the vital ingredient if [people] are to learn'" (pp. 20–21).

Brookfield (1990) suggests that the ideal of the teacher is a mix of humanistic empathy, critical questioning, and sharp, contextually appropriate humor. Teachers continually strive to become this perfect being rather than ask, "How well did I help people learn today?" (p. 7). This chapter will explore the concept of the

teacher as an element in the teaching-learning exchange by looking
at the teacher as a human being, examining the characteristics of
a "good" teacher, asking if teachers really make a difference, and
seeking authenticity in teaching. Finally, we will examine what a
teacher does and how the person becomes the same as the teacher.

Exploring the Teacher as a Human Being

Becoming a teacher is a process of growth and development that
continues throughout the teaching career (Heck & Williams, 1984).
Just as with life, this process is ongoing and changing. It requires
that teachers spend time getting to know themselves, whomever
they may find.

The self is a "system of ideas, attitudes, values, and commit-
ments. Self is a person's total subjective environment; it is the distinctive center of things" (Jersild, 1955, p. 8). The challenge for the
teacher, as with anyone, is that many different situations compris-
ing his or her world are superimposed on this inner world of the
"self" (Heck & Williams, 1984). The "teacher" may also be a parent,
a child, a friend, a colleague, a partner, a spouse, ad infinitum,
depending upon the moment and the situation. Through all these
roles, it is still the same person who, in that other context, is called
"teacher."

This is not to say that being a teacher necessitates "knowing
thyself," though it would certainly help. Rather, because we humans have many interests, experiences, and facets to who we are,
there is value in looking at *who* the teacher is in the teaching-
learning exchange. We use this concept of "estimating self" because
full knowledge of self is not likely for most of us.

What a teacher is cannot be separated from who the teacher
is, except, of course, on paper in a generic job description. But any
of us who have observed colleagues or talked with co-workers can
attest that a job description gets played out in ways that vary from
individual to individual. What teachers need to seek is not a job
description but a framework for understanding personal beliefs
about who the "teacher" is in the exchange so that they can ultimately work toward fulfilling that vision of self.

You can examine yourself as a teacher in many different

ways. Kozman, Cassidy, and Jackson (1967) construct four estimates an educator could use to examine self:

- Estimate yourself as a human being by describing yourself over-all. Are you a self-directing person; a person with broad cultural and social interests; a cooperative person; a person with good communication techniques; a healthy being?
- Estimate yourself as an educator by assessing level of knowledge, listing areas of exceptional ability, and examining both formal and informal preparation for teaching.
- Estimate yourself as a member of a profession by asking why you are a teacher and examining your knowledge of organiza-tions, opportunities, and demands of the profession on the in-dividual (for example, ethics, committee obligations, other re-sponsibilities).
- Estimate yourself as a member of the community by looking at yourself as others see you. Or ask people who will be open with you to provide you with their estimates of who you are.

Perhaps the starting point for most of us is to critically ask ourselves, Why do I teach? What do I like about teaching? What do I dislike about teaching? Being human, we tend to be driven by both internal and external rewards that fit our individual system of values or worth. Highet (1989) suggests that two major rewards of teaching are to be in a profession where the mind can function on valuable subjects and to have the joy that comes with "making" something—in this case, learning. It can be argued that only the learner can "make learning," but there is a joy associated with being a part of that process.

Individual experiences, past and present, influence the pro-cess of growing as a teacher. The roles an individual plays outside of teaching influence how that individual will act and react in the teaching-learning setting, and how members of the group act and react to that individual as the teacher. In the same way, how much "self" a teacher puts into the instructional exchange is directly re-lated to the level of commitment from the learners (Lowman, 1990). Enthusiasm can only be contagious when it is authentic, and au-thentic enthusiasm only occurs when an individual is wholly present. In naming the personal factors that affect role behavior of adult educators, Robinson (1979) includes the social roles of the educator outside of the teaching setting, personal goals of the individual, and individual needs of acceptance, achievement, and dominance.

We know that what the teacher does speaks volumes about who the teacher is. This makes the teacher part of the "hidden curriculum," or the message that is conveyed beyond the content (Bloom, 1976; Heck & Williams, 1984). All aspects of a teacher—the whole teacher—are conveyed in some manner in the teaching-learning exchange. Growth is knowing what messages you send as a teacher, in content and in context, consciously and subconsciously.

But a teacher's growth or change, like most people's, is an ongoing process. If the teacher grows, so will the learner. If a teacher is bored, enthusiastic, happy, or sad, learners will be the same. Identify three very different teachers who will let you observe them teaching. Before you watch them, make an observation checklist of behaviors you believe will reveal the beliefs that educator holds about teaching. Are the three teachers' behaviors the same? Different? How so? Why do you think this may be? Do their behaviors reveal information about who they are as individuals? Are they aware of this revelation?

Reflecting on the Characteristics of a "Good" Adult Educator

Many taxonomies of teacher traits are offered in the literature (see, for example, Boone, 1985; Conti, 1985; Robinson, 1979; Ryans, 1970). Underlying teaching activities, however, are human qualities of the teacher that, as Heck and Williams (1984) suggest, separate good teachers from great ones. They include trusting, caring, and sharing of self beyond the facts of the curriculum; dealing with real feelings; sharing experiences and feelings with peers; being a person-oriented individual; and being authentic and honest while maintaining professionalism and leadership. These characteristics imply there is an art to what we call teaching.

In 1932, Ruediger suggested that teaching is both an art and a science. The art relates to the positive traits of the teacher, including creative and courageous imagination, mastery of information skills and previous work, enthusiasm for high standards and ideals, and a projection of personality. The science of teaching is not in the content but in using the scientific process to construct the learning setting. Requisite characteristics for a teacher might be knowledge of the subject and teaching techniques, a willingness to learn from students, intellectural integrity, broad cultural perspective, freedom from prejudice, an interest and belief in students, a warm and sympathetic personality, and a sense of humor (Lenz, 1982). Lenz also suggests that these characteristics flow from the idea that teaching is an art, not a science or business. One might add that these characteristics, along with enthusiasm for the subject, define a great teacher. Other assets are a good memory and will power, although these are not necessities (Highet, 1989).

Generally, most teachers and students would agree that good teachers are enthusiastic, kind, agreeable, accommodating, cooperative, patient, optimistic, inspiring, tactful, clear-thinking, courteous, sympathetic, knowledgeable, and responsible. On the other hand, poor teachers could be labeled as sarcastic, conceited, snobbish, selfish, profane, intolerant, sloppy, unenthusiastic, and indifferent. Note that these traits do not relate much to the content taught but speak more clearly to who the teacher is. Behaviors often separate those teachers identified as good teachers from those identified as lesser. In the same way, work habits, ethics, professional attitudes, courage, mental honesty, and punctuality are taught intentionally and unintentionally by example (Skilling, 1969).

Eble (1983) identifies the seven deadly sins of teaching as arrogance, dullness, rigidity, insensitivity, vanity, self-indulgence, and hypocrisy. Arrogance can come from possessing much knowledge but little experience. Dullness heaps abuse upon learners. Rigidity and insensitivity deny learners something they deserve by nature of being human. Vanity is the elevation of self above the learners' demands. Both self-indulgence and hypocrisy create conflicts within the learning setting that separate the educator from the learners.

Alternatively, Wilkinson (1984) suggests that positive behaviors in a good teacher support a learner's choice to learn, stimulate the learner to become curious, facilitate the initial drive of learners, help learners develop a critical thinking approach, use a variety of teaching methods to address diverse learning styles, and encourage the learner's independence from the teacher.

All these considerations of what makes a "good teacher" could lead to a never-ending cycle of self-analysis without action. We suggest each educator create two personal "sets" of criteria from the types of characteristics defined above. The first set provides a means of assessing who the educator is now and current performance. This is the stage of introspection concerning teaching. The second set of standards is the "ideals" by which each teacher measures personal growth or expansion. This second set of standards can also be the interteacher comparison we all do intuitively when we react to another's teaching—positive, ambivalent, or negative.

As educators of present and future teachers, we believe that teaching has never changed and will never change. It is based on the human instincts of experience and recall (Hill, 1981). Whether one is a parent with a child or an instructor standing in front of a group, one has a human instinct to teach. Individuals grow and learn; teachers are there to help.

Do Teachers Really Make a Difference?

"It is a mistake to assume that all learning occurs in the classroom. . . . What, then, does the teacher contribute to the process of learning that students cannot supply on their own?" (Wilkinson, 1984, p. 1). What, indeed, does the teacher contribute?

A 1950s study suggested that students learned as well *without* a teacher as they did with one (Hodgkinson, 1973). For this study, a group of students were assigned either to a teacher-present class or to independent study for a quarter. At the end, the independent study group scored slightly higher on an achievement measure than those who attended the class. Student reactions to the experience were mixed. The conclusion of the study surmised that better teaching is not the crucial issue in education and that the individual instructor working in isolation and at odds with colleagues is relatively ineffectual. Therefore, as Siegel has said, "prescriptions for 'how to teach effectively' are about as outdated as leeching" (Hodgkinson, 1973, p. 6).

So does the teacher make a difference? In answer to this question, Wilkinson (1984) suggested three things that the teacher offers as the intermediary between learners and a body of knowledge:

- *Structure.* The teacher can help learners structure their random learning experiences into a meaningful sequence.
- *Evaluation.* The teacher is the critic and stimulator of dialogue.
- *Support.* The teacher's interest and encouragement is crucial for creating an environment that enhances motivation.

If all an educator did was to present information, then perhaps the value of the teacher would be no more than for any other mode of content delivery. The argument is that the teacher enhances learning, which goes far beyond content presentation. The teaching-learning exchange suggests that teaching and learning can be related and are brought together when the elements of the exchange are all present. Teaching is not exclusively "information presenting," and this is in part what distinguishes an educator from a public speaker, a salesperson, or a nightly news anchor.

Bloom (1976) asserts it is the *teaching* and not the *teacher* that is central to learning. What the teacher does is more important than the small percent of the variation in student achievement outcomes explained in various studies by the traits of the teacher. We suggest that the traits are not as important as the congruence of the traits within each educator.

Teaching does make a difference. One reason many studies suggest that the effects of instruction are low is that many of these studies relate not to the management of learning but to the management of the students (Jackson, 1968). Teachers are not responsible for the differences in abilities of the learners, but they are responsible for creating the desire in all students to learn, to do their best, and to learn to enjoy learning (Bloom, 1976).

Teaching can excite and incite—without teaching, learning is reduced to repeat and recite. Teaching is the human connection between the content and the environment and the learners. The masterful teacher is the one who conveys to the learners "the message that one must reach beyond the knowledge of things that is merely knowledge, to the knowledge of others that is wisdom, and thence to the knowledge of self that is enlightenment" (Fraher,

1984, p. 127). The only way to lead learners to this type of outcome, the epitome of what a teacher can do, is to be there oneself. The teacher is the connector of the elements of instruction, and to allow the elements to function fully, the teacher in this exchange must be authentic.

Authentic Teachers

Rogers (1983, p. 23) asked, "As a teacher, can I be myself?" One way of saying "be myself" is to describe how authentic or genuine the teacher is as a human being in the classroom. Brookfield (1990) suggests that characteristics related to authenticity are (1) making sure behaviors are congruent with words, (2) admitting error, (3) sharing aspects of self, and (4) respecting students.

Congruence is what authenticity is about. Do my behaviors as a teacher truly match what I say, what I espouse as beliefs, and what I want to do? Am I consistent in the model I present and the expectations I express? The teacher is set apart from learners by nature of the culture of learning groups (Van Tilburg and Heimlich, 1987). Being consistent in word and deed is ultimately the only way to truly be yourself.

Additionally, "being oneself" can mean admitting mistakes. Brookfield (1990) tells us "learners seem to warm to teachers who acknowledge that they don't have all the answers and that, like their students, they sometimes feel out of control" (p. 168). Who we are will inform us as to how we admit our mistakes. Since teachers are all different, there is no set way of "confessing." All teachers must learn to be vulnerable in a manner that is consistent with their life patterns, not by a preconceived phrase that will make them appear "human."

Brookfield (1990) encourages teachers to build trust with students by revealing personal aspects of their personalities, experiences, and backgrounds. This technique of "autobiographical metaphor in teaching" (Tarule, 1988) helps students see the teacher as a real person and thereby increases rapport and trust. That the teacher is a person is never in question; what is in question is how that person chooses to share self with the learners. Characteristics of the individual, including intellect, interests, emotions, attitudes, character traits, social adjustment, and influences, cannot be abstract and depersonalized "things" but are tools for the teacher to use in understanding learners as developing organisms in a dynamic interaction with the elements of instruction (American Association for Applied Psychology, 1942).

The behavior of a teacher can be measured by observation, self-report, or preference measures. The intent is to seek consistency between intentions and teaching actions (Flanders, 1970). To do so, the intent of the teacher must be known. Unfortunately, how many of us can explain all our actions in a normal length of teacher-learner discourse? The more we learn about ourselves, the more we find that we don't know why we do some things. So our first step is to understand our own intentions in the teaching-learning exchange, whether they are products of intuition, expediency, or regression in terror. Merrill and Gregory (1974) include this in their discussion of the importance of measuring oneself as a teacher when they list the need to measure abilities and limitations, values and aspirations, and all the people and forces (both positive and negative) that are part of teaching.

The teacher is "the hub" of the instructional event (Humphrey, Love, & Irwin, 1972). To be able to react honestly to situations, teachers must listen to concerns, suggestions, and problems and through that listening show learners that they are partners in the exchange. Being yourself means recognizing, respecting, and taking others seriously—allowing them to be themselves as well. Of course, there are pitfalls in being yourself in the classroom. You may have to say, "I don't know." You may find that you like some students more than others. You may find out that learners aren't satisfied with your teaching. You may have to do things you don't want to do. But at least it's *you* in the classroom, and not a facade.

What a Teacher Does: The Balancing Act

Is there a way to balance personal and professional? Purkey and Novak (1984) identify a four-pronged approach to this question: be personally inviting with oneself, be personally inviting with others, be professionally inviting with oneself, and be professionally inviting with others. As an introduction to this approach, they indicate that "a major goal of invitational education [or quality education] is assisting teachers to become beneficial presences in the lives of others. . . . [This] requires a certain perceptual orientation, a particular stance, and a consistency in behavior. . . . [To do this, we need to look] at the person in the process and consider what is necessary to sustain the desire and energy to function at an intentionally inviting level—to develop the stamina and courage" (p. 72).

Perhaps the easiest way to understand the balance of what a teacher does is to examine how learners see a teacher and what they expect or demand of a teacher. We can do this by looking at ourselves as learners. How do we imagine the role of the teacher—both in and out of class? More specifically, what are the functions of the teacher that we believe would most contribute to our own successes as learners? As learners, we know the behaviors and attributes we expect from teachers, and we know what attributes we believe make quality teachers. On the basis of the Florida Key, an inventory of student behavior related to self-concept, Purkey, Cage, and Graves (1973) identify four concepts on which they believe teachers must focus in order to help students perform, or four behaviors that the teacher can help encourage within each learner: relating, asserting, investing, and coping. *Relating* has to do with the level of trust and appreciation that individuals show toward others. *Asserting* pertains to the ability to accept control and responsibility for one's actions and reactions. *Investing* is the willingness to take risks and to speculate on future outcomes or ideas. *Coping* includes possessing an image of oneself as able to maneuver through school requirements. How do teachers bring themselves into the teaching-learning exchange and balance who they are with the expectations of them? How do *you* handle this challenge?

The key truly is balance: balance in knowing who you are as a person and what you expect of yourself as a teacher; balance between what you believe about learners with the reality of teaching and the real-world problems of distractions, interruptions, maintenance tasks, and diversity in the group; balance between being aware of yourself and being aware of the learners; balance between creating comfort necessary for learning and creating the tension that incites enthusiasm and energy around learning. The teacher is a human being who holds the scales of polar concerns. He or she can easily tip the balance; or just as easily can combine the weights on either side of the scales to create a unique blend of instruction that is, for that individual teacher, just "right."

How teachers reach this balance often comes through discussion with other teachers. For example, we led a workshop recently in which we were discussing a study by Borich (1990) about how little time is spent on content in traditional classrooms and about the hundreds of exchanges a teacher has during a typical hour. One of the participants brought up the question of why. Why spend so much time on social relations, regulatory behavior, administration, and monitoring? Why not spend more time on content? Another participant suggested that if we understood how these things occur, perhaps they could become manageable. Then another offered the idea that we need to relate all these demands to the content, whatever it may be. Another participant stated that we just need to know that these things occur and to be aware of them when they do, rather than attend to them as routine. After much discussion, we finally arrived at the realization that each of us must find the way to secure a balance that is right for us. For some there is a structure that will handle such annoyances. For others, creating opportunities out of the interruptions is ideal. There is no universal measure or scale, only what works best with who each of us is.

Teaching is a skill and a gift, a talent and a technique. It is learnable and intuitive. Teachers must approach the balancing act from their personal perspective and create what is congruent for them between themselves as "teacher" and each of the other elements of the teaching-learning exchange.

The Teacher and the Person: Making Them the Same

How would you describe the ideal teacher? What characteristics of that ideal do you hold? How many characteristics of the ideal are not you? Why? In a class on teaching style, we all became aware of how many texts, books, and articles had prescriptions for how a teacher should act, dress, think, or behave. So we held a teacher fashion show in which each participant chose one of the writings and then created an "image" of the teacher posited in that writing.

Costumes and props, gestures and descriptions were stereotyped and caricatured concepts from the writings. It became obvious to us all that the "ideal" teacher is just that—an ideal. But how do we each meet our own potential rather than someone else's prescriptive ideal?

An interesting paradox of being human is that we often overlook the many gifts we have because, if we have them, we believe everyone must have them—be able to do those things, think in that manner, and so forth. The paradox is that we then admire someone who holds a different set of skills or gifts simply because of the difference. We move toward congruence by letting go of the desire for abilities that are not ours and developing those many skills we each have.

Although teachers can continually strive to expand the personal repertoire of techniques and seek to continually improve, they must begin the growth process by first working on those skills that are inherent. This is the essence of style. Teachers must first know what they believe and value and then develop the skills that enhance and further those beliefs and values before embarking on exploring what is, for them, uncharted territory.

The process of exploration, reflection, and application must occur on two levels. As discussed earlier, there is the introspection of determining who the teacher is and level of current competency. There is also the interteacher comparison of "how I'd like to be" against current performance. Both sets of standards are crucial in working toward congruence while moving toward growth/ expansion.

Eble (1983) discusses the craft, science, and art of teaching. The craft of teaching is the utilization of personal abilities: the guile, or tricks of the trade; the humility, which Eble refers to as intimate, caring, and personal attention paid to materials; the utility, or the encouragement of growth beyond practical skills to the shaping of lives; and honesty in work and deed. These are elements of the craft of teaching. The science of teaching comprises what is independent of the teacher's style: the technological, philosophical, and psychological foundation for the transfer of knowledge, skills, attitudes, and behaviors. The art of teaching involves a creativity that moves beyond technique. It involves "developing a certain wholeness of character from which the details of one's teaching will flow . . . 'giving style to one's character—a great and rare art'" (Ganrose, 1980).

The teacher faces the challenge of applying knowledge from many and diverse fields into every moment of the teaching-learning exchange. A teacher must apply psychology, principles of learning, methods of instruction, sociology, communication arts, communication strategies, philosophy, and cultural anthropology—and all this to be able to convey some other subject! Teaching is a natural process; all humans have an instinct to share information, experiences, and ideas with others. We do this with children, with friends, with co-workers. The formalization of this natural process is, however, rife with obstacles and opportunities that contribute to the "books" each of us could write on our own experiences in teaching.

What is the teacher? To the learner, a teacher is not who the teacher believes him- or herself to be but who the learners think the teacher to be. The teacher is one complex element in the whole teaching-learning exchange. A teacher's beliefs regarding the relationship of the teacher to the other elements define what that teacher must be.

On the dimension of centeredness, the teacher is somewhere in the middle. Teacher-centered educators approach instruction from a base of "self." Who am I and what do I expect from this teaching exchange? The content, the environment, and the learner and group are integrated into the instructional plan through the awareness of the teacher concerning the outcomes and structure that best suit him or her. A teacher-centered instructor is often the type to provide an answer when asked a question instead of showing learners how to look up the answer themselves.

In teacher education, much attention is given to the learner. However, teaching-learning is not directed simply "from teacher to learner" but is truly an exchange. Therefore it is equally important to consider the teacher as an individual both inside and outside the instructional setting. Much of this is subconscious. We know when we're having a bad day and we know how to cope. But do we share with the learners in the same manner that we expect them to share with us? The depth to which any educator chooses to reveal self to students is a matter of personal choice. However, the teacher must maintain an integral honesty regarding what affects the educational moment and how can that be used to improve the opportunities for learning.

For example, a leader of a twelve-week training program was approached by a participant who said she would miss some initial sessions because her father was getting out of the hospital and she felt the need to be there. Expecting resistance, the participant was surprised when the group leader simply said, "Fine, thanks for letting me know."

The leader, a friend, also had a father who was ill. But he did not disclose that to the participant. His position was that the participant already held the right to attend or not attend the sessions; she did not need "permission" from an instructor to do something she already had the freedom to do. Also, the participant did not approach him for empathy or comfort; she had done so merely as a courtesy. Discussing the illness of his father, something he had trouble talking about with even his closest friends, was not necessary. At the same time, it was his experience as a son that allowed him to identify quickly with the participant's dilemma and react in a professional, and human, manner.

No human interaction is value-free. We all have beliefs and opinions about everything. All teachers have valence around the content, the environment, the group, and the individual. A teacher working toward congruence of thought and action does not necessarily change these values but becomes aware of them and aware of how they are present in the teaching and learning that do (or do not) occur in the setting.

For some teachers, the task of making the teacher and the person the same may seem insurmountable. The key is to understand the way you relate teaching to the other elements of instruction. How does the teacher relate to the environment, use the environment, and build the environment? Who are the individual learners to the teacher, and what is their role in the exchange? What is the nature of this group assembled together with the teacher at the helm? How can the teacher take this "stuff" of facts, ideas, processes, skills, or information and create an opportunity for it to be meaningful to the learners?

The questions are not easy. The answers are always changing. What we can do is continually aim for that point where what we do is in line with what we believe, even though tomorrow we may learn something that shapes our beliefs a bit differently. This process is inherent in working with adult learners. When dealing with children, adults often feel they must have all the answers. It may be easier to step off that pedestal when dealing with other adults, even in a teaching-learning exchange. In this way, we can be more honest with ourselves and about ourselves with the other participants, and we can help each other discover the answers to how we relate teaching to the other elements of instruction.

Teaching is an art, a craft, a science, a technology—and teaching is what a teacher does.

Chapter Seven

The Learning Community

Adult educators spend much preparation and practice with the issues surrounding individual learners. The *collection* of individuals that make up the group of learners, however, carries with it a very different yet equally important set of considerations for the teacher. The following personal recollection recounted by Booker T. Washington in *Up From Slavery* illustrates the complicated nature of belonging to and interacting with a community of learners.

> At the school for the first time, . . . I found that all the other children wore hats or caps on their heads, and I had neither hat nor cap. In fact, I do not remember that up to the time of going to school I had ever worn any kind of covering upon my head, nor do I recall that either I or anybody else had even thought anything about the need of covering for my head. But, of course, when I saw how all the other boys were dressed, I began to feel quite uncomfortable. As usual, I put the case before my mother, and she explained to

me that she had no money with which to buy a "store
hat." . . . She accordingly got two pieces of "home-
spun" [jeans] and sewed them together, and I was
soon the proud possessor of my first cap [Washington,
1965, p. 21].

This chapter explores the cultural concepts related to learning communities in the teaching-learning exchange. Readers can
reflect on how these concepts relate to learning and to their teaching. Suggestions for application strategies are focused on achieving
congruence between the teacher's beliefs and the behavior within
the exchange specifically related to the learning community.

Defining Culture

As we talk about a learning community or group, we begin to
discuss the language, habits, ideas, beliefs, customs, social organization, inherited artifacts, technical processes, and values that the
individuals within the group share. These elements comprise the
artificial, secondary environment that is superimposed by humans
through human nature on the natural (Niebuhr, 1951). Whenever
a group forms, the potential exists for these factors to become clearly
unique for the specific group. In the example above, the community
of learners was bound together through certain shared characteristics, with the outward symbol of membership being an article of
clothing, a cap. The language through which it is possible to talk
about groups is the language of culture.

The Language of Culture

Culture develops, maintains, and determines the closeness of
any group (Turner, 1974). The patterns that emerge from the group
as behaviors specific to that group become the customs, institutions,
and traits of that group of people (Benedict, 1935). Those who study
cultures analyze individual acts that contribute to the group. Actions that define a culture are extrinsic, or outside an individual's
consciousness; coercive, or expected and required; interdependent
upon others and self; and replicable (de Carvalho-Neto, 1965). We

are defined as individuals by our actions as part of a group or groups.

Some definitions of culture parallel the assumptions used in discussions of organizational culture. Blake and Mouton's (1969) definition of culture within an organization illustrates the transferability of the concepts to groups: patterns of interactions, values and attitudes derived from traditions, precedents, and past practices— the assumptions and beliefs by which people live.

Characteristics of Culture

Niebuhr (1951) suggests five characteristics of culture that contrast to nature: (1) culture is tied to society; it is always social; (2) culture is distinguished from nature by human achievement; (3) all human behavior addressed to culture is for a specific end or purpose; (4) pluralism is a characteristic of all culture; and (5) we cannot escape culture. We can apply these five characteristics to the concept of the learning community.

Unique Grouping. The first characteristic suggests that the essence of culture is the organization of human beings into groups. In learning settings, the group is often self-selected. And within the group, a cultural identity can form. What shared beliefs brought these disparate individuals together? What common goals might these individuals hold? How do these individuals see themselves as set apart from the rest of the world? These common bonds form the basis for the group identifying itself as a group with a relationship to the outside world (Spengler, 1961).

The view of the group as a separate identifiable unit also allows the group to begin to identify how it is collectively influenced by outside sources of change that alter how the group views the world (Kearney, 1984). A learning group has the potential for sharing an identity, depending upon how the educator allows the group to function.

To illustrate this first characteristic, use a cohort to which you belong and get various members to answer each of these questions: What are five things that bind the group together? What behavior(s) emanates from the group to illustrate the culture? Are there any words or phrases that mean something unique to the group? Do we have any group jokes or shared humorous experiences? Do we share any trauma or tragedy? List five behaviors that are part of our group.

When you have the input, compare the comments. Are they consistent? How cohesive would you say the cohort is? How likely is it that there is any other group, formal or informal, exactly like this group? It is the culture of the group that makes it unique.

To further illustrate this point, bring any group of people together and ask them what they all have in common. Sooner or later, a list will emerge. The longer the group is together, the more shared characteristics they will discover. In fact, the passage of time and shared experiences allow the opportunity for the group to create its own culture so that the culture that emerges is a combination of original shared characteristics and new ones developed by being together.

Human Involvement. The second characteristic, that culture is distinguished from nature by human achievement, is a given in an educational setting. Humans coming together to learn may or may not be natural, but as Niebuhr illustrates, "a river is nature, a canal culture. . . . Culture is the work of minds and hands" (1951, p. 33). Education is the process of work with the human mind, and the application of the knowledge is the work of human hands.

A tool we use to clarify the concept of culture versus nature is to have teachers seat themselves in any environment, inside or out, and make two columns on a piece of paper: "culture" and "nature." They record tangible evidence of each in the appropriate column. Next, they each spend some time in one of their teaching environments and repeat the activity, but adding a third column, "educational culture." They then compare which column has the most entries in the educational setting and why.

Focus. If characteristic three is true, that all human behavior addressed to culture is for a specific end or purpose, education becomes a process of culture. Govan, Faber, Prins, and Mangold (1972) tell us that the group processes at the sensory level, and that this is below the level of consciousness: we become a group, we do not necessarily set out to be a group. Education in a group setting has a specific end or purpose. Sometimes it is knowledge acquisition. Sometimes it is change in attitudes or behavior. Sometimes it is even the intent with which the educator enters the learning exchange! When the group assumes a common purpose, the potential to become a cohesive body is established.

The world of culture is a world of values. Individuals hold values, and many of the values each person holds come from somewhere and are learned. Groups form with purpose, and the activities of the group serve the shared beliefs of the individuals. Primitive art, for example, indicates human interest in color, shape, and rhythm. Our judgments of what is beautiful, right, good, or appropriate are perceptions of value. In a group, our perceptions become our reality (Sanchez, 1987). What is valuable becomes valuable through the group—which, perhaps, is why sports stars make millions while teachers often make subaverage wages.

What the group values becomes unquestionable and "is." Values ascribed to culture are generally those for the good of humankind as defined by the group; this explains why in some cultures certain behaviors are acceptable and even encouraged that to someone from another culture seem barbaric.

Pluralism. The fourth characteristic is that of pluralism. Individuals within the group hold many values representing their particular interests (men, women, adults, children, haves, have nots). These diverse values do not always align. The culture seeks to hold together a group with disparate views. This is similar to what de Carvalho-Neto (1965) means when he says individual acts contribute to the total. The culture will unify the individuals at the greatest common denominator or the most abstract of the value levels.

Inevitability. The bottom line in the discussion of culture is the fifth characteristic, that we cannot escape culture. Culture exists, and many levels of culture interact in the learning setting: the dominant culture under which the program is conducted, the many different cultural representations of the individuals within the group, and the potential emergence of a well-defined cultural unit of the group itself. This last possibility is the learning community to which this chapter is dedicated.

To gain further insight into the idea of culture of a learning community, gather some adult educators with whom you work or share similar responsibilities. Discuss the relationship of each of Niebuhr's characteristics of culture in relation to the cultures students form in your educational settings. What are some implications for you as you approach the culture of your various learning communities? To enhance the discussion, pick an environment in which to meet that has a clearly defined culture of its own, such as an art museum or the local zoo. Next time you gather together, change the environment to a very different culture, for example a day care setting for older adults or preschoolers. Did the change of environmental culture change the nature of the discussion? How? Why?

The Mini-Culture of a Learning Community

In the realm of education, working with groups of individual learners is working within the "mini-culture" of the learning community. In the observation activity described above, the third column, "educational culture," represented the mini-culture of the learning community. The choice of the word *mini-culture* versus *subculture* emphasizes the size of the group, not its marginality or the nature of its culture. All groups of learners form learning communities with a unique mini-culture. The coherence of a learning community and the strength of its culture are determined by the subconscious belief system of the group (Jung, Von Franz, Henderson, Jacobi, & Jaffe, 1964), the values inherent in these beliefs (Knowles, 1970), how the group learns, its beliefs about the dominant culture generally and education specifically (Parsons, 1966), and the past history of the group with education in general and the specific content.

Interaction with the Greater Culture

A belief is held by the mainstream or dominant culture that if it is to maintain its predominance, its beliefs and practices must prevail and be incorporated by any smaller culture (Smelser, 1963). In some cases, the mainstream culture is more technologically and scientifically advanced and thus rationalizes that it can "help" or "aid" the "disadvantaged" through education.

This type of education is often directed toward alignment of behaviors such as nutrition, hygiene, sanitation, and aesthetics to coordinate the individuals within the social system (Turiel, 1983). Or, as is likely the case with smaller cultures not bound by geographic or heritage unities, the behaviors of that culture are seen as deviant from the major culture so that the major culture has the right to "corrective" education. Although these cases seem extreme, they are not out of the ordinary.

A student in a seminar shared a letter she received from a friend involved in an international assistance program. The friend told her about the hard time the assistance team was having in getting people to understand what they were trying to teach them. The friend shared stories about the resistance to doing it "the right way" and how the team often had to repeat the same information over and over. This is a good illustration of the concept that unless a lesson has meaning within the cultural framework of the learning community, it either will not be learned or will be short-lived.

Types of Learning Communities and Mini-Cultures

Three types of learning communities can exist in adult education settings: the artificially formed learning community, the preexisting learning community, and the contextually based learning community. Each will potentially have a very different type of mini-culture.

Artificially Formed. The artificially formed learning community is one that before coming together for the purpose of a specific educational activity did not exist. The one thing all members have in common is that they are members of the newly formed learning community. A mini-culture will arise from the artificially formed learning community through sets of experiences the members have during the teaching-learning exchange. Every time this concept is discussed in our presence, the authors think of the following example of an artificially formed learning community and mini-culture.

Several years ago we found ourselves in a car going south through the Great Smoky Mountains. We were with two other adult educators all headed to an adult education conference. Even though we shared an interest in adult education, our mini-culture really formed through the experience of riding together through the mountains, each one taking a turn at negotiating the steep hills and sharp curves. Evidence of the culture that was formed included jokes about the one and only air bag in the car, tall tales of the bears we didn't see, and a longing for oat bran pretzels. Only the four of us would understand these elements of our mini-culture—the "you had to be there to appreciate it" phenomenon. The same phenomenon is present in a learning community that comes together for the sole purpose of learning.

Preexisting. The second type of learning community is one in which the members already have group membership in common. The example used in Chapter Three was a civic club that also included educational experiences for its members. The learning community that is formed in a situation like this has many more shared qualities binding its members. Many times, learning (and teaching) is really affected by these preexisting bonds.

Take, for example, the civic club. Any teacher who enters into a teaching-learning relationship with that learning community will be dealing with several issues, the least of which is a clear hierarchy (or pecking order) of members. The educator will also most likely experience resistance to anything remotely resembling change or new ideas. The club members have been together for years, and the mini-culture of the club has many years' worth of experiences to bind it together. Both good and bad experiences and their memories support the mini-culture.

Picture yourself in this situation and imagine how you might approach it: You are invited to teach a three-hour seminar on "you name it." What would you do to prepare, and in what order would you do it? What would you do specifically to address the mini-culture of the group? What would be your greatest concern with this particular assignment? How would you plan to overcome this concern? Your answers to these questions might very well suggest that a preexisting learning community presents multiple challenges for the adult educator.

Contextually Based. In this situation, the educator comes in contact with a group of learners who may never have been together before in this exact configuration but who all share some very unifying personal or contextual characteristic(s). The example of the Amish community, again taken from Chapter Three, presents the kind of situation that adult educators must often negotiate.

Whether the shared characteristic is geographic, demographic, or something else, it is probably not the major reason for the current grouping of learners. It is, however, quite relevant to the educator to know about these contextual bonds because they will certainly play a major role in the forming of the mini-culture of the learning community. And they will most likely have an influence on the success of the educator in interaction with that community's mini-culture.

The Adult Educator and the Learning Community

In many adult educational settings, the teacher is, at least initially, the individual tagged with the responsibility for identifying what is necessary or appropriate for the learners to gain within that setting. By its very definition, the action of teaching involves a cultural exchange between the learning community and the dominant culture, and the dominant culture is represented by the educator. So although any group has the potential to become a well-defined mini-culture, the extent to which it does depends at least somewhat on how the educator works with the group to facilitate or constrain this natural occurrence.

Sensitivity

Adult educators may see great value in utilizing the culture of the group to assist with teaching and learning. To be able to include unique cultural characteristics in the planning, implementation, and evaluation of the teaching-learning exchange, the teacher must be aware of just what these shared characteristics are. Sensitivity, as defined in Chapter Two, represents a teacher's beliefs related to the importance of knowing about the learners for the purpose of interaction with the learning community. An educator who possessed sensitivity would spend time and energy learning all he or she could about the learners. One of our mentors spends at least a quarter of the time with learners gathering information about them. He uses information sheets, one-on-one interviews, and small and large group discussion to encourage learners to self-disclose about background, goals, and desires. Then he searches for the shared characteristics among the individuals that bond them together as a community. It is these cultural characteristics upon which he focuses.

Inclusion

A second dimension, inclusion, refers to the beliefs of the educator about the importance of involving the learning community in all phases of the learning experience. Teachers who practice inclusion often ask learners to contribute to all phases of the teaching-learning exchange. Our mentor not only spends time learning about the learners but also encourages the group of learners to participate in the planning and implementation of the educational exchange. He forms teams of learners who are then responsible for a specific portion of the class. Each team not only plans the methods to be used but frames the exact content to be addressed. He releases control to the group of learners in such a way as to empower the group. Notice that for this adult educator the focus of empowerment is not on the individual student but on the learning community.

Combining Dimensions

All adult educators vary in the importance they place on knowing about the mini-culture of the learning community. They also vary on the utilization of that mini-culture in the teaching-learning exchange. Some teachers believe that it is very important to know about the mini-culture but do not believe that they need to involve the group to any extent in the teaching-learning exchange beyond the role of receiver of information. This type of adult educator might be called a *provider* because he or she spends the necessary time getting to know the mini-culture so the correct decisions can be made about their instruction. Learners might describe this teacher as caring, supportive, and nurturing because their needs (as the teacher has diagnosed them) are being met.

A teacher who, on the other hand, doesn't know about or care to know much about the mini-culture but who releases much control to the learning community might be labeled a *facilitator*. This person approaches all learning communities as similar entities but believes in shared control. This type of teacher has been described as open and flexible because the learning community has control over its actions.

We have all had the opportunity to experience the educator who has both low sensitivity and low inclusion, the *expert*. When the educational need at hand is immediate, complex, detailed, important, and massive, the expert may be just the type of adult educator called for. The expert enters the teaching-learning exchange, knows what the learners need, gives the learners what they need, and then exits the exchange. Adult educators who exhibit "expert" characteristics are often referred to as specialists, authorities, masters, or professionals.

Adult educators who, like our mentor described above, are both highly sensitive and highly inclusive, might be labeled as the "perfect adult educator." A term we have selected is that of *enabler*. The enabler empowers or capacitates the learning community by knowing about and involving the group to the fullest extent.

When discussing dimensions such as sensitivity and inclusion in the context of congruence, we suggest that educators focus on matching philosophy with behavior rather than expanding beyond current boundaries. Much adult education literature claims that there are better and worse places to "be" on these dimensions. For example, many believe that the enabler is a better educator than the expert. We, however, continue to remind ourselves that the best adult educators we can be, at this point in time, are congruent in philosophy and behavior. Getting to know ourselves as educators is the first step in growth. Moving toward congruence is the current challenge; moving beyond congruence is a lifelong endeavor.

Teaching Within a Mini-Culture

No two groups are identical; thus what works for one group will not necessarily work for another group (Verner, 1964). Not only is this a prescription for teaching; it also suggests that no two groups will "learn" in the same manner. Reflect on various teaching experiences where the same content has been taught to two different groups. No matter how "identically" the information is shared, the result is usually very different. Each group, with its own characteristics, learns in its own way.

Considerations of Mini-Cultures

Mini-cultures of learning communities share several characteristics. These cultures are fragile and exclusive, yet they can play an important role for individual learners.

Fragility. Learning groups are fragile mini-cultures. They often do not have a long history of existence, and many times their purpose for being a group is temporal and quickly satisfied. Consequently there are special considerations for learning groups. For example, changes in membership of relatively informal groups can radically alter the group's personality and in some cases, can negatively affect the relationships within the group (Applbaum, Bodaken, Sereno, & Anatol, 1974). Through an event as simple as a person's leaving the room, the dynamics of the learning setting can change.

Even more threatening to many groups in formative stages is the introduction of a new person to the group. Not only is the individual often reluctant to commit to the group, but the group may not be willing to share some of its "language" and experiences with the new person until he or she has demonstrated a certain "worthiness" to belong to the group.

Most of the information needed for planning for instruction is related to societal (group) influences (Knox, 1987), and an educator must assess the strength and potential of the mini-culture in planning for group involvement. How much and in what ways the group is considered in the planning and preparation process for the learning setting might depend on how well defined the mini-culture is. The extent to which an educator includes the group in defining its own values, beliefs, and outcomes can contribute to the building or demise of group cohesion. This is true for both short- and long-term groups, for example, one-time workshops or semester-long continuing education classes.

Exclusivity. The culture of the group creates a challenge for an educator because the leader is not a member of the student culture and therefore is not a member of the group. Stories abound of individuals who "go off to school" and return home to work within their community (poverty-stricken inner-city or rural areas, for example), only to discover that they are no longer viewed as they were before they left—they are now part of the establishment or the "other side." The saying "you can never go back" has tremendous implications for adult educators who choose to work with groups to which they once belonged.

An adult educator can, however, have successful interaction with learning communities in spite of their exclusivity. For example, the Appalachian culture holds friendliness in high regard; an educator who is "all business" and insists on starting a workshop at precisely the stated starting time will not engender much good will with participants. Someone who knows enough to sit and chat for fifteen or twenty minutes will foster much more participant involvement in group outcomes. That teacher is working within the mini-culture of the learning community; he or she is not part of the mini-culture but does understand it *and* respects it.

To further clarify the exclusive nature of the mini-culture of the learning community, try the following. Recall a situation in which you were the teacher and there was a clear mini-culture of learners—one in which you were not a part. What behaviors (of the participants) gave you the indication of the mini-culture in operation? What were your reactions to their behaviors? What were your feelings? How successful was the teaching experience? How comfortable? Were you able to navigate the mini-culture? How?

Now assume yourself to be a member of the learner mini-culture in this class. What values, beliefs, experiences, traditions, and artifacts illustrate the characteristics of the mini-culture? How did this phenomenon come about? Why is the teacher not a part of this mini-culture? What problems might the teacher encounter because of exclusivity? What strategies do you suggest for the teacher to navigate this culture?

Necessity. Learners clearly benefit from the formation and existence of a learning community with a unique mini-culture. "When speaking of surviving education, the factor that is recalled as being most crucial is a supportive learning community. . . . Whatever its size, however, this community functions as a support network of learners who reassure each other" (Brookfield, 1990, p. 55). Teachers who recognize the importance of the community to individual students will want to foster that community. Strategies might include distributing students' names and addresses, having students share a list of their concerns about learning and also their special skills, using learning groups and peer teaching, and encouraging cooperation and discouraging competition (abolishing letter grades, for example) (Brookfield, 1990).

Additionally, helping to build a shared vision among learners and encouraging a systems thinking approach to interaction can contribute to the growth and development of the mini-culture (Senge, 1990). Members of the learning community can develop group process skills to enhance the formation and fostering of the group. These skills include gate keeping, standard setting, expressing group feelings, diagnosing problems, compromising, harmonizing, consensus testing, and following (Fessler, 1976). Various tasks undertaken within a group such as information giving, information seeking, opinion seeking, coordinating, recording, and expediting are also life skills that support the development, maintenance, and growth of the group. These roles occur naturally within any group; functional roles change among members of a group, with any member performing different roles during a single exchange. An educator who makes explicit the roles and the process supports the group and encourages the solidification of the group into a functioning whole.

Using Mini-Cultures in Teaching

One approach to understanding culture within the classroom is to select an analogy that makes sense and use its parameters for assessing and then navigating (not manipulating) culture. The "inviting family" analogy (Purkey & Novak, 1984) suggests that there are at least five basic characteristics present in a functional, inviting family: respect for individual uniqueness, cooperative spirit, sense of belonging, pleasing habitat, and positive expectations.

The analogy is expanded as "the inviting family school" and is described with the same underlying characteristics applied to a school setting. In adult education settings, leaders' and participants' actions can be evaluated by how well they foster those ideals. Whatever the analogy, the teacher's role assumes a different shape when considered in light of the group rather than the individual student.

Building on the social dimensions of the teaching-learning exchange, one approach to enhancing instruction using a mini-culture is that of "collaborative learning." A description of what would take place in a collaborative learning situation is presented by MacGregor (1990): "Students are working with each other, and frequently alongside their teachers, to grasp subject matter or to deepen their understanding of it. In the process, they are developing their social skills, and their intellectual skills as well. Students might be interpreting, questioning, creating, synthesizing, inventing, doubting, comparing, making connections, puzzling, or doing myriad other sorts of active, visible intellectual tasks. But this active learning takes place publicly, in partnership with others. Students and their teachers are involved in a common enterprise: the *mutual* seeking of understanding" (p. 20).

A key assumption in collaborative learning is that the teacher can, at least superficially, become a functionary in the learners' culture. At the very least, the teacher interacts as a special member of the group for a period of time. Experiential learning, student-centered instruction, cooperative learning, learning community, and problem-centered approaches such as case method, guided design, and worksheets or workshops are all methods of instruction that encourage and support the formation and utilization of the group and the culture of the group in learning.

Of course, simply applying a particular method to the teaching-learning exchange will not guarantee the desired outcome. The educator must identify personal beliefs regarding mini-cultures and, in particular, a learning group related to the elements of instruction. This is the first step in achieving congruence between beliefs regarding the group and behaviors in the teaching-learning exchange.

Understanding Membership

What groups do you belong to? If we ask that question of someone, of anyone, the list becomes huge! People typically participate in so many groups that they often fail to see them as groups—social circles, committees, ethnic groups, task forces, boards, professional organizations, and on and on. Because all people are members of many groups, some fascinating things begin to happen that affect groups in learning settings.

One challenge all people face in various degrees of intensity throughout their lives is that the beliefs and behaviors appropriate to one group to which they belong are not necessarily appropriate to another group. Most people have, at some point, experienced discrimination of some sort. Discrimination is often the clash of values between groups, and often both parties in the interaction belong to some larger culture. All people belong to many mini-cultures and larger cultures at the same time. In some settings, the conflicts between values of the groups will arise.

Another interesting concept in multiple group memberships is that the shared beliefs and values among groups often are held only in the abstract. Many of us profess strongly held beliefs, only to "change" our minds after additional information is provided to us. Truly strong beliefs are not changed through casual transfer of information between friends or teachers and learners. An interesting exercise is to get a group of people together who "agree" on a controversial topic. Have the group try to identify where they disagree on the topic. It is often much closer to the surface than we would expect, suggesting that shared beliefs are shared on abstract levels, not in specifics.

Because of multiple memberships in mini-cultures, individuals may have different ways of understanding an issue, depending upon the "hat" they are wearing. We consciously change hats when we say things like "as an educator . . ." or "if I were an economist, I would . . ." or "speaking as a . . . " How often do we neglect to change hats when we are in learning settings?

To help untangle this discussion on multiple group membership, readers may want to round up a few friends and try this activity. Each person should create a three-dimensional model of the relationship to the various groups to which he or she belongs. Now with the others, join your models together to represent an artificially formed learning group. Look for intersections in areas other than the learning group.

Clarifying Philosophy

Educators will want to examine their values, beliefs, and attitudes in relation to the mini-culture of the learning community. This process includes an examination of the learning community as both a single element and a player in the larger picture.

Importance of the Learning Community

The first belief to be clarified regards the importance of the group in the teaching-learning exchange. How do you view the group? How do you work with the group? Why? We might assume that the group is important, but the question is, how much and how soon in the considerations of teaching does the concept of the group become important to the individual educator? Teachers who tend toward content or instruction centeredness may hold a central belief that the group is important for the receipt or the process of content.

Some educators believe that groups are instrumental in the process of learning. In teaching settings, they structure different groups for different tasks to force the process to work. These are the group leaders who say, "Talk to the person behind you for three minutes about . . ." or "Everyone with a blue note card go over to this corner; those of you with yellow, over here. . . ." The group is used for the process more than the process for the group.

Other educators look upon the group as a unit that deserves

gentle nurturing. To foster cohesiveness, they structure group activities to enhance total group growth. Activities are functions of the group working together and becoming increasingly identified as a group. This is accomplished by using activities that reveal who the individuals are within the group, then seeking a group understanding.

Both methods can be effective but reflect differences in beliefs about the process of education. Similarly, another belief each educator must define is how much value to place on the development, maintenance, and growth of the group versus that of the individual, the content, the environment, and the teacher. As educators, we cannot agree on an absolute of importance of a group in learning. Each educator holds personal biases; the challenge is whether we act on them in a manner that supports these biases.

Most students express dissatisfaction with "group projects," even in some informal settings as well as more formal settings. Yet in the spirit of cooperative learning or team building or collaborative learning, most educators structure group projects. So why do we do this very thing we dislike as learners? Intuitively, educators know how valuable the experience can be, even when frustrating. The question is, do we do group projects to enhance the group, or do we do group projects simply to do group projects? Learners can always tell the difference.

How aware are we of our own life experiences in relation to the myriad groups to which we belong and the many settings in which we function? As with any of the elements, to truly understand our belief system we must challenge what we assume to be our beliefs. Are the beliefs we espouse consistent with the beliefs that are reflected through how we perform? Congruence is achieved through questioning ourselves over and over again. How much power does a group have, as opposed to an individual? What about the individual who is only tangentially involved in the group? Is learning enhanced by group functions? Is that true for all learners or only certain types of learners? Are you threatened by a cohesive group of learners? What about when they decide that your instruction is not appropriate?

Questioning our beliefs about groups means probing below the answers that seem to "pop out" of our mouths almost by rote.

For some of the questions, we may not have answers. In time, given questioning, experience, trying out different behaviors, and dialogue with colleagues and ourselves, educators can define beliefs regarding the group and learning.

Relative Importance of the Learning Community

We achieve congruence when our behaviors match our beliefs not only about the importance of the group but about how the group interacts with the other elements of the teaching-learning exchange. An educator who believes that group learning is usually a better means of learning than individualized instruction will use group process over individual assignments, even though individual assignments may be a part of what is necessary for the group to function. An educator holding a polar view will use group process as a means of allowing individuals to develop and refine skills necessary for their individual progress. The method appears the same, but a different belief system is in operation. The result is a different experience for the learner in both settings.

As we begin to understand what we believe about the group, we can begin to explore how we can use the group in a manner that is congruent with our beliefs. All individuals are in some potential state of internal conflict. Individuals in groups may share beliefs, but only on the most abstract levels will the whole group share the belief. Still, all people can understand an issue from different personal perspectives. These aspects of a group are the canvas for the "picture" the educator will paint with the group. Given the personal understandings and beliefs about a group, the subculture, and learning, the canvas may be abstract, expressionistic, realistic, deconstructionist, or whatever style you paint in.

Do you encourage the individual to confront internal conflict? Do you support conflict among learners (challenging the shared values)? Do you prompt learners to explore the affect from all aspects of themselves? How the educator uses the group relates to how inclusionary he or she is. Inclusionary practice involves the learners not only in determining their own learning outcomes, pace of learning, meaning, and the like, but also in allowing the group to function as a group within the teaching-learning exchange. A highly inclusionary educator will use process as a primary tool in teaching; an educator with less inclusionary practices will control the group to guide it to his or her desired outcomes.

Again, reflect on the many groups to which you belong. List five groups in which you have membership (for example, family, religion, school cohort, professional groups, and social circles). For each group, describe your role in each group in five to ten words. Look at the descriptions. How consistent are the words you used to describe your role in each group? What makes the variability, if anything? Now, for each group, describe in five to ten words your feelings toward the reason you belong to each group. Do these statements have more congruence with your role?

Now assess how you view the group of learners in the teaching-learning exchange. The degree of variability with which you view the group may indicate how much you believe the cultural behavior of the group is part of the teaching-learning exchange. Culture is more than art and artifacts; culture in the learning setting is the group with whom you work.

Conclusion

Adult educators seeking further understanding about the formation of a mini-culture and the resulting conflicts and issues born from that formation may want to try the following activity. The authors have used it with many different groups of adult educators and have found that it always produces great discussion and debate.

Gather a group of at least ten adults together. Separate into two groups based on marital status, "marrieds" and "singles." Marital status is the characteristic we have used in a variety of adult education settings to establish an artificial "major or dominant culture" and a "mini-culture" (Heimlich & Van Tilburg, 1988). Rationale for marital status is based upon the assumption, which still holds at the writing of this book, that for adults in the United States, being married is the norm for the major culture and being single is the deviant status.

Distribute to both groups the directions for the activity (Resource C). The directions are different for the two groups, but group members assume that they are all working on the same activity.

Each group works through its assignments: the major culture develops an educational program tailored to the mini-culture while the mini-culture discusses shared values and beliefs and how these might inhibit or promote participation in an educational program.

After thirty minutes, the two groups come together and discover that they have indeed been doing two very different things. The "marrieds" unveil their educational program, and the "singles" react to it based on the values and beliefs they discussed.

Interesting things can happen as the discussion evolves. The topics selected for the educational program usually represent stereotypic thoughts about the values and beliefs of single people. For example, one group of marrieds selected birth control methods as the content of the educational program because "after all, they are swingin' singles!" Of course, this mini-culture of singles took offense at some of the assumptions the major culture made about singles' values and beliefs. The ensuing discussion highlighted many of the issues discussed in this chapter and in fact brought these issues to life for the participants.

As adult educators we must continually be aware of the impact of the community of learners on the other primary elements of the teaching-learning exchange and vice versa. Whether the community is newly formed or has been in existence in a similar or the same configuration, it will develop a unique mini-culture.

The extent to which we as teachers take notice of the mini-culture and then utilize it in the teaching-learning exchange represents our sensitivity toward and inclusion of the learning community. Even though much literature in adult education suggests that focusing on the individual learner is preferred, many excellent teachers choose to focus on the community of learners. The quest for readers is to identify beliefs, values, and attitudes related to the learning community and mini-culture and to seek congruence among those attributes and behavior.

Chapter Eight

The Learner

Picture yourself standing in front of a group. Look at each face in front of you. Now, make these faces "learners." Perhaps, for a bit of ambience, add some fog, perhaps a couple of colleagues. Then "Fillet of a fenny snake,/In the caldron boil and bake;/Eye of newt and toe of frog,/Wool of bat and tongue of dog,/Adder's fork and blindworm's sting,/Lizard's leg and howlet's wing,/For a charm of pow'rful trouble,/Like a hell-broth boil and bubble" (*Macbeth*, Act 4, Scene 1).

Maybe being a teacher is like being one of Shakespeare's witches or a "mad scientist." We have a cauldron bubbling with some potent elixir. We add just a touch of some other highly potent chemical. What we hope to produce is some sort of life.

However, if we are adult educators, the "containers" we teach are nearly full. We add just a few drops of knowledge, perhaps even some wisdom, to the previous knowledge, beliefs, and opinions of our learners. What happens? Sometimes nothing. The addition does nothing to the total cauldron. Sometimes disaster. The little bit we add causes an adverse chemical reaction. But once in that wonderful while, magic does happen. The experiment succeeds; learning does occur, and the content we shared becomes an integral part of the individual.

Each individual is like every other individual in some respects: we all belong to the human race. Each individual is also like some specific individuals as a result of belonging to a specific cultural group. "The cultural group serves as the basis for individuals to become humanized. Each individual becomes fully human through the process of participating in a cultural group or groups" (Locke, 1992, p. xiii). Each individual is also unlike any other individuals in some respects—we differ from everyone in the entire world on a multitude of characteristics. "What these three identities mean for teachers and counselors is that they must be aware that each individual is seeking a personal identity, to a greater or lesser degree, by acknowledging an identity with a cultural group while living in a world community" (Locke, 1992, p. xiii).

As educators, the choices we make affect the learning opportunities for our participants. Methods, techniques, the arrangement of the room, and the selection and organization of the information itself are all elements the teacher can control—the drops the teacher adds to the cauldron. The more cognizant we are of the choices we make as teachers, the more likely it is that positive learning opportunities will occur. Yet as educators we are placed in the inevitable and unenviable position of having to work with that most nebulous and ethereal of factors—other human beings. The old image of learners being empty vessels into which the teacher can pour knowledge simply is untrue for most of us. We must remember that what we add is only a small part of each learner's "cauldron" of knowledge.

Human beings are wonderful and complex. In this chapter we discuss how this wonderful, awful, exciting, terrifying, delightful, frightening phenomenon called the learner ingratiates itself into the teaching-learning exchange. To examine how the individual fits in the teaching-learning exchange, we will look at how individuals learn about learning, reflect on the role of the learner, and consider achieving a balance between beliefs and behaviors related to the individual learner.

The Learner and Learning

There are myriad ways of exploring who the learner is in the teaching-learning exchange. In order to keep the focus on the learner in relationship to the other elements of the exchange, we have elected to examine the dimension of the learner from four perspectives: characteristics of adult learners, prior experiences with learning, motivation to learn, and outcomes for learning.

Characteristics of Adult Learners

The arguments for and against a theory of androgogy (adult education) are well established. Knowles (1970, 1980), Darkenwald and Merriam (1982), Brookfield (1986), Kidd (1973), Freire (1973), Knox (1986) and others have put forth eloquent discussions on characteristics of the adult as learner. The importance of this literature notwithstanding, we challenge the reader to consider not only the concepts of the adult learner but also the well-documented research in human learning from the field of applied psychology. For our purpose, we will assume the characteristics of the adult learners and focus more on the role of the learner in the teaching-learning exchange.

We cannot separate the individual learner from the life of the individual: "learning, schooling, and education are experiences of the whole person" (Richards, 1980). This inseparability of the learner from the adult, the family, the cultures, the profession or occupation, and the emotions of being human creates the rich tapestry of the individuals who appear in our learning settings and say "I want to learn," "I have to learn," or "Teach me."

Learning cannot exist without a learner. Likewise, meaning cannot exist without a meaning-maker (Postman & Weingartner, 1969). Educators are often in the role of creating meaning from chaos, data, ideas, and energy. Meaning, ultimately, comes from our perceptions of the things and people around us, and our perceptions come from us (Postman & Weingartner, 1969). Solomon and Solomon (1993) note that learners are seekers after meaning, not information processors. They further the discussion by stating, "One does not get an education by memorizing the Denver telephone directory, even if it is filled with useful information" (p. 19). The characteristics with which we usually examine the learner often relate to the steps of information obtaining and digesting rather than the process of learning.

There is tremendous value in understanding how a learner learns if what we truly value is the act of learning and not the knowledge, skills, attitudes, or aspirations that result from the learning. How a learner thinks, how the learner regulates the learning process, and how the learner takes responsibility for his or her own learning are learner characteristics that are useful to the educator to know (Twining, 1991).

Each learner is truly an individual, and the total personal style of learning is unique. Lovell (1987) suggests that individual learning skills; social learning; personality differences and cognitive styles; and individual differences in age, experience, motivation, and self-perception are factors that make each adult a unique learner. We can aid in our understanding of learning by examining traits of learning and taxonomies of learning styles. The tools by which we can measure various learning preferences of learners are revealing, but they reveal only limited dimensions of the learners and not the whole. The more we accept the adult learner as a complex, individual entity that will never be fully understood, the more we can focus on how we are affecting the learning potential of each individual.

Prior Experience with Learning

Learning occurs when previous perceptions of reality are not in harmony with current experience, creating dissonance (Mezirow, 1977). Learning is the act of aligning perceptions of reality with empirical or sensory data and occurs because there is real benefit in having knowledge. The earliest training is familial training. Few remember, or probably care to remember, much of their earliest learning. Who, for example, wants to remember potty training, the struggle to learn to communicate, or the lesson that when told the stove is hot, one should trust the teacher? Social training and early experiences are full of learning about self and for self. As Gagné (1970) pointed out, "Human skill, appreciations, and reasonings in all their great variety, as well as human hopes, aspirations, attitudes, and values, are generally recognized to depend for their development largely on the events called learning" (p. 1). But somewhere along the line, the concept of what constitutes learning changes in three distinct ways.

The first change occurs because learning is not based on interests. "Whys" don't get answered, resulting in three outcomes: (1) the realization that all grown-ups are dull, stuffy, and unable to enjoy the wonders of the world; (2) the loss of hope about understanding the world and a loss of interest in learning; and (3) a gradual withdrawal from family communications (Highet, 1989). The earliest learning is sensory: the child empirically comes to understand what holds meaning or makes sense from the world. The senses can be trusted, the human animal knows. Then school, day care, or other programs begin to instruct in "non-sense": the learner is trained, instructed, and educated for the mind but not the senses (Schrank, 1972). This act places learning outside the self, and the learner is told that perceptions are sometimes "wrong" or incorrect. Sometimes this correction is neither gentle nor persuasive but mandatory and imposed. "You don't know that." "How would you know?" "That's not important." These phrases give the strong understanding that perceptions are not to be trusted and that trust in what is to be learned must be placed in the external.

The second change is that learning occurs at school. This is a part of the perpetuation of any culture; the purpose of schooling is primarily to adapt human potential to the dominant culture, not to develop human potential (Schrank, 1972). The purpose of education has never been to free the human spirit and mind but to bind them (Lindenfeld, 1973). Conformity, obedience, and acquiescence are the major subjects learned in school (Lindenfeld, 1973). Ideally, learning is about the learner's meanings—the learner's psychological needs and desires to know something. If this happens, learning is not a contest between the learner and something outside the learner, but is internal (Postman & Weingartner, 1969). Does this happen? Sometimes, but more often learning is equated with tests, grade cards or report forms, honors or lack of honors bestowed, and the continuation of sports competition into the classroom (spelling bees, history downs, Suzy's poem being selected as the best one, the one to be read aloud in class). In the adult setting, this continuation relates to job performance, continuing education requirements, performance criteria, and even "being best" in the group. Even the term *curriculum* at its roots refers to "race track," and in school, one's success is only at the cost of another's failure; "the nightmarish fear of failure comes to haunt those socialized in our schools, even at the heights of any later success" (Lindenfeld, 1973, p. 41).

The third change is that learning is related to the powerful and highly individual vantage points of our own pedagogical experiences. In school, the student gradually comes to understand what "teaching" is. Each student experiences models of instruction, both good and bad, and grows to believe that what teachers do is teach. Perhaps the actions of the teachers constitute the entire spectrum of what the student believes to be "teaching." Learning is experienced as being given information that the teacher holds. The teacher has the answers, and the student's role is to accept them from the teacher. Perhaps some dialogue occurs and some projects are even completed independently of the teacher, but the student learns that the real teaching occurs when the teacher explains what one needs to know to pass tests, to get through the class, and to get the diploma or certificate.

What happens then to the adults who have internalized the concepts of learning discussed above? Learners accept the premise that learning occurs most and best when the educator talks about what the teacher knows best. The role of the learner is to take notes, ask questions for clarity, respond to questions with the *right* answer, and absorb that which the teacher gives. In so doing, the learner affects the posture of learning: nod the head at the right time, look puzzled when necessary, appear to be busy to avoid being called upon, raise a hand to ask a question, and accept the rules given by the trainer, organization, or program, and other rules of school.

These rules are carried unconsciously by adults into all learning situations: Don't go to the bathroom except when given permission (like a scheduled break in a program). Walk up stairs on the right side. Don't talk when you're learning. Don't chew gum or eat or drink while you're learning. Stand in line. Stand in line. Stand in line.

These "rules" of school help the young learner get through the formal education system. Every adult who has been through school knows the rules, or boundaries of acceptable behavior, established as norms for experience. To different extents and applications, all people learn to operate under certain behavioral expectations; rules are imposed and acted upon as if the rules themselves have meaning. Adults have a much broader understanding of "power" and who's in charge than children, yet they carry with them the complex realization that the rules learned in school appear to be the rules for learning (Carlsen, 1988).

All the rules learned in school also have "subtextual rules," or deeper levels of real meaning. These subtextual rules include messages about gender differences (Best, 1989), race (Kimloch, 1979), and power (Solomon, 1989). Here is an example of one of these rules in action from a male colleague:

> In fourth grade, once a week we attended art class. One day, returning early from art, two girls and I were giggling in the hall. Well, the girls were giggling and I was laughing. Loudly. Out of the classroom stormed my teacher who grabbed me by the ear, hauled me into the classroom and put a sign around my neck that read something like "obnoxious." As the rest of the class returned from art, I had to stand in the front of the room. It was humiliating. As an adult, I can look at the situation and realize that the lesson I was supposed to learn was that one should not make a disturbance in the halls when classes are occurring. What did I learn? 1) learning cannot be fun—you shouldn't laugh; and 2) girls can giggle, boys can't.

Motivation to Learn

In the learning setting, participants are influenced by many things: the teacher, the physical environment, the books, other learners (Hill, 1963). The "learning" that the teacher believes is the purpose of the exchange is compounded by the other lessons that simultaneously occur. These complex lessons are often integrated into the individual as part of the learning setting.

Adults carry "rules" with them as part of what they hold as entry behaviors, knowledge, skills, abilities, or attitudes to the instructional setting (Cranton, 1989). Teachers of adults often expect adult learners to behave differently from children, yet again and again the behaviors of "school" are apparent in adult teaching settings. Draves (1984) revisits this point when he reflects that for many people, formal schooling was less than successful and that adult structured learning environments or situations are inevitably associated with the pedagogical experiences.

Adult learners carry with them the baggage of their expectations of learning derived from formal schooling. Expectations grow from internalized, sensory learning and, though unspoken and sometimes subconscious, are powerful influences on the teaching-learning exchange. This baggage is in part the "because of" or "in spite of" why adults participate in various learning settings.

Considering this, the work Cross (1983) conducted on why adults participate becomes even more revealing. Unlike the formal learning settings of "school," most adult education programs are in part choice based. Training for employment and court-required programs are perhaps the only truly mandatory education programs for adults. What drives adults to participate in education programs? And what will turn the adult from participant to learner? The distinction is one labeled as "motivation" and is that which prompts humans to use habits or learned behaviors (Deese & Hulse, 1967).

No single factor in the teaching-learning exchange determines the motivation of a learner to learn. In adults, the incentive, the reinforcer, the relevant drive, the behaviors for seeking the outcome, and all the thoughts about action and responses are intermingled in complex behaviors described by motives (Hill, 1981). Motivation to learn is not learning, and motivation to learn may or may not be within the teacher's realm of control with any individual in any particular situation.

Motivation theory addresses why people choose to act, the intensity of their actions, and the persistence toward those actions (Schaie & Geiwitz, 1982). Why is one learner driven to acquire information while another in an apparently similar situation is not so driven? Why is an individual a committed learner in one setting and a barrier to information in another? Why, indeed. The best one can do is to work toward one's potential.

Outcomes for Learning

One of the concepts of teaching adults is to allow learners to be equal partners in the exchange, or as nearly equal as learners can be with a teacher. To do this, teachers must know how much control they are willing to release and why. The person with the "control" is the one who determines what the outcomes for the particular teaching-learning exchange will be. According to Mocker and Spear (1982), educational exchanges can be identified as formal, informal, nonformal, or self-directed on the basis of who controls the objectives for learning and the means of obtaining the objectives. Formal learning occurs when the educator controls both objectives for learning and means of learning. Nonformal and informal learning differ in that the learner controls the objectives and the teacher the means in nonformal learning, whereas in informal learning the educator controls the objectives and the learner the means. In self-directed learning, the learner controls both the means and the objectives of learning. Control is an issue with which our society at large struggles.

For many of us, the idea of totally releasing control to the learners is terrifying. We think that total release of control would be walking into a learning setting, sitting down, and saying, "So what do you want to do/learn/try?" As Draves (1984) points out, "It just doesn't happen that way." Yet the educator who does release control completely to learners believes learners are fully partners, with the responsibility for learning being the learner's, and the responsibility for teaching remaining the teacher's. The degree of comfort one is able to find with this balance is a function of individual preference, beliefs, values, and experience related to the student. Even those of us who are not oriented toward such a release of control can at times function well in a real partnership. We just may not prefer to remain there.

Releasing control to learners is more than finding out what they want to gain from the exchange. True empowerment of learners provides them with the resources to define their need to know, what to know, how to know, and when to quit. This is what Freire (1973) discusses when he tells us that dialogue is entered into by someone with someone about something and that something constitutes the content of the proposed education. The educator who acts according to this belief consistently and congruently is releasing control to the learner.

Releasing control also suggests the relevance of the content to individual needs for power, identity, and competition (Glasser, 1986). An educator who believes the student is central does not make the meaning for the individual—that is, tell the learner why the content is important in the learner's life—but allows the content to fulfill the meaning "needs" in the learner. True release of control allows learners to cull appropriate data and identify for themselves the patterns and processes of their need for information in the process of realizing meaning (Carlsen, 1988). A teacher with a low need for control allows discovery rather than requiring learners to repeat facts and figures. Further, as much as we would love to ensure learning, learning will always remain the prerogative of the learner. It is up to the individual to decide how thoroughly or extensively anything relates to his or her fundamental beliefs and needs (Kline, 1971).

For many teachers, this concept is terrifying! What happens if every learner wants something different? What if none of the learners chooses to do what we have planned or would like to do? What if we cannot fulfill their needs?

Interesting, isn't it, that when we go to the extreme (in this case the release of control to the individual), we can begin to see our own beliefs more clearly. Those of us who may be very high on inclusion would expect this diversity and have concepts for how to allow individuals to structure learning, based on each other's needs and wants. The biases we have assumed through the inculturation into adult education theory are strong: learners must be responsible for their own needs, learners must define the outcomes of their learning, and learners must direct their own learning. So the question arises: what do I really believe, and from that belief, what do I really do?

An effective teacher does not forget that the learner may not have the information, experience, or ability requisite for the answers being sought. Addressing this potential gap is one of the roles of the teacher. But needs are highly personal and individual. A content-centered teacher may allow discovery on the individual level, but the focus remains on what is being learned. An environment-centered educator maintains the climate for learning even if the individuals are paramount in the process of teaching. High inclusion does not and should not universally demand student-centeredness. They are different functions. Inclusion focused on the individual may or may not be based on individual-oriented teaching.

On the other hand, a truly sensitive teacher may operate with a great deal of control. Have you ever heard someone say, "I really want each participant to understand this" or "I really care about each student—I know what each needs from this workshop/course/seminar." Extremely high sensitivity to the individual does not necessarily mean that the educator allows the process to contain the individual's ongoing input beyond questions and suggestions.

However, it might. Few models exist for us regarding a focus on the individual with high inclusionary practice. Some radical community education theory operates from this perspective. But few of us have really experienced this type of teaching, even though many adult educators claim the beliefs that individual focus and individual input are very important in their teaching activities (Heimlich, 1990; Seevers, 1991). The risk in being individual centered is that not all individuals will be given equal or equitable treatment or attention. The risk in releasing control to the individual is that the program may not fulfill the expectations of the organization or sponsoring body.

But if the concepts of inclusion and sensitivity to the individual are strongly held in your beliefs, the returns will be tremendous if you act on these beliefs. The challenge is to make explicit personal beliefs about the learner. Who is the learner? What is the learner's role? What is the teacher's role with the learning exchange?

Reflecting on the Learner in the Teaching-Learning Exchange

How teachers choose to ignore or to address the "rules of school" that each adult learner carries into any learning environment relates to the teacher's orientation toward the human element of instruction and to the level of control released to the individual learner. "There is no way that a teacher can 'learn' a student. Students choose to learn, just as they choose *not* to learn in the face of ridicule, embarrassment, or coercion" (Purkey & Novak, 1984, pp. 40–41). The teacher can reinforce the old rules of school or violate these rules without realizing that this is occurring.

The old rules of school can affect both teachers and learners. Have you ever noticed that in workshops or seminars for adults (including a lot of training programs), the presenter or moderator often makes a statement to the effect of "there are refreshments in the back, the restrooms are down the hall—if you need anything, feel free to get up and get it." These things are often said but seldom meant. Nearly every teacher I know is thrown for a loop when learners leave the setting early. Usually we, as presenters, become tremendously uncomfortable when participants get up to stretch their legs or even lean on a chair rather than sit. We begin to wonder, "What did I do? Don't they like me?" We personalize these routine actions of learners as commentary on our teaching.

Perhaps the real challenge in this is to begin to separate ourselves from our teaching setting. We cannot separate ourselves from us as teachers, but we can examine the situation as one that is not totally within our control. What are five things that you like as a learner in a teaching-learning setting? What are five things you do not like as a learner in a teaching-learning exchange? Think of your last several teaching events. Compare the methods you used against your likes and dislikes as a learner. One of the keys to successful teaching is to utilize methods so that the outcomes are as positive for the learner as possible. We can use ourselves as learners as a first step in examining the complex relationship of the learner to the elements of the teaching-learning exchange.

From the adult learner's perspective, previous educational experiences have a tremendous influence on the effectiveness of any new learning (Lovell, 1987). Success breeds success, and past successes are often the determinant of current achievement, as is the level of expectation of both the learner and the educator. A classic example of this is revealed in studies that show students' success to be predetermined when their teacher is made aware of their previous record. A "slow" learner whose file reflects this label is often placed with slow learners in the next class even before the teacher knows the student. Likewise, students with high grades in previous years encounter higher expectations, which they often meet.

From communications theory, we can extrapolate the concept that given limited initial data, we all place people into narrow boxes called stereotypes. The first segment of time together is spent trying to decide if the person fulfills the expectations of the stereotype or not. This is not all bad; it is done subconsciously and constantly. For example, many of us have experienced the sense of "knowing" someone really well almost immediately—or thinking we do. Maybe the person reminds us of a favorite aunt or uncle, or a best friend from years gone by. Whatever it is, something in what the person says or does "clicks" in us, and we project a positive stereotype upon the person. Negative stereotypes work the same way.

What a teacher needs to know to feel adequate with the collection of individuals defines his or her level of sensitivity. Some teachers are more sensitive to individuals. They are not satisfied with limited sources of information and often go to great lengths to allow participants in the teaching-learning exchange to reveal much about themselves. Other teachers are more sensitive to the group. The concentration is on understanding the similarities rather than the differences among the learners. Still other teachers are more sensitive to themselves; teacher-centered instructors believe they must know themselves and the situation before learning can begin. The teacher who is learner centered is willing to commit to knowing the issues behind the individual that may affect the teaching-learning exchange. Those who are not learner centered may be threatened by knowing too much about the individuals: knowing them means having to deal with the information about their lives. In any case, those teachers who have figured out where they fall on the dimension of sensitivity can design effective, efficient teaching-learning exchanges in terms of their own teaching. Others often waste their time on routine "getting to know you" exercises that are never used again or, on the other extreme, do not place enough emphasis on such exchanges and feel frustrated in their level of understanding of their participants.

Take, for example, the experience of two colleagues who led a series of seminars for leaders of an industry group. They agreed to ask participants to keep journals as a component of the seminars. They agreed on the journal assignments and were excited over the way the journal keeping encouraged a depth of consideration around the topics being discussed in the sessions. Then the participants turned in the journals. It seemed that for every comment that was positive about an activity, there was a negative comment. The leaders learned about the history of participants, about strong beliefs participants held regarding racism, sexism, military action, family life, pain in the participants' lives, joys they were going through—it was all there. One of the leaders soaked up the information. This was just what she was looking for to understand each participant. The other read the journals and panicked. He felt a need to defend himself and the seminar.

Together, they decided how to process the information they gathered from the journals within themselves and with the class. But the difference was strongly illustrated: one teacher's minimum need to know about the individual may be too much information for another teacher.

Achieving Congruence

One danger for teachers who center their concentration solely on the individual learner is that the concern for the individual may obstruct awareness about the functioning of the group. An individual with an issue may blind the instructor to the needs of the group to move on with the content. This individual/group conflict is very real and can be viewed in classrooms where the teacher patiently works with the participants who "still don't get it" while the rest of the group chatters, drums fingers or pencils on tabletops, or starts to work on other things. As with all orientations, it can be so easy to rely on the strength of the center that we fail to observe the interactions with the rest of the model.

The individual is an important part of the instruction but is only a part and is not necessarily the greatest part. We say this again to reempower those of us who are not individual learner centered but have felt that there is something wrong with us because we don't quite believe what some of the literature has told us we should believe.

The individual is an important part of the instruction and is only a part, and is not necessarily the greatest part. We say this slightly differently to reempower those of us who are individual centered and need to utilize this strength without ignoring the other elements operating in the teaching-learning exchange.

Create a lifeline of yourself as a learner. Using a rope, string, paper, poster, or whatever, identify the significant events of your career as a learner by drawing, attaching, or symbolizing the events on the lifeline. (If you can, get someone else to do this too and compare your lifelines.) What did you see as significant incidents in your learning history? How did these "learnings" relate to the content, the group, the teacher, or the environment in which they occurred? Not only our learning preferences but also our learning histories makes each of us truly unique.

Because individuals are so complex, teachers can get a peek into a potential gold mine of resources and problems when they allow the individual to become a part of their awareness in the teaching-learning exchange. In early efficiency studies, humans on factory assembly lines were viewed as devoid of purpose or outside interests and concerns while they were at work. We now realize that no matter what the responsibility, individuals bring to work with them all that is going on outside the work environment. It may be suppressed much of the time, but the rest of their lives is with them there. We can say the same for the learner. A bad day for someone is a bad day for that person no matter how hard we try to teach. In teaching education classes, we often use the following extreme example to make the point:

> I get the news this morning that a dear friend is very
> ill/has died. Then I have a fight with my spouse/
> partner/best friend. On the way out of the house, I get
> a phone call, but trying to reach the phone, I trip over
> the dog and spill coffee all over my just-cleaned
> clothes. Then the car won't start and I can't get a tow
> for two hours. Then I have to fight a traffic jam. So
> I walk into class and am instantly ready to absorb

everything the teacher wants me to know about some
obscure subject that I am studying only because I need
the stupid credit hours.

A similar example can be imagined for all adult learners, whether
in a one-time workshop, a job training program, a series of seminars, or a church study group. Is this individual ready to learn, or
is this a person overwhelmed with the realities of the outside world?
    We believe that instruction will be improved if the teacher
knows something about each individual in a learning group. The
duration of the program, the situation in which the learning is to
occur, and all those other confounders limit or facilitate the depth
to which we are able to "know" individuals. What is vital to remember is that individuals are present and acting as individuals in
every learning setting, no matter what *our* constraints may be.
    And what does this mean for the individual learner? Whether
the individual is the educator's primary concern or not, an awareness of the individual and an understanding that the individual is
functioning in the learning setting can determine that individual's
level of success. Although writing about writers, Rubin (1990)
makes a powerful point regarding the role of the individual in the
teaching-learning setting when the teacher is aware of the element
of the individual: "I do not mean [they] did not already possess an
aptitude . . . or had failed to demonstrate incipient . . . talent. . . .
Given the talent, given the innate inclination, however, it is possible for the teacher to happen along and make the student heed the
inclination and perfect the talent" (p. xi). Awareness of the individual in the teaching-learning exchange is being open to the individual talents and unique contributions each learner can make to your
teaching-learning exchange.

Part Three

Integrating Teaching Concepts with Teaching Style

Chapter Nine

Matching Methods
to Teaching Style

So far we have explored individual philosophical bases, questioned beliefs and behaviors, and identified the elements of instruction. What ties all these things together into an identifiable instructional event? What can we point to and say, that is effective teaching?

We are at a place in our exploration where we can examine the relationship between teacher behaviors and learner achievement; we can understand that a teacher's behaviors that result from certain beliefs and attitudes are somehow related to how an individual learns (Rosenshine & Furst, 1971). Whether we choose to focus on the management of learning or learners (Bloom, 1976) or on instructional variety and its many dimensions (Borich, 1990), we can look at observable, measurable behaviors demonstrated in the teaching setting. Teacher behaviors appear to overlie the entire model of the instructional moment. For lack of a more inclusive term, these behaviors have been called *methods* of instruction, *strategies*, and *techniques*.

Perhaps it will help at this point to explain what this chapter is not. This is not a "how to" chapter. There are many excellent texts on the application of teaching methods (see Resource D). These and other texts are highly recommended for both the student of adult education and the practitioner. Additionally, this is not a chapter on evaluating, comparing, or ranking various teaching techniques. Those issues are best left for another discussion.

The first goal of this chapter is to provide a framework for exploring the various teaching techniques that can be used by a style-focused teacher. A second goal is to provide an opportunity to reflect on how we choose our strategies for teaching. A final goal is to consider how to become more congruent in teaching by adapting methods to individual teaching style.

In any setting, the educator has a great deal of control over what occurs in the teaching-learning exchange. Perhaps most notable of these educator-controlled elements is the method of instruction. We find, however, that methods are often selected by precedent, routine, or a cursory examination of the situation.

The choices we make as educators affect the learning opportunities for the learners. The more cognizant we are of the choices we make and how they relate to us as teachers, the more likely it is that positive learning opportunities will occur.

Methods of Instruction

Reed (1939) describes three phases of the learning process: a goal, a method, and a content. The first condition of effective learning is to have a goal; learning is effective only when there is something to work on, or content. But Reed suggests that the psychology of learning is focused upon methods, techniques, or a group of techniques by which learning works toward its goal.

Methods are the collections of tools we have available to us to use in our instruction. We each have a wealth of experiences in learning, and from these experiences we can pull unlimited numbers of ideas about how to tie the elements into a cohesive whole. Smith (1966) describes teaching as a creative activity, and creativity as "sinking down taps into our past experience and putting these selected experiences together into new patterns, new ideas, or new products."

Our methods are the sum of observable behaviors that we as teachers undertake in instruction. Whether we know it or not, these behaviors are visible as a whole for any single instructional event.

One explanation of predilection for a particular teaching style is that an educator prefers particular teaching methods to garner specified learner outcomes. In this approach, the educator as a person and as a medium is a part of the unique message to the learners (Thompson, 1984). The choice of teaching method can suggest the degree of involvement of the group in determining its relationship to the subject matter, teaching methods, media, and outcomes (Darkenwald & Merriam, 1982).

Simply knowing that different methods are suggested does not guarantee that each teacher will be able to use the different methods with equal skill. The personal and the social characteristics of the teacher are manifested in the teacher's classroom behaviors (Ryans, 1960).

Most methods texts suggest that instruction can be improved if a teacher uses diverse methods. But no one can possibly be equally competent and proficient in all methods. Style is what a teacher is; method is the planning, carrying out, and evaluating of specific classroom activities (Lovell, 1987). How do we go about planning, carrying out, and evaluating activities in a way that is congruent with who we are?

Understanding Methods

Methods for instruction may be best defined as the *intentions* of the teacher. In a broad view, "method" is how you, the teacher, decide to take the content in the environment and reveal it to each learner and the learners as a whole. This is how the elements are tied together, and the observable part of this process is labeled *method*. The purpose of the instructional event, the purpose for pulling the elements into a unified whole, should drive the instructional event.

Some teachers at a college in the South Pacific we were working with were struggling with the concept of methods. What is the difference between a method and a technique or strategy for instruction? One of the teachers shared a concept that clarified the topic for all of us: plans for construction of a building. The method is the original design. Whether the planned building is a house, an office, a shed, a store, or whatever, the original design tells us its purpose. But we cannot build without more specifics. Enter the blueprints, our "techniques." Even here, however, we will run into construction problems unless we have elevated drawings that give us specifics of measurements, fittings, wiring, plumbing, and so forth. These are our strategies. The techniques and strategies may be the same from construction to construction, but they are put together in different ways depending upon the purpose of the design.

It is possible to begin our exploration of methods by looking at them as input/output transactions. A purpose-driven approach would focus methods on the outcome or the learner, not on the input or the teacher/content. This may challenge the paradigm of "method" that many educators are taught. Graphically, a standard approach to the teaching-learning exchange would look as shown in Figure 9.1. Note how the model is input oriented. The decisions stem from the perceptions of the teacher related to content.

An alternative approach that provides more flexibility for individual teaching styles might look as shown in Figure 9.2. Although this model is also driven by the teacher's perceptions, content is moved to a level equal to a consideration of the interactions of the elements. Method emerges as a result of the interactions of the elements of the teaching-learning exchange.

This view of method can generate a taxonomy of methods

Figure 9.1. Input-Oriented Model.

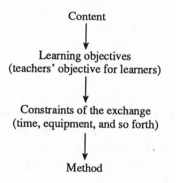

Content

↓

Learning objectives
(teachers' objective for learners)

↓

Constraints of the exchange
(time, equipment, and so forth)

↓

Method

Figure 9.2. Alternative Purpose-Driven Model.

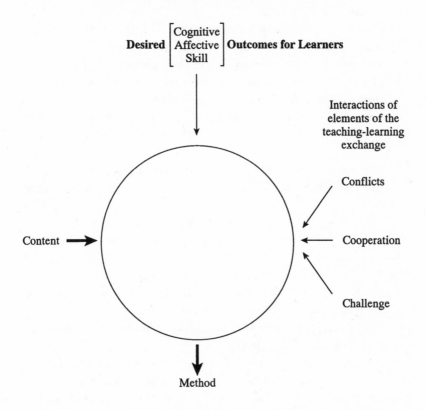

that is purpose driven. Such an approach is consistent with Verner's (1962) definition of method as "the relationship established by the institution with a potential body of participants for the purpose of systematically diffusing knowledge among a prescribed but not necessarily fully identified public" (p. 9). Although our own working definition examines the specific "teacher" rather than the institution, both definitions rely upon the purpose of the instructional session. Verner furthers his definition by focusing on whether the orientation of the instructional purpose is individual or group centered, thereby making his definition of method learner based.

Let's look at six purposes of instruction from the orientation of the teacher:

1. Cognitive learning through efficient delivery of a large quantity of information
2. Experiential learning, or integration of learning through the teacher's imposition of an experience on the learner
3. Attainment of self-understanding through the content
4. Affective learning through a process the teacher constructs
5. Sensory learning through image orientation
6. Cognitive learning in a large or dispersed student population, through efficient and consistent delivery of information

These six purposes can each be given a label. We can start to build a matrix of methods with these purposes identified (Table 9.1).

Knowing one's own philosophy of teaching-learning can help an educator to identify the "purpose" of an instructional event and consequently to choose his or her approach to that event: a concept of revealing content in an environment to each learner and the group. The taxonomy of methods used here is not technique or strategy bound: no specific means of structuring learning lies solely or entirely under any method. The method is the broad purpose; we can get into specifics a little later.

In this taxonomy, method contains the "key" to information exchange. Who has the information the learners want? How do the participants gain this information? In a presentation method, the teacher holds the information and "gives" it to the learner. In an experiential method, the teacher imposes experiences on the learner;

Table 9.1. Teaching Methods and Purposes.

Method	Purpose
Presentation	Efficient delivery of a large quantity of information
Experiential	Imposition of an experience on learner
Discovery	Self-understanding through experience
Games	Affective learning, psychological/physical stimuli
Media	Sensory learning
Teacher Absent	Efficient delivery to a dispersed population

the teacher still holds the knowledge and allows the learner to acquire it by controlled experiences. Discovery methods suggest that the learner ultimately holds the knowledge but must discover it through some guided activity. In methods using games, the teacher structures activities that allow knowledge to be assimilated into a new level of understanding within each learner. Media methods are used to create a sensory learning environment or to share sensory experiences that the educator cannot provide (for example, experiences related to a faraway geographical location). And teacher-absent methods, whether computer-based instruction, distance education, or concurrent data presentation, make the teacher the holder of information that is shared through some medium.

This framework suggests that the method is not the *what* but the *why*. Moving the discussion of method to this level allows the teacher to bring personal beliefs, values, and philosophy of teaching and learning to the application of the method. Further, it suggests that teachers do more than employ an array of techniques; they adapt these techniques to their own teaching style. Like a well-coordinated wardrobe, methods can be mixed and matched, all suiting the individual teacher well.

Reflecting on Methods

A brief explanation of each of the methods may help focus on the relationship of method to teaching style. For this initial discussion, we will simply examine the "pure" concept of each method. Later, we will look at how they work together in being adapted to a teacher's teaching style.

Presentation

Presentation methods are methods of "giving" information to the learner. The teacher presents concepts and information. Most of us are very comfortable with presentation methods and often use them in routine teaching situations. Teaching strategies often included in "pure" presentation methods are lectures, lecture-demonstrations, visually supported lectures (overheads, slides, charts, chalkboard), guest presenters, expert testimony, panels of experts, and resource panels. Presentation methods are an efficient means of getting information to people, a powerful tool for inspiration, and a good means of establishing interest. Motivational and after-dinner speakers, comedians, and storytellers all use presentation methods. Although much maligned, presentation methods have an appropriate place in education and deserve to be given due attention, refinement, practice, and respect.

Presentation methods rely in part on the development of effective interest approaches, careful structuring of the material, and appropriate use of visual aids. There are numerous ways to structure information, and a well-done presentation method uses an appropriate model: simple to complex; cause to effect; specific to general; problem to solution; pro versus con; chronological; concept to application; or familiar to unfamiliar.

The role of the educator is to present the information clearly, concisely, and simply (Lovell, 1987). The teacher is the vehicle for the information and is responsible to observe the learners and respond to their informational needs. When done well, a presentation method is a good means of supplying information to learners in a directed, teacher-to-learner manner.

Experiential

Experiential activities are those that draw on the learners' prior life experiences and, through imposition of an activity, allow the learners to "experience" the information we want them to gain. Technical training uses experiential learning through simulations. Therapists use experiential activities to allow clients to identify the patterns of their behavior or the foundations for their beliefs.

The key to developing experiential activities is to ask, "What experiences do I want the learners to have? What are the values that they should use?" Experiential methods are often inextricably linked with critical thinking. Another skill often required in experiential methods is decision making. In fact, any time we want transferrable knowledge to be the outcome of teaching, we should consider experiential activities. Values clarification, self-discovery, diversity, and change are all words that key into experiential methods. Experiential methods are not limited to physical behaviors but apply to affective and cognitive learning equally well.

The role of the educator in experiential methods is to devise, plan, implement, and organize the learning event. Experiential methods frequently require much more preparation than do presentation methods. The educator must identify *what* the learners are to gain, *how* the learners will experience this information, *when* information will be released, and *why* this activity is used. Evaluation of the method is often more difficult since internalized learning, a desired outcome of experiential methods, is less cognizantly realized by the learner than presented information at the time of the learning.

Discovery

Allowing learners to find in themselves what they already know or have the ability to know is called "discovery." Inevitably, whatever form the actual discovery takes, a significant component of discovery learning is the processing of the learning: challenging one's assumptions, sharing concepts with others, pooling knowledge. Discovery learning can utilize games, experiments, or a multitude of process activities. What ultimately sets discovery learning apart is that the outcome is not ensured by the teacher. What happens as an end is less important than what leads to the end. Discovery learning is process oriented.

Because processing "what happens" is important, discussion is an important component of any discovery-learning situation. Far too often, however, discussion is employed as a learning tool only after a presentation, as in "Now we'll break into groups and discuss what we've learned." This makes discussion nothing more than the "doing" part of a more formal presentation. Discussion should be an opportunity for learners to bring into the learning setting their own knowledge, beliefs, values, and experiences. In adult education we often profess that adult learners bring a great deal of information with them to the learning, and discovery methods, when correctly applied, allow this input.

Discovery learning also works well in situations in which learners know more than the teacher. For example, a volunteer at a science museum was asked to fill in at a Saturday afternoon workshop for advanced-level chemistry students. The volunteer knew something about the topic to be covered—polymers—but little about chemistry. After some initial discussion, the group leader decided to ask participants to put on their scientist's hats. In this role, they outlined what they would need to look for in a laboratory analysis and, after some prompting, suggested procedures for the tests. The leader then split the participants into groups, and the groups went to the lab, where they conducted all the tests possible in that lab in the manner they had identified. The discovery was total for all: about the lab, about the testing processes, about experimentation, about polymers, and about how much the pa. .icipants already knew about how to discover.

How an educator uses discovery should reflect his or her teaching style. There is no right or wrong way to conduct a discovery session. It is an individual factor of control whether the teacher sets constraints or parameters for the group or allows the group to set them; whether the teacher creates the learning activity or allows the group to do it; or whether the teacher structures the dialogue or allows it to emerge.

Many of us hold discussions, as is evident by the variety of constructed discussion methods: fishbowl, rap sessions, art projects, observation, buzz groups, task evaluation, brainstorming, Nominal Group Technique, Modified NGT, Phillips 66, task-oriented project groups, Participation Training, Friends meetings, support group process, and others. The key is to allow the group time to establish itself. Understanding ground rules, knowing limits and boundaries, and having a purpose are ways to improve this method of instruction.

The role of the educator is to construct the discovery setting and turn the learning and the process over to the participants. Facilitation skills are often undervalued by educators and in the situation of a discovery become invaluable tools. Two vital skills the educator needs are (1) to understand the use of silence and (2) to know when to end an activity. Conflict utilization is a skill that can also help improve discovery methods in the teaching-learning exchange.

Discovery learning is an exciting yet frustrating process. Setting up situations in which learners discover information that is necessary for the curriculum, the topic, or the situation is challenging and time consuming. The process of discovery itself is fast, but the time necessary in a teaching-learning situation may be extremely long because the initial developmental processes for learning through discovery may be time consuming. Discovery methods are exhausting—and tremendously rewarding.

Games

Long ago, most of us learned that learning may not be fun. We talk about making learning enjoyable, yet in our adult programming we are afraid to allow play to be a part of the learning process. The use of games in the learning setting is invaluable in creating trust, facilitating group learning of other members, creating group culture, and structuring informal learning opportunities.

There are many reasons to use games in education. Anderson, Elliot, and La Berge (1972) identify seven purposes:

1. To participate in structured situations in which various skills are employed
2. To increase awareness of surrounding space
3. To increase ability to use appropriate patterns in ever-changing situations (transfer)
4. To understand the organization and rules (process) of the games
5. To learn to work together and develop strategies
6. To learn boundaries
7. To participate as an individual with the aim of contributing to the group

Humphrey (1980) defines games as active interactions in competitive and/or cooperative situations. Games use the concepts of competition/cooperation, knowledge/skill transfer, and individual/group as their driving forces.

Many commercial games are available for learning activities. Unfortunately, these games rarely teach exactly what we want to teach in our educational setting. As educators, we can create our own games or adapt existing games to our specific needs. The key to creating effective games for learning is to ask ourselves not what we want the learners to "know" from the activity but what we want the learners to experience—to feel, to act, to react, to believe. Think of all the games you played as a child and as an adult. Rather than attempting to "create" a game, it is often more effective to adapt a game by using situations and relevant content. Games include drama, simulations, challenges, and fun.

The role of the educator is to plan the game, construct the rules for play, initiate the game, and monitor the progression. As with experiential learning methods, it is important for the learners to understand that they have indeed learned through the game. A debriefing session following the game is an important if not vital component of using games in education.

Games are created or adapted by working backwards. The educator first identifies desired outcomes, then considers a situation using conflict (intra/inter/inner), then applies necessary skills and knowledge to the situation, and finally creates the environment for the game.

Media

The use of media provides an educator with an opportunity to allow learners to use their senses to gain information. This sensory learning is achieved by removing the educator from the role of presenter and making the learners responsible for garnering what they need to learn from the media presentation.

Increasingly, teaching repertoire relies more heavily upon media than in the past. In contemporary society, all people are exposed to multiple media daily. Television, movies, and radio are common. These media can be effective tools in a learning setting. The question to ask ourselves is "Does this media piece present the information I want it to present?" Further, we need to seriously examine each medium and use each when appropriate rather than because it is available. Knowing the content of the piece, understanding the technology, and having all equipment prepared and preset are important elements of using media well.

The role of the educator in media use is to prepare learners for the medium and the information that the piece contains. Knowing and applying basic rules of media (for example, size of screen, size of projection, level of volume, lighting and control, and equipment use) are part of the requirements for the educator. In media methods, the key words are "appropriate use." Is the medium appropriate? Is the message appropriate? Is the use of the equipment appropriate? Although a danger of being "upstaged" by the medium exists, media provide opportunities the teacher could otherwise not present: people prominent in the field; visual, auditory, tangible documentation; sensory experiences; and first-person views of history, geography, nature, and so forth.

Teacher-Absent

Entire books and courses devote themselves to the concepts of individualized learning, programmed learning, and distance education. All of these learning approaches have something in common: the teacher is not present or is not necessary to the learning tasks in real time. Newspaper articles, correspondence courses, newsletters, displays, computer-based instruction, satellite programs, and project books are all common teaching activities in which the teacher is absent. The intent of teacher-absent methods is to provide information to the learner when the learner needs or wants to gain the information without the teacher having to be present.

In developing teacher-absent programs, it is critical to consider the learner in the teaching-learning exchange. Why would an individual wish to devote time to this content? Is the content absolutely clear so that clarifying questions will not be necessary? Have we provided enough images and activities so that we can satisfy a variety of learning styles? Improving teacher-absent methods requires careful and critical analysis of what we are trying to teach, how the information will be assimilated, and what will be done with the information we present. In many teacher-absent settings, it behooves us to consider that this may be one of the major learning projects of the learner for the year (Tough, 1979). The ability of the distance-education or individual learner to simply "quit" is far greater than when there is the pressure of a real person leading the session and other people (learners) present.

The most obvious role of the educator in teacher-absent methods is the development and dissemination of the materials. Another important role is the availability of the educator to respond to questions or inquiries regarding the information. This is true whether the teacher-absent strategy is a newsletter, a satellite program, or a home study course. Teacher-absent methods remove the human interaction from the contextual learning and rely on the interaction between the student, the materials, the concept of others, and the environment in which the learning occurs. The teacher's absence from the immediate setting does not remove the learner's need for some type of human interaction with the teacher, whether by letter or by telephone.

In selecting methods for teaching, we all use our own experiences. Methods in which we have been learners as well as methods we have tried before contribute to our tools for teaching. Our challenge is to expand our repertoire of methods and then devise a system by which we can select strategies to implement our methods in various teaching situations.

You as the teacher are given a situation in which you are to instruct a group. You have information that somehow you want to share with the learners. How you choose to organize information is the method (Seaman & Fellenz, 1989). The means by which you implement this organization is the teaching strategy, and the specific teaching activities can be called techniques.

Strategies and Techniques: Tools for Adapting Methods to Style

Draw a line down the center of a page. On the left side, list your strengths as a teacher. On the right side, list those areas as a teacher where you feel you are weak. Across the bottom of the page, describe what you most frequently do as a teacher. Is there a relationship between your strengths as a teacher and what you do? Is there a relationship between what you do not do and what you perceive as your weaknesses? The purpose of teaching is to allow learning to occur. Given that different learners prefer to learn in different ways, can you teach in ways that utilize your strengths while developing those areas in which you perceive yourself as weak?

One common flaw in discussing methods is that we often do not have the experience to know how or when to use various methods. We may understand how different methods may be more or less appropriate in a specific situation, but we do not know how to adapt a particular approach to a specific learning situation. We need to know how to use the various methods by adapting them to different situations. We need a framework for the educator to use in determining what method will work in a given situation. We can label such a framework as a process of determining strategy.

Teaching strategies are the specific activities selected to further the method of instruction. Strategy is the activity through which the educator assists the adult learner in the acquisition of new knowledge skills (Seaman & Fellenz, 1989). Just knowing different methods does not guarantee successful implementation. Careful consideration must be given to various factors surrounding the teaching-learning exchange. Seaman and Fellenz offer four factors that determine teaching strategies: the learner, the teacher, the organization, and the content. We'll look at the four factors and then begin to explore how concepts of strategy fit with teaching methods.

Each of these four factors has aspects of both needs and preferences. We often talk about the needs of client groups but forget that the instructor, the organization, and the content also have needs. The interrelationship of needs determines, to a great part, the specific strategies to be employed. Likewise, instructors, learners, and organizations all have preferences about what strategy would serve their needs most effectively.

We often ask ourselves what outcomes we want from a program. Usually the answer is in terms of learner needs. But the organizational needs for this program might include fulfilling the goals of the sponsor reaching new client groups, and being visible in the community. The needs of the teacher might include contacting a great number of people quickly, balancing time on other projects, satisfying sponsors, and conducting a program he or she enjoys. Needs dictated by content might range from a need to discover the information one-on-one to mass educational efforts. Content can dictate methods, but no more so than can the learner, the teacher, and the organization.

It is easy to see how needs and preferences between factors might conflict. Method evolves as teachers compare their teaching objectives with the objectives for the learners, the content, and the organization. Teachers can then identify multiple strategies that would effectively present the information to the learners in order to meet as many of the diverse objectives as possible. Various strategies that might satisfy those needs and preferences can then be identified. A strategy can use techniques from more than one method! Teaching is most effective when it is complementary mix-and-match.

In identifying the needs and preferences of these factors, you begin to remove some of the rationale for using the methods that are most familiar. You also can begin to see how different strategies for teaching will satisfy different needs for learning. This is the empowering part of understanding methods and strategies. Practice and experience make up the rest.

Many times, teachers just have to learn from mistakes, as a colleague has. He put together a program—hastily, due to other time constraints—on the need to change educational behaviors in community education programs. Unfortunately, he didn't have the time to think out his approach. He used a presentation method, which seemed to work fine. Many people participating in the program were pleased with what he presented, or so they said when they sought him out after the program. But something didn't feel right. He realized he felt hypocritical. A longtime proponent of the position that one should teach as one believes, he realized that he didn't teach in that manner at all that day. He used no strategy that allowed any of what he professed to be shared, except in his own words. Looking back, he could see dozens of ways he could have brought in experiences, activities, or games to that presentational method and still have operated under the constraints that led him to originally decide to use a presentational approach.

There are many ways to utilize strategies from various methods in your teaching plan. You might, for example, decide that the learners' needs are best met through a general guided discussion of a problem. This discussion might be followed by a video from a group that had addressed a similar problem. Finally, you might end the program with a presentation using overheads or slides. In this one educational program, you would be using many techniques to "mix" your teaching strategies.

Teachers develop certain skills. These skills are often the tools we use, which are in turn often how we are defined as teachers. It is in the techniques that we can observe our teaching behaviors. Do our strategies for instruction truly match our beliefs, our values, our philosophy of teaching-learning? If you are going to conduct a program that you have taught several times before, challenge yourself to approach it from a different methodological point of view. For example, if you normally use a lecture technique, is there some other method (or even technique) that might be appropriate? Media? Games? Make a commitment to yourself to use another strategy. This does not necessarily mean that you must discard the way you have taught in the past, but you can supplement what you have done before with a new technique for teaching, creating a different strategic mix.

We often rely solely on our presentations to give information. For many educators, this is the biggest barrier to congruence. We tend not to rely on learners' life skills, formal and informal knowledge, and interests for meaningful information sharing. This concept goes beyond the idea of "starting where an audience is" related to knowledge. To reinforce a positive image of informal learning, we need to allow the learners to teach each other and themselves. As Socrates illustrated with an uneducated slave, even complex geometric and mathematical concepts can be culled from the knowledge and understanding inherent in each human.

As educators, we are constantly seeking ways to improve our teaching. It is easy to get into ruts. The danger is that once we are in one of these ruts, we become method bound. We fail to use any method but that with which we are most familiar. To improve our instruction, we need to commit to trying something new in every program we conduct. This does not mean we must make major changes in all our programs but that we accept small risks constantly.

By taking small risks ourselves, we invite learners to also take risks. In this risk taking, the opportunities and outcomes for applicable learning increase. When we try something new, we need to examine it closely. If it works, it goes into the bag of tricks we call teaching tools. If it doesn't work, we need to examine why—did we try to control the outcomes of an experiential activity? Did we rely too much on an understanding of concepts that the learners didn't have? Did we present more information than the learners could grasp? We can decide if the activity might work for us in another situation and discard those activities that simply won't work for us. But here we must be careful. It is easy to discard an activity because we are uncomfortable with the teaching, not because the activity might not or did not work.

One way to see how method bound we are is to create a matrix of the teaching methods and strategies we use. Across the top of a paper, label columns *presentation, experiential, discovery, games, media,* and *teacher-absent.* The left side rows should be labeled for each of the last several teaching sessions you conducted and spaces for upcoming teaching programs. As you reflect on the programs you conducted and plan programs for the future, put a check in the column that best describes your objective in the teaching-learning exchange. Beside the check, describe the strategies or techniques you use or are planning to use. After you have completed a series of programs, examine your chart. Do you tend to rely on certain teaching techniques? Is one method the dominant method you use? This is not to say that what you do is right or wrong; rather, it is a way of exploring how method bound you might be.

Variation simply for variation's sake may not always be appropriate either. Here's an illustration from our notes from an extended training program on teaching adults:

> We had decided to use as many experiential and discovery methods as possible. We allowed time at the beginning of each seminar to process the preceding seminar (often, much more in depth and time consuming than we had planned). The intent was to "lay bare the elements of the teaching-learning exchange." Well, it was sometimes *really* bare.
>
> We found that early in the seminar we were defending the validity of the activities we chose to use—nondominant hand drawing, collages, games,

fingerpainting, journaling. The participants were sometimes unsure as to what they "were to get" from the activities, and even more so, they were unsure as to "what do you want us to do? I mean, what *exactly* is it you want from us?"

Interestingly, as the workshop progressed, we began to defend our activities less as some of the participants began to defend them for us. A few of the learners argued throughout the sessions that the activities were unfruitful. Yet the quality of all the learners' work was impressive throughout and gained in depth and thoughtfulness as time passed.

We spent many hours wondering if we were on the wrong track. In retrospect, we can see that we simply moved too much too fast. At the beginning, the activities did not provide information that the learners needed, wanted, or believed in. We often wanted to scream, "Look! See how you are really learning! Look at your faces, you're intent. Look at your bodies—you're involved. Can you see how much fun you're having? Don't you realize that it's only when you leave here and begin to assess the activities based on your preconceived notions of learning and what it means to be 'grown up' that you question the learning you had?"

Well, we learned. Discomfort comes not only during an activity, but in the postprocessing that we tend to do in our society. Move *with* the learners—continually press, but avoid warp speed.

The discomfort you feel in trying something new will also be present in some learners. When we stretch ourselves as teachers, we force the learners to stretch. Change is always uncomfortable. But change is also the only way real learning can occur. We are aiming toward a blending of individual characteristics with the "teaching plan" (Robinson, 1979) that is congruent with our beliefs and philosophies about teaching and learning. That is, ultimately, teaching style.

We can improve the very essence of our teaching by increasing and diversifying our use of methods and techniques or strategies. By examining the methods we commonly use and seeking to add additional tools, we can meet the learning needs of increasingly more learners while still operating in a manner that is true to self. We each must learn our own means of selecting strategies and developing programs that satisfy the situation, the learner, the content, the organization, and even the teacher, the self.

Chapter Ten

Developing a
Personal Style

"**A**ll teachers should recognize that a good style is essential to their rising above the veriest of mediocrities, [that] . . . its acquisition is a whole and lifetime process, and that, though style may manifest itself in skills and techniques, the development of style involves much more than these" (Eble, 1980, p. 1).

Eble reminds us that developing a personal teaching style is important to all educators. It is an ongoing and never-ending process of exploration, reflection, and application that includes much more than what we can merely observe during the teaching-learning exchange. Even though we have come to the final chapter of this book, we hope it can be viewed not as an ending, but as the beginning chapter of a sequel—one that each of us writes for ourselves. We all have within ourselves the best teacher we can be. To reach our potential, we must continually dig deep within ourselves.

Locke says that knowing and understanding one's own values, beliefs, attitudes, and behaviors can "enhance one's sensitivity toward other cultures" (Locke, 1992, p. 2). Doesn't it follow, then, that knowing one's current self enhances the probability that

177

that same kind of sensitivity for others' needs and differences can be applied, as well, back to self? We think so. Knowing the current self provides a starting point for greater depth in our understanding of who we are and greater breadth through the expansion of our boundaries and the enhancement of our experiences as teachers.

We have examined our philosophical and behavioral boundaries related to the teaching-learning exchange, questioning our motives, our understanding, and our belief system that supports those boundaries. Now it is time to assemble all the information we have collected about ourselves and prepare to make changes toward a more congruent self and a more skilled, knowledgeable teacher.

Along the way to congruence, however, we may discover that we possess unfounded beliefs or that some of our behavior is outdated. In other words, our philosophy does indeed match our behavior, but either one or both are no longer desired. These are the times when we will choose to expand beyond our current belief system and behavioral repertoire to a more desired belief and corresponding behavior. This is the situation we have described in Chapter One as growth through expansion.

Movement Toward Congruence Versus Expansion

We have investigated our current values, beliefs, attitudes and behaviors, which, in combination, present the whole picture of who we are as teachers—our teaching style. We may suspect that there are some specific areas in which we are not congruent, in which our philosophy does not match our behaviors or vice versa. We are now at the point where we can begin to take those inconsistencies, once identified, and address them in one of three ways. We can discard the part of our philosophy that does not match our behavior (congruence through a philosophical shift). Or we can discard the behavior that does not match our philosophy (congruence through the reinforcement of philosophy). Or we can discard both the current behavior and the current belief and select new, matching beliefs and behavior (expansion). The last choice represents stretching current boundaries beyond congruence toward a more desired style. Even though the focus of this book has been congruence, the authors agree that expansion may be the best growth choice in many cases. Consequently readers are encouraged to consider all three choices when exploring, reflecting on, and applying new strategies related to teaching style. To illustrate these three possibilities, here are descriptions of three types of teachers.

Teachers who decide to reevaluate the importance they place on content and ultimately change their beliefs about the role that content plays in how they conduct the teaching-learning exchange are shifting their philosophy, or changing their beliefs to match behavior. Teachers who begin asking learners to identify *their* objectives for their participation because the teachers believe strongly in student input and participation in planning are reinforcing their philosophical base, or changing behavior to match beliefs. Teachers who decide that both their beliefs and their behaviors related to physical environment arrangement are faulty are actually expanding both philosophy and behavior by changing beliefs and selecting matching new behaviors. This third group has realized that even though their beliefs and behavior are congruent, neither is valid anymore.

Whether making a shift in philosophy, reinforcing philosophy, or expanding beyond both, the way to begin is by clearly defining where you are now. You have already initiated that activity as you investigated your beliefs, attitudes, and values throughout the previous nine chapters. You have thought about what you mean by teaching and learning; you have defined teaching style; you have assessed how you view content, environment, the teacher, the group, and the individual student and the relationships among them. It is now time to clearly articulate an individual philosophy of teaching and learning and to describe your behavior surrounding the teaching-learning exchange. Finally, it is time to make some initial decisions about your current self (congruence of philosophy and action) and, ultimately, your desired self (expansion).

Articulating Your Philosophy

A philosophy of teaching and learning can encompass implicit theories (personal theories, tacit knowledge) as well as principles taken from formal theories such as social, cognitive, and motivational theories (Rando & Menges, 1991). Throughout this book, the assumption has been that teaching philosophy is based upon beliefs, attitudes, and values, many of which have been adopted from individual interpretations of explicit knowledge. We believe that although implicit knowledge is valid, it can be analyzed through a process of reflection and questioning, applying beliefs to real life, determining appropriate behavior, and then "finding a rationale that links the belief and the behavior" (Rando & Menges, 1991, p. 11). The blending of personal (implicit and explicit) and formal theories produces an individualized yet solidly grounded philosophy of teaching and learning.

Whether based on personal theory, formal theory, or the blend of the two, certain questions will help teachers begin hammering out a philosophy of teaching and learning. Ask yourself: What keeps me teaching? What are the most important qualities a teacher must have? What are the most important characteristics of the teaching-learning environment? What kind of relationship does a good teacher have with the group of students and with each individual student?

More specific questions related to the elements of the teaching-learning exchange provide specific information to help crystallize your philosophy. Again, ask yourself: What is important to me in content? How does content relate to teaching? To what degree should instruction be controlled by content?

These values related to the element of content can then be stated as beliefs: "I believe that content is ———— to the teaching-learning exchange." When you repeat the process with each of the other four elements of instruction—the environment or climate, both physical and emotional, yourself (the teacher), the culture of the learning community, and the individual learner—relationships among the elements will begin to emerge.

Defining a personal philosophy can be done in a number of ways. In a continuing education class on teaching adults, a major assignment is the development of a personal philosophy of teaching and learning. Students develop their philosophy during a ten-week process of writing, reflection, and revision. The first product resembles the raw data that would be gathered from extensive responses to the previous questions. The next step is to reduce that information to a set of principles related to teaching, learning, and the elements of the teaching-learning exchange. Students are asked to limit their principles to no more than twenty-five. From this set of principles, a formal philosophy of teaching and learning is developed. The formal philosophy must be able to fit on one 8 1/2"-by-11" typed page. Like an organizational mission statement, it can be reduced to a clear, concise descriptive statement that is easily memorized and recited at will.

We also like another, very different approach to articulating philosophy that Brookfield (1990, p. 7) illustrated in *The Skillful Teacher*. He described the elusive "perfect teacher" that many teachers strive to be as a combination daytime talk-show host, news reporter and comedian—each role illustrating a critical component of this ideal (humanistic empathy, critical questioning, and sharp, contextually appropriate humor). Although Brookfield presumes that the quest to become a "perfect teacher" bypasses the more important question, that is, "How well did I help people learn today," a process similar to his selection of roles and ideal qualities could help teachers articulate a written philosophy of teaching and learning. Try picturing a combination of people that you know (or know about) who, in total, would represent the perfect teacher. What are the characteristics that each possesses that cause you to include that particular person? Your answers can lead you indirectly to your philosophy. This technique by itself may not give enough information, but you might want to try it as one approach in combination with others to discovering and articulating your philosophy.

Regardless of the form your philosophy of teaching and learning takes, prepare to revise it regularly, using the results of this process of assessing congruence and the results of living and learning.

Examining Your Behavior

Examining behavior surrounding the teaching-learning exchange is really an integrated two-step process. The steps include initial collection and organization.

Collecting Information on Behavior

Using a variety of inputs, describe your behavior related to the teaching-learning exchange. Ideas include videotaping a series of your teaching experiences (Lewis, 1991), allowing peer or mentor observation, accepting mini-teaching opportunities and then reflecting upon them (Ishler & Ishler, 1980), requesting expert observation, and keeping an ongoing personal recollection journal (Brookfield, 1990). Notice that verbal and nonverbal behavior and technical skills are included in these ideas (Ishler & Ishler, 1980). Be sure to gather information from as wide a variety of teaching settings as you can. Include typical teaching situations, ongoing teaching situations, one-shot teaching situations, atypical settings and content, atypical students, unusual environments, and so on. You might also want to complete questionnaires and inventories you have come across in your teaching that relate to behavior. This process helps you develop your own "instructional awareness" (Lewis, 1991, p. 69). What we tell learners during the process of collecting data is to use multiple sources. The sources should be both objective and subjective.

Organizing Information on Behavior

Information on teaching behaviors can be organized in a variety of ways. We have identified four different procedures to organize information about your behaviors. The first two use a deductive approach, in which categories are predetermined and behaviors are identified that fit into these categories. The third is inductive in that the categories of behavior are established using the information after it is collected. Our fourth suggestion for organizing information on behavior is an integrated approach. All approaches are useful when managing the information you collect about your teaching behavior, so select the one you prefer. Remember, the purpose of gathering information on your behavior is to assess congruence as well as judge appropriateness for you.

Deductive Approaches. A framework proposed by Ganrose (1980) lists behaviors under six categories: (1) "choosing" (what did you choose as textbooks, assignments, format, methods, and so on?); (2) "preparing" (how did you study, organize your thoughts, and otherwise prepare for the exchange?); (3) "speaking" (be sure to include what you speak about in and out of class); (4) "listening" (again, include how you listen both in and out of class); (5) "responding" (in and out of class); and (6) "testing and grading."

Another method of categorizing your behaviors includes "planning," "communication," and "evaluation behaviors." Once again, it is important to include teacher behaviors related to the teaching-learning exchange before, during, and after the exchange. Behavior can be verbal, written, physical/nonverbal, or a combination; it includes what a teacher says and does. Table 10.1 illustrates how to categorize behaviors under this system.

In this categorizing system, planning behaviors include selecting an approach, conducting needs assessment, formulating objectives (selection of needs to be addressed), developing curriculum (identification of information required to address needs), selecting methods and strategies (how to address needs), and sequencing activities (planning the most appropriate sequence to address needs). Communication behaviors include all those that relate to interaction between and among individuals, including those relating to tasks (strategies to accomplish the purpose of the instruction, which are detailed in Chapter Nine) and process (motivation, care and support, feedback, guidance, climate building, and information sharing). Evaluation behaviors include both formative evaluation (for improvement) and summative evaluation (for judgment) of a variety of evaluation objects, including the learner, the teacher, the

Table 10.1. Categories of Teacher Behavior.

Time Frame	Planning	Communication	Evaluation
Before exchange			
During exchange			
After exchange			

teaching, the learning, the learning community, the environment, the content, the process, the interaction of any of the elements, or other objects related to the teaching-learning exchange.

Inductive Approach. An equally effective approach for organizing the behaviors you have identified is to allow the categories to emerge from the data. This approach, similar to several techniques used in the analysis of qualitative research data (Miles & Huberman, 1984), is more personalized and ensures that all behaviors fit into the framework because the framework comes from the set of behaviors. Qualitative research methods texts contain some ideas for organizing data by emergent themes that can easily be adapted for this process.

Integrated Approach. Some teachers will want to organize teaching behavior by categories directly related to components of their articulated philosophies. To do this, reorganize your philosophy in such a way as to allow specific behaviors to be matched to certain parts of your philosophy. A structure that works well is to take your written philosophy and break it back down into simplified statements or principles of teaching and learning. Teachers might end up with fifteen to twenty principles. For each principle, then, list behaviors that would directly relate to that principle (Table 10.2). For example, the teacher might hold the principle that "each student should be recognized for his or her own unique contributions in and out of class." (This principle would represent a highly individual-oriented approach.) Yet one of his or her behaviors (as recorded by peer observer) might be that only three of seventeen students were included in class discussions during the hour and that no attempt was made to draw others into the discussion. Thus the teacher would recognize a lack of congruence between this behavior and his or her principles: "I can't recognize unique contributions when I do not encourage all students to make them. But I don't like to call on quiet students." Another behavior (as recorded by teacher in syllabus) might be the provision of learning contracts as an option for all students. Here the teacher would recognize congruence: "By encouraging learners to identify what they want to

Table 10.2. Integrated Approach.

Principle	Behavior	Congruence
Unique contributions of students are of value	Ignores some students	N
	Uses learning contracts	Y

learn and how, I can enhance the unique interests and abilities of each student."

When using any of the first three approaches described above, the next step is to review all the information about your behavior and try to identify trends across settings, students, context, and content. Identify unique behaviors as well—those that only occur in certain situations. Then compare both unique behaviors and behavior trends with philosophy to assess congruence. The integrated approach incorporates the comparison of philosophy and behavior right into the organization of behaviors.

As a teacher, you can develop your own format for comparing philosophy and behavior and make it as simple or complex as you like. Once inconsistencies in behavior and philosophy are identified, you can make the decision to change the behavior or shift philosophy.

Making a Philosophical Shift

Of the three possibilities of change, changing our philosophy to match specific behavior is probably the most difficult. Our systems of values, beliefs, and attitudes have been established and reinforced over the span of a lifetime. Our culture, ethnicity, previous experiences, and a host of other influences all interact to build an understanding of our immediate world and the world beyond. When trying to change the very basis upon which we have formulated our day-to-day actions, we may experience a wide variety of emotions: guilt, fear, confusion, doubt. However, sometimes we must realize that what we have always believed is somehow not "good enough" anymore; the test of time has finally proven the belief untenable.

The question then becomes, "How (in the world!) do I change what I believe, feel, or value?" We would encourage teachers to spend less time in guilt, confusion, and doubt and be aggressive in discarding of outmoded beliefs. We recommend eliminating old beliefs with gusto. In a discussion of theory as a tool for more fully understanding the world, Schaef (1985) suggests that "when a particular theory fits a particular observation, we should go ahead and use it. When it does not, we should throw the theory out!" She also comments that "our most productive opportunities for new growth and understanding may come during times when our theory just does not work" (p. xxii).

One approach to eliminating beliefs is to use the beliefs (values, attitudes) analysis process mentioned in Chapter Two. Begin by discovering the bases—explanations, reasons, possible causes—on which your beliefs, values, and attitudes have been laid. Possible bases would be culture (major or subculture), experience, education, traditions, or family influences.

A good example of a "base" is what Schaef (1985) calls the "White Male System" (p. 3). The system "controls almost every aspect of our culture. It decides what is knowledge and how it is to be taught. Like any other system, it has both positive and negative qualities. But because it is only a system, it can be clarified, examined, and changed, both from within and without. . . . We all live in it, but it is not reality. It is not the way the world is. Unfortunately, some of us do not recognize that it is a system and think it is reality or the way the world is" (Schaef, 1985, p. 3).

If some of your behaviors do not fit with what the "White Male System" teaches and yet you accept the system as part of your reality, you are setting yourself up for conflict. The joy is in the freedom you have to decide whether to change your behaviors or to reject that belief system for one that fits you better.

After identifying where the belief comes from, we can make a judgment about the current validity of the base. Does it still "hold water"? Did it ever? It is more comforting to reject the base of a belief as something external to ourselves, as opposed to the belief itself, which is a real part of ourselves.

One of the finest adult educators the authors have ever known recently experienced a major shift in philosophy. We knew right away when she had made the decision to change her thinking about teaching and learning. Not only did she speak differently about issues, but the quality of her behavior in and out of the teaching-learning exchange was heightened.

When asked about the shift, she described the series of emotions she experienced.

> First I was confused about what I did and didn't believe. I spent a lot of time sorting all of that out. I finally made a list of what I truly believed about teaching and learning. I noticed that the list was quite a bit shorter than I had expected. The reason was that I only knew for sure that a handful of beliefs were really mine and the rest must have been "borrowed." After I identified a set of beliefs that I could really say were mine—that I owned them—then my confusion turned to panic. I realized that everything I had been doing in my teaching was really based on just a few personal principles and a truckload of someone else's! It was almost like starting over in my philosophy. Panic subsided and I got down to business examining what I actually did—how I behaved—in the classroom and in workshops and seeing how that did or didn't match my little list of beliefs. Strangely enough, most of the behavior I described fit with what I said I believed. Amazed as I was, I realized that by tightening up my philosophy and making somewhat of a shift, I became a much better teacher.

Reinforcement of Philosophy

Changing behavior may not really be that much easier than changing philosophy, but it certainly has been a more popular approach. Research on behavior and its modification fills the annals of social and behavioral science libraries everywhere. It seems that everyone from B. F. Skinner on has addressed how to modify, eliminate, introduce, or otherwise adjust behavior.

Before discussing approaches to changing behavior to match philosophy, let us examine, in a bit more depth, the various categories of behavior that appear in Table 10.1.

Planning Behavior

Planning behavior includes selecting an approach, conducting a needs assessment, formulating objectives (selecting needs to be addressed), developing curriculum (identifying information required to address needs), selecting methods and strategies (planning how to address needs), and sequencing activities (planning the most appropriate sequence to address needs).

Selecting an Approach. Selecting, articulating, implementing, and monitoring an overall approach includes the identification of an operational paradigm that best matches your educational philosophy. This paradigm sets the philosophy in motion and includes rules for planning, communicating, and evaluating that represent your values, beliefs, and attitudes toward the elements of the teaching-learning exchange. An important part of this process is, of course, the monitoring of implementation (assessing congruence). Are you acting as you have identified you would?

Most teachers develop their own paradigm from which action comes. There are many preidentified paradigms from which to select, however, so for illustration we have outlined four different paradigms from different areas of the field of education. The first, the *problem-solving approach,* is most like what we might find in a formal classroom of adults or young adults. The second, *praxis,* mentioned in Chapter One, has been identified and used extensively in both formal and informal adult education settings. The third approach, *educere,* may not be as familiar as the other three and presents a very different paradigm for action. The fourth approach, coming from Brookfield's *The Skillful Teacher* (1990), is the *critically responsive approach*—again familiar to many adult educators. Remember that educators can pick and choose from existing paradigms but will most often formulate their own using bits and pieces of others.

One specific approach to conducting the teaching-learning exchange is the problem-solving approach (Newcomb et al., 1986, pp. 65-74). Steps include the interest approach, establishing group objectives, identifying questions to be answered, generating problem solutions, testing solutions through application, and evaluating solutions.

Steps in the learning process that correspond to each step in the problem-solving approach are described in brackets after each step. This six-step process is known as "Dewey's Steps in Reflective Thinking," "the chain of reasoning," and "the scientific method" (Newcomb et al., 1986, p. 65).

1. The *interest approach* consists of creating the necessary provocative situation that draws the attention of all the students to a common point as well as helping to create a felt need [experiencing a provocative situation]. It makes students aware of their experiences that relate to the content to be addressed. It also sets the stage for establishing group objectives. Some techniques to use include raising questions, showing samples or specimens, presenting a case study, giving a demonstration, showing pictures of before/after, giving in-class assignments, role playing, and doing computer exercises. The key in the interest approach is to help students see that they need to know the information to help them succeed in the future.

2. The next step is *setting group objectives* based on student and teacher input [defining the problem]. The teacher asks students for their objectives, conducts a discussion, and then generates a list of the group's objectives (visually). This step is the first half of "defining the problem."

3. The teacher and learners *identify questions* that need to be answered so that they can reach their objectives [defining the problem]. This process is the second half of "defining the problem." If learners do not feel comfortable articulating what they need to know, then it is the teacher's job to facilitate enough discussion to identify areas of need.

4. "During this phase of problem solving, (*problem solution*) the teacher seeks to assist the class in obtaining, studying, and evaluating facts, concepts, and skills necessary to answer the questions, solve the problems, and develop the conclusions needed to master the unit of instruction. In essence, the teacher and the students cooperatively decide on the content to be studied" (Newcomb et al., 1986, p. 71) [seeking data and information;

formulating possible solutions]. Many possible strategies exist, including lecture, discussion, demonstrations, field trips, role playing, resource people, supervised study, independent study, experiments, use of student notebooks, and other handouts.

5. *Testing solutions* through application is the "premier doing stage of the process" (p. 72) [testing proposed solutions]. The learners put into practice what they have learned to "test it out": Does it work? Why? How? This phase allows learners to practice new skills and reflect on new knowledge, helping them to become more proficient. Application can occur anywhere— in a classroom, laboratory, or field.

6. *Evaluating the results* of the testing phase is the last step of the problem-solving approach. "Students try what they have learned and decide if it works. They use their knowledge and new skill and determine if it produces the results they had come to expect it would" (p. 73) [evaluating the results]. Along with evaluating the results of the solution, they also can evaluate their own progress. Additionally, the entire process provides information for the adult educator to use in student learning evaluation. Various techniques to use include paper and pencil tests, checklists, project work, records, and other instruments.

Try listing some of the underlying beliefs, attitudes, and values related to the elements of the teaching-learning exchange that support the problem-solving approach. Does this approach "fit" your philosophy?

A second approach, *praxis* (Bateman, 1990; Brookfield, 1990), is "one of the most frequently espoused principles of skillful teaching." Praxis is "ensuring that opportunities for the interplay between action and reflection are available in a balanced way for students. Praxis means that curricula are not studied in some kind of artificial isolation, but that ideas, skills, and insights learned in a classroom are tested and experienced in real life. Essential to praxis is the opportunity to reflect on experience, so that formal study is informed by some appreciation of reality" (Brookfield, 1990, p. 50). "The Circle of Praxis involved taking a closer look at part of society, reflecting on it in discussions, revising your own opinions, doing this over and over again, and gradually coming up with a world view closer to the observed facts. The circle involved alternating periods of observation and reflection and discussion" (Bateman, 1990, p. 167).

Bateman (1990) has described what he calls *inquiry teaching* (a form of praxis) as "you give those big-brained students of yours a chance to use their big brains . . . by giving [them] a set of facts and slip[ping] the leash. They speculate, they create new concepts, they apply old concepts, they test, they reject, they ask for more evidence. And the more of this process you can have the students verbalize, the more conscious students will become of the way they are learning to infer, to test, to reject, to accept, and to help each other learn" (p. 18). This description is very similar indeed to the problem-solving approach described earlier. List some of the underlying beliefs, attitudes, and values related to the elements of the teaching-learning exchange that support the praxis approach. Does it "fit" for you?

The third approach, *educere* (Greenberg, 1974), from the Latin, "to lead out," "does not describe an act of imparting to the student what the instructor knows. Instead it is a process of leading out, with the emphasis on what is in the student, not what is in the instructor. The student grows, develops, blooms; [he or she] does not acquire, receive, collect. . . . All learning is a development and growth of the self. None of it comes from the outside. It cannot be taken or received from others, nor memorized from authorities. All learning comes from within the learner" (Greenberg, 1974, pp. 19–20). A basic assumption of this paradigm is that human beings are "basically good, positive, moral" and "when left to [their] own, . . . will seek not only [their] own good but the good of others as well." Thus "if education is defined as leading out what is inside the individual, then we must have faith that what is in the individual is growth-oriented, positive, good. If education instead is defined as acquiring knowledge from others, then the learner's basic nature is at best ignored, at times rejected, and often considered irrelevant if not downright interfering, immature, or disobedient" (Greenberg, 1974, pp. 21–22). Other assumptions include: "Everyone is great and beautiful!"; "Each student is unique—and learns in [his or her] own way"; "Students learn out of curiosity, wonder—not from rewards and punishments"; and "The only true source of positive feelings about the self comes from within the self" (pp. 23-37). The teacher is described as expressing love toward the students, and love manifests itself in the following behaviors: "[He or she] gives of [him or her] self . . . feels affection, concern, acceptance; responds positively, strives for honesty, communication, understanding. To do this [he or she] must be [him or her] self . . . be sincere, real" (p. 41).

List some of the underlying beliefs, attitudes, and values related to the elements of the teaching-learning exchange that support the *educere* approach. What is your opinion of *educere* as your paradigm of choice? Are there elements that fit you?

The fourth approach is the *critically responsive approach* described by Brookfield (1990). "Critically responsive teaching aims to nurture in students a critically alert, questioning cast of mind" (Brookfield, 1990, p. 24). To do this, "Critically responsive teachers are not tied to some predetermined methodological stance. They are ready to mix small-group work with lectures, to alternate collaborative approaches with teacher-led projects, and to develop materials in cooperation with students as well as using standardized exercises. Responsiveness means that teachers judge whether or not to use a particular approach, method, or exercise by one criterion—whether or not it helps people learn" (p. 24). List some of the underlying beliefs, attitudes, and values related to the elements of the teaching-learning exchange that support the critically responsive approach. Is this your paradigm?

Review the rest of the description of planning behavior below. Visualize how the planning process would differ among these examples. How would the communicating and evaluating behavior differ? What does this indicate to you about the importance of your paradigm of operation?

Conducting a Needs Assessment. This part of planning behavior includes delineating and obtaining information to be used in the identification of "a discrepancy or gap betwen some desired or acceptable condition or state of affairs and the actual or observed or perceived condition or state of affairs" (Witkin, 1984, p. 6).

In other words, ideally, the question becomes what the learners should be able to think, feel, or do; to what extent they already possess these abilities; what the gaps are between the existing conditions and the ideal, if any; which gaps are priorities for addressing; and, given this set of priorities, what the curriculum should address.

Steps of a needs assessment include identifying the desired state, identifying the existing state, assessing the gaps, and prioritizing the gaps (importance, size, immediacy, requirements). Step 1, identifying the desired state, is usually the most straightforward part of the needs assessment. Many educational opportunities are designed with desired end results in mind; in fact, requirements for degrees, licensure, professional standards, and other criteria are common desired end results. Most often, it is the organization providing the educational opportunity and not the educator that sets the desired end results. For example, in a college or university setting, academic departments establish desired end results for specific courses that are approved through a hierarchy of academic affairs committees.

Criteria for educational end results are usually both normative *and* absolute (they are compared to "what everyone else has or is able to do" as well as to the societal "accepted and desired" state)—"Everyone should be able to read; it is a God-given right!" so they are usually spelled out at a higher level than the individual teacher or class. In other words, the teacher seldom has a choice about the desired state.

What are some sources of information on the ideal state for your students, or, to put it differently, what should the end results of the educational activities be? How do you sort out that information and decide needs to be addressed in your educational activities?

Step 2, identifying the existing state, is conducted at individual and learning community levels. Brookfield (1990, p. 31) suggests, at the individual level, that having students record critical incidents in their learning experiences and then keep learning journals will help the teacher assess where the students are and to what extent they are growing. With regard to the learning community, Brookfield indicates that current research on the specific type of learners can give a good measure of the current state of affairs. He also suggests that teachers investigate their own experiences with learning to help with an understanding of learning potential and blocks to learning.

Additional methods of assessing the existing situation with

the individual members of the group and the group as a whole include standardized tests, surveys, questionnaires, and other quantitative "needs assessment tools" (Hiemstra & Sisco, 1990, p. 95) measuring specific knowledge or attitude levels, general aptitude or ability, and learning style and motivation potential. Additionally, Hiemstra and Sisco advocate small group work to facilitate not only the teacher's assessment of the existing state but students' own assessment of their facility with the "three R's": "relationships with each other; relationship with the instructor; and relationship with the course content" (p. 100).

Pintrich and Johnson (1990) suggest two standardized assessments that can give the teacher information on cognitive style, motivation level, and strategy preferences of students: The Learning and Study Strategies Inventory (LASSI) and The Motivated Strategies for Learning Questionnaire (MSLQ). This information can be used as grouped data to provide a "snapshot of the class" or as an individual profile for each student.

Bonham (1989) developed a comparison table synthesizing learning style theories and instruments for teachers to use in assessing existing learning style preferences of students. Lenz (1982) suggested "developing a learner profile" as a helpful way for the teacher to obtain a "rough estimate of the kind of people for whom you are designing your course" (p. 57). She states that a needs assessment should assess not only the existing state of the student's cognitive skills but the potential for success in the learning situation: learner ability, motivation, expectations, reasons for participation, and so on.

Step 3, assessing gaps, is simply assessing the extent to which the existing situation matches the desired state. Gaps will vary in size, importance, and immediacy. Note that if there are no gaps, then the educational activity is not needed. Have you ever found yourself in that situation as a student? as a teacher? What could/ should have been done to prevent that "unneeded" educational activity?

Step 4 involves prioritizing gaps (translating them into existing needs) to be addressed. Many sources of information may be sought: professional opinion or standards, students' wants, teacher's beliefs and preferences, societal goals and norms. After the gaps have been sorted out and prioritized, the next phase of planning, developing objectives, takes place.

Developing Objectives. This step includes selecting the needs to be addressed and translating them into observable, measurable student behaviors (cognitive, affective, psychomotor). Beard and Hartley (1984) make a distinction between aims, goals, and objectives: "Aims are broad general statements of intent . . . which attempt to set the scene for later, more detailed statements which will specify how these aims are to be achieved" (p. 24). "Goals explain how aims are to be achieved . . . specifically directed to the more immediate ways in which one might start to try to achieve the aims" (p. 25). "Objectives provide specific statements of what students will be able to do at the end of instruction. . . . If aims are general statements of interest, and goals state how that intent may be realized, then objectives provide statements which enable one to assess whether or not that intent has been realized" (p. 26).

"Most objectives contain three elements . . . a description of what the student should be able to do or to produce [or to feel] after the instruction; a statement of the conditions under which the student should be able to do this; [and] a statement of the criteria, or standards of performance that will be used to judge what has been done" (Beard & Hartley, 1984, p. 26). As indicated, objectives can be affective, cognitive, and psychomotor. Referring to cognitive learning, Newcomb and Trefz (1987) have organized a vocabulary into four categories of cognitive levels to help in the writing of objectives. Those four levels—remembering, processing, creating, and evaluating—were condensed from Bloom's (1956) taxonomy of cognitive behaviors: knowledge, comprehension, application, analysis, synthesis, and evaluation. There are, of course, pros and cons of using behavioral objectives (Beard & Hartley, 1984, pp. 34-35). On the positive side, they provide a guide to planning, a means of exposing underlying assumptions, a stimulus to thinking, a help with communication, a guide to teaching methods, a guide for learners, and a guide for assessment. But on the negative side, the process of developing objectives is time consuming and vague in directions; furthermore, objectives are prescriptive and inflexible, appear to be directly related to behaviorism and its weaknesses, and can limit student-teacher interaction. What is your opinion of using behavioral objectives? Who should select the needs to be addressed and consequently develop the objectives to guide the learning activity? When should they be developed? Should the learners have a say in what they will be taught and what they subsequently may learn?

Developing Curriculum. The next category of planning behavior includes the identification of the specific content to be used in the meeting of needs, as indicated by objectives and the organizing of that content into the overall teaching-learning exchange. Newcomb et al. (1986) describe this phase as developing the course of study and suggest that needs and their corresponding objectives be grouped into problem areas. These problem areas can be assessed to determine what information and skills (and experiences) the students will need to address the problem. Curriculum materials (content) can then be obtained.

Selecting Methods and Strategies. This step is a crucial part of the planning process. Chapter Nine has thoroughly addressed methods, so we will refer back to the previous chapter for information about this step.

Sequencing Activities. Included is the immediate sequencing of the specific teaching-learning exchange activities as well as the sequencing of the overall plan (fitting the specific into the general, such as which course or workshop should follow which others, and so on). Newcomb et al. (1986) suggest that specific problem areas be sequenced using logic, calendar restrictions, schedules of facilities and resources, and needed variability in content.

Maximizing the Chance for Learning to Occur. In this step, teachers perform planning behaviors that directly serve to enhance process communication, teacher behavior related to facilitation of the learning processes (see below). Examples of this type of behavior are planning a physical room arrangement or incorporating process time into, or eliminating it from, the sequence of activities.

Planning behavior can occur before, during, and after the

teaching-learning exchange. It is the teacher, however, who decides when, how, and by whom the planning will be conducted, monitored, and managed.

Communication Behavior

Communication behavior includes task communication and process communication. This category includes all the behavior related to interaction between and among individuals. Other terms that might represent this type of behavior would be *facilitating the learning process, delivering the content, motivating students, developing and maintaining the climate, teaching, communicating,* or *conducting class.* The key to this category of behavior is that it involves at least two individuals interacting to further the task (purpose) of the instruction or to facilitate the process.

Task Communication. This behavior includes use of methods and strategies to accomplish the purpose of the instruction. We once again will refer to Chapter Nine for an in-depth discussion.

Process Communication. This second type of communication includes motivation, care and support, feedback, guidance, climate building, and information sharing. All these categories of behavior serve to facilitate the teaching-learning exchange.

Teacher behavior associated with *motivation* is that which creates opportunities for enhanced motivation within the learners. "Motivation cannot be directly measured. . . . Most psychologists use the word *motivation* to describe those processes that can energize behavior and give direction or purpose to behavior" (Wlodkowski, 1990, p. 97). Therefore motivation is under the control not of the teacher but of the individual student; the most the teacher can do is to manipulate conditions so that the student's ability and desire to motivate him- or herself is maximized.

There are many teacher behaviors related to supporting motivation. The following are just a few to consider.

1. Ensuring success in learning (quality instruction, concrete feedback, and continued feedback)

2. Making the "first" experience with education, the topic, and the teacher a safe, successful, and interesting one (first impressions are important)
3. Communicating clearly the amount of effort needed to guarantee success
4. Making the learning goal as clear as possible
5. Making the criteria of evaluation as clear as possible
6. Promoting the student's self-determination within the learning experience [Wlodkowski, 1990, pp. 107-112].

Caring and supportive behavior has been addressed in a variety of ways in the literature. Purkey and Novak (1984) described it as "being with" and indicated this category of behaviors as one of the most important categories of teacher behavior for the success of their "inviting approach" to education: "being inviting is a special way of being with people" that involves the skills of "developing trust, reaching each student, reading situations, making invitations attractive, insuring delivery, negotiating, and handling rejection" (Purkey & Novak, 1984, p. 58).

In *To Educate with Love*, Greenberg (1974) answers the question of what the teacher does in the teaching-learning exchange by suggesting that the teacher "expresses [his or her] love." He illustrates his philosophy with the following: "I support students in feeling whatever they honestly feel. I encourage a student to leave class if [his or her] inner concerns are so powerful that [he or she] cannot attend to the class discussions. . . . I accept student feelings as relevant for learning, making it unnecessary to hide them or deny them" (p. 45).

In the book, *The Complex Roles of the Teacher*, Heck and Williams's (1984) chapter entitled "The Teacher as Understander of the Learner: A Nurturing Role" suggests that one of the many roles a teacher can play is that of caregiver and supporter. They point out that to be able to care for and understand the individual student, the teacher must have knowledge of the complete environmental context from which the student is operating: "family context, the school-community context, and the many social contexts such as clubs, athletic teams, and church groups" (p. 50). Add to these contexts of children the additional environmental influences and constraints of an adult student and the complex becomes even more so. Heck and Williams suggest that "within these multiple contexts, the [child's] self-image is formed" (p. 51). And for an adult, that image is not only continuing to be formed but is re-formed and reinforced as well.

Teacher behavior that supports the role of the teacher as nurturing includes attentive behavior apart from the teaching-learning exchange, extra time involved in "getting to know" the learners, becoming aware of cultural differences among groups and individuals, and creating what Heck and Williams call "a learning environment that focuses on the development of the total person" (p. 60). This type of environment is one in which "the pupil assumes the basic responsibility for learning but uses the teacher as a guide, a consultant, a resource person, and many times as a 'navigator' (Hunter, 1976) for the learning effort" (p. 60).

In an environment addressing the total person, we would see much one-on-one interaction, much small group conferencing, and many opportunities for social involvement. Heck and Williams also suggest that "the learning environment needs to reflect a basic understanding of the integration of social, emotional, and cognitive development," (p. 62) without forgetting "physical development needs" as well (p. 62).

What teacher behaviors do you associate with care and support? Name some of the behaviors you possess which relate to this process communication behavior. Think back to a teaching-learning exchange in which you purposely used these behaviors to accomplish something. Describe the situation.

Feedback behavior involves assisting with self-assessment and utilization of that information to make positive changes. Think of a mirror. Learners look into the teacher's mirror and get either a distorted or an accurate picture of themselves. Feedback should serve to provide an accurate picture of the student. Can and should feedback be objective? Should the teacher provide the accurate picture but not *evaluate* what is seen? And can the teacher help the individual to evaluate what she or he sees without biasing the learner's picture of him- or herself?

It is possible for the teacher to serve in the role of mirror, providing a picture and even providing guidance for changing that picture without attaching value to what is seen. The value of objective feedback is that the student receives an accurate picture of reality but can decide on the need for changes. Control is in the hands of the learner.

Guidance can be illustrated by the metaphor of a highway map. A map provides guidance for the lost driver. The map offers alternatives for traveling and finally arriving at a destination. The map gives information on obstructions, distance and length of time, and opportunities along the way. The map does not offer the end result, just assistance for the process. Teacher behaviors in this category of process communication help the student to see options, provide information on the positive and negative attributes of each alternative, and help the student decide on an alternative; they facilitate the process. The difference between feedback and guidance is when it takes place in the process. Feedback takes place after the learner has selected an alternative and has moved toward it. Guidance is provided before the selection has been made.

The behaviors involved in *climate building* are those that the teacher uses to create, communicate, and maintain the maximum learning environment. Climate, as the local weather person would describe it, involves temperature, pressure, moisture, wind, and a host of other meteorological phenomena. Climate in the classroom involves many concepts as well.

What are some of the various characteristics of classroom climate? What behaviors can the teacher use to help create and communicate those to the learner? Use the following chart (Exhibit 10.1) to help identify the kind of learning climate you prefer in a typical adult education setting. Place an "X" on each continuum as to what you perceive your actual classroom climate to be. What would be the corresponding teacher behaviors for the climate you have described?

Information sharing behaviors are objective and are meant to receive and provide information related to the maintenance of the teaching-learning exchange. Examples are giving directions, making announcements, collecting and distributing assignments, and opening and closing the exchange.

As with planning behavior, communication behavior can take place before, during, and after the teaching-learning exchange.

Exhibit 10.1. Assessing Climate Characteristics.

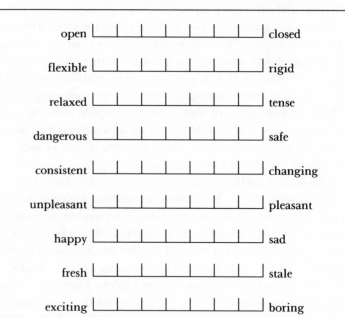

open	closed
flexible	rigid
relaxed	tense
dangerous	safe
consistent	changing
unpleasant	pleasant
happy	sad
fresh	stale
exciting	boring

It is the teacher, however, who decides when, how, and by whom communication behavior will be integrated into the teaching-learning exchange.

Evaluation Behavior

Evaluation behaviors include formative evaluation and summative evaluation of a variety of evaluation objects. Evaluation objects can include the student, the teacher, the teaching, the learning, the environment, the content, the process (as in the evaluation of process communication), the interaction of any of the elements (student, group, teacher, content, environment), and many other objects related to the teaching-learning exchange. An important first step in evaluating behavior is to identify just what the evaluation objects are.

An important second step is to determine whether the evaluation will be for formative or summative purposes. Who wants the information and for what purpose?

Formative evaluation has as its purpose the improvement of the evaluation object. Most often, formative evaluation will come before or during the teaching-learning exchange and can involve almost any evaluation object, such as student learning, teacher behavior, classroom environment, or level or appropriateness of content. Teacher behaviors in this category include interim assessments, asking questions, holding group discussions on process, assessing student opinion, and asking for peer review to help with adjustment of curriculum and methods.

Summative evaluation has as its purpose the placing of value on the evaluation object. Most often, summative evaluation occurs at specific junctures in the teaching-learning exchange: midterm, end of term, delayed follow-up. Student learning and teacher behaviors are usually the objects of a summative evaluation. The value judgment is placed upon the assessed by using grades, certificates, degrees, awards, salary adjustments, and so on. Formative evaluation information should not be used in a summative way. Summative information, however, can be used to help improve future teaching-learning exchanges.

As in both planning and communication behavior, evaluation behavior can take place before, during, and after the teaching-learning exchange. And once more, it is the teacher who decides who will be involved and when and how evaluating behavior will occur.

In summary, then, teacher behavior includes planning, task and process communication, and evaluation behavior. All types of behavior can take place at any point in the teaching-learning exchange. The purpose of all teacher behavior is to accomplish what the teacher believes is the purpose of the teaching-learning exchange.

Methods of Reinforcement

When one is identifying an inconsistency between belief and behavior and subsequently deciding to change behavior, it is important to have a selected, new behavior "waiting in the wings" to adopt. Eliminating unwanted behavior assumes replacement with a more desired and consistent behavior (consistent with philosophy). The practice and final adoption of behavior concludes the process of paradigm reinforcement.

For example, we have talked with many teachers of adults who would like to abandon their podiums (and lecture-style teaching) for something less classroom-like and more informal. But lecturing is the behavior that they learned as new teachers, and it is the method "everyone" uses. Their current behavior does not illustrate their beliefs.

In the past year, one of those teachers, a community college professor, has been yielding his lecture podium in one class for a seat in a circle of students. He is attempting to learn a new, more appropriate method of teaching adults (more appropriate because his philosophy says so). He could not have abandoned his podium without having an alternative style to adopt. He is now talking to other teachers to come up with other ideas and see if they "fit" him even better.

Reinforcing philosophy can also involve some individual and/or group creativity in generating alternative behavior. Adult educators in a local public service agency have participated in in-service activities designed to improve creative thinking for on-the-job problem solving. This educational program, however, addressed their ability to solve problems not only out of the teaching-learning context but in it as well. Some rather unorthodox approaches to public adult education have been developed and well received—all stemming from the techniques learned through this creativity in-service.

One activity, Morphological Forced Connections (Koberg & Bagnall, 1974) proved to be an excellent approach for this group of educators as they sought new and more appropriate individual behaviors. What they did was this: as a group, they listed the attributes of a particular adult education context. Then they generated a list of alternatives for each attribute and arranged the alternatives in columns. Finally, each teacher randomly connected an alternative with other alternatives under each attribute (see Exhibit 10.2). By randomly connecting, for example, "audio," "unorthodox," "peer tutors," and "sender," a particular adult educator created a

Exhibit 10.2. Morphological Forced Connections Example.

Content	Environment	Learning Group	Learner
audio	traditional	works together	active
visual	unorthodox —— peer tutors		passive
detailed	diverse	separate	sender
general	mixed	hierarchical	receiver

teaching-learning exchange in which he could try out a variety of new behaviors that were actually generated from these new characteristics of the exchange. Can you picture the new behaviors he discovered?

Sometimes adult educators, like everyone else, can get stuck in a rut of old "worn out" behaviors, and thus need a new perspective on how things can be done. The philosophy is solid, but the process of implementing it is a little stale. Creative approaches like the one described above can help us all gain a broader spectrum of appropriate behaviors for the teaching-learning exchange.

Expansion—Teaching Style Reformation

Whether choosing to discard both philosophy and behavior because of an inconsistency between the two or choosing to eliminate congruent but no longer appropriate philosophy and behavior, the reformation of teaching style moves teachers beyond the activities of congruence and on to expansion. By matching philosophy and behavior, we become the best teachers we can be *at the present time.* Style reformation, however, moves us beyond congruence to "a higher plane," helping us expand our boundaries and encompass new ideas, new techniques, and new understandings of process and its relationship to product.

Through expansion, teachers can move from their "current best" to a "desired best." The process of expansion requires the teacher to participate in continual learning and to seek a diversity of experiences in the teaching-learning exchange. Deciding to discard old beliefs and behaviors for new ones assumes knowledge and opinion about those new beliefs and behaviors. In fact, teachers who do not remain open to widening their boundaries are usually those who do not take in new knowledge or seek new, diverse experiences.

Learning about new ideas, perspectives, and techniques can be accomplished in a variety of ways. Talking with and observing others is a practical way to gain information for consideration (Svinicki, 1990). Reading books on teaching, taking formal courses, participating in workshops, keeping up with current research on teaching by reading professional journals, participating in formal and informal roundtable discussions with other professionals, joining and participating in professional organizations, and subscribing to newsletters and magazines are other possible ways to learn about potential new perspectives and behaviors related to teaching and learning (Weimer, 1990).

However, be forewarned: it is very easy to become so inundated with new ideas that challenge gives way to perplexity and overload. In his video on paradigms, Joel Barker (1985) suggests that paradigm (or for us, style) paralysis comes when we are close-minded to other opinions and approaches. However, paralysis can also stem from overexposure. Svinicki (1990) warned us that "change should always be approached with caution, lest it overwhelm the instructor" (p. 5). Moderation in any new venture is wise.

No matter how we gain new information on prospective change, the most important thing to remember about expansion is that belief and behavior must both change. It is not enough to learn a new behavior and adopt it into a repertoire. The teacher must also value and believe in that behavior and accept the underlying assumptions about the teaching-learning exchange that accompany it.

The concept of expansion does not assume a "right" teaching style, a perfect style that all teachers should adopt. Rather, expansion suggests that once teachers accomplish congruence within their current self, they might want to begin to expand, moving toward a different, more desirable self. For example, a habitually disorganized teacher might have developed a set of behaviors to compensate for the disorganization and the belief that "it's okay to be disorganized." However, that person might one day decide that it would beneficial to change both that belief and those behaviors to become a more organized, effective teacher. A key point here is that the desirable self will differ for each individual teacher, just as the current self differs from individual to individual.

The Process as an End in Itself

Do not get hung up on striving to be the perfect teacher (Brookfield, 1990). By the very nature of the cultural systems in which we have grown and continue to interact, the focus is on the product, not the process, the end and not the means. The process requires and deserves more attention. Process includes identifying philosophy, describing behavior, matching the two, moving from one state of congruence to another, expanding boundaries, trying new techniques, and questioning philosophical bases. To reach the end of the process would mean the end of growth. By accepting that we can and should continually challenge ourselves to become better teachers, we must also accept that we will never be perfect. That is a small price to pay when the benefits are so great.

Resource A

The Van Tilburg/Heimlich
Teaching Beliefs Scale

Instructions: Please check only the items with which you completely agree. If you have never been in a teaching situation, react to the items as you believe a teacher should act or believe. Thank you very much!

☐ A. To really make instruction successful, students need to know the relevance of the topic to their lives.

☐ B. The selection of teaching methods should depend mostly on the nature of the content being taught.

☐ C. I always learn from my students.

☐ D. A group learns better when a principle or concept evolves from the group.

☐ E. My methods of instruction usually depend upon the make-up of the group.

☐   F.   I stick fairly close to my teaching calendar.

☐   G.   My teaching objectives pretty much dictate my teaching strategies.

☐   H.   I make it clear to students, right from the start, that I am the teacher and they are the students.

☐   I.   Sometimes, I include the group of students in decision making related to course content.

☐   J.   I am almost always behind in my teaching calendar because students ask too many questions in class.

☐   K.   If students are not participating in class, I try to draw them in rather than letting them "do their own thing."

☐   L.   If I try to understand the students' culture, I lose the respect of the students.

☐   M.   There comes a point in my teaching where the subject has to be more important than individual student needs.

☐   N.   My prior experience with similar teaching situations tells me all I need to know about my students.

☐   O.   I usually do not have time to spend on individual concerns in class.

☐   P.   I do not let my care for the students interfere with my teaching.

☐   Q.   I let the students know I've been in their shoes.

☐   R.   I want to know "where the students are coming from."

☐   S.   I use different teaching approaches within any class depending upon the experiences and life-styles of the students.

☐ T. I can easily diagnose why a student is having trouble.

☐ U. As soon as I can in a class, I find out who the students are as individuals, as separate human beings.

☐ V. I try to encourage the students by establishing a close relationship with them.

Scoring

Inclusion:

A–9 B–5 C–11 D–10 E–7
F–2 G–3 H–1 I–6 J–4 K–8

Sum ___ ÷ Circle ___ = ___

Sensitivity:

L–2 M–4 N–1 O–3 P–5 Q–7
R–9 S–11 T–6 U–10 V–8

Sum ___ ÷ Circle ___ = ___

	Inclusion	
11		
10		
9	Facilitator	Enabler
8		
7		
6		
5		
4	Expert	Provider
3		
2		
1		

Inclusion (vertical axis): 1 2 3 4 5 6 7 8 9 10 11

Sensitivity (horizontal axis): 1 2 3 4 5 6 7 8 9 10 11

Sensitivity

Resource B

The Norland/Heimlich
Teaching Values Scale

Code Number _____

Please respond to the following situations by *ranking* each of the five responses for each situation.

> Use the number one (1) for your *first* choice, two (2) for your second choice, and so on. If there is a response that you *completely* disagree with, please place a zero (0) in the blank but be sure to rank the others in the set.

1. You receive a telephone call from a colleague asking you if you would be able to fill in for him or her in a class (s)he is teaching tomorrow. Assuming your schedule permits your participation, in what order would you ask the following questions?

_____ a. What am I expected to teach?

_____ b. May I see the roster of individual students?

_____ c. Where is the class to be held? What are the facilities available?

_____ d. What is the group of students like?

_____ e. Are there specific methods to be used?

2. Rank the following situations in terms of your level of excitement for each.

_____ a. The book you ordered two months ago, on your favorite subject matter, finally arrives.

_____ b. That student who "just didn't get it" finally "got it" in terms of a concept you have been teaching.

_____ c. You learn that you have the "honors" of being the first one to teach in the new classroom/laboratory, complete with updated equipment you have been struggling without for a number of years.

_____ d. Your class is interacting so well together that they hardly notice when time is up and the bell rings.

_____ e. The one method of instruction you have been most uncomfortable with finally becomes "like second nature" to you.

3. When _planning_ to teach a class, rank the following activities in terms of what you focus on the most.

_____ a. Learning about each individual student's needs and skills.

_____ b. Obtaining and reading as much information on the subject as is available.

_____ c. Making a list and securing all needed equipment and arriving in plenty of time to arrange the classroom.

_____ d. Being sure that there are activities planned for each session that help students get to know one another.

_____ e. Planning to use the methods of instruction with which you feel the most comfortable and experienced.

4. During a particularly heated class discussion, rank the following actions you would most likely take to "defuse" the situation.

_____ a. I would have planned ahead and arranged the room (physical arrangement) such that discussion could be "controlled" when needed.

_____ b. I would exert my authority as teacher and ask that we "move on."

_____ c. I would speak individually with the students involved to get a better perspective on the issues at hand.

_____ d. I would address the class, as a group, to see what they preferred to do with the situation.

_____ e. I would call the class's attention back to the subject and have them refocus on the content and lesson. After all, that's what they're there for.

5. When selecting textbooks for a class, rank the following criteria as to what is most (to least) important.

_____ a. The text is the most comprehensive available.

_____ b. The text is the most appropriate one for the level of the group of students.

_____ c. The text uses multiple approaches to various concepts.

_____ d. The text is written by your most respected scholar(s).

_____ e. The text has high quality print and photographs.

6. When determining the *course objectives,* rank the following sources in terms of importance in your decision making.

_____ a. Direct input from the individual students enrolled in the course.

_____ b. Your knowledge of the kind of students who will enroll/are enrolled.

_____ c. Your opinion of what is important to learn in that particular course.

_____ d. The potential resources available (physical, personnel, equipment, etc.) to engage the learners.

_____ e. The nature of the content to be taught.

7. When selecting *methods of instruction,* rank the following sources in terms of importance in your decision making.

_____ a. Your particular expertise in using various methods.

_____ b. The learning styles of individual students.

_____ c. The nature of the content to be taught.

_____   d.   The kind of physical environment in which the class takes place.

_____   e.   The expressed preferences of the group of students.

8. You have been asked to teach a mini-lesson for a group that you have never taught before. You have received the confirmation letter that gives you the specifics. When you arrive for the class, rank the following in terms of which would be *most bothersome* for you.

_____   a.   The location has been changed; the room is not at all what you expected; the equipment you needed is not available for your use.

_____   b.   The subject matter of the lesson has been changed. You are familiar with it but not prepared for it.

_____   c.   The group of people shows up and to your surprise, they all know one another well—an element you did not expect nor plan for.

_____   d.   The group of people shows up and they are not at all the kind of individuals you expected in terms of background and demographics.

_____   e.   The time frame you were given has been altered and you have significantly more/less time.

9. Picture yourself the first day of class in a course that is a new assignment for you. Rank the following in terms of what you would do first (to last).

_____   a.   Ask the class members to share their goals for their participation.

_____ b. Conduct an activity to get members to know one another better.

_____ c. Introduce the subject of the class and try to get some enthusiasm going for the topic.

_____ d. Physically rearrange the room for maximum learning potential.

_____ e. Introduce yourself and share about your background and experiences.

10. Rank the following in terms of the impact each has on your decision making as a teacher.

_____ a. The content you teach.

_____ b. The environment in which you teach.

_____ c. The needs you experience, as a teacher.

_____ d. The nature of the group of learners.

_____ e. The nature of the individuals you teach.

Code Number _____

Extension Educator Version

Please respond to the following situations by *ranking* each of the five responses for each situation.

> Use the number one (1) for your *first* choice, two (2) for your second choice, and so on. If there is a response that you *completely* disagree with, please place a zero (0) in the blank but be sure to rank the others in the set.

1. You receive a telephone call from another educator asking you if you would be able to fill in for him or her in a program (s)he is teaching tomorrow. Assuming your schedule permits your participation, in what order would you ask the following questions?

_____ a.   What am I expected to teach?

_____ b.   May I see the list of people who signed up to attend?

_____ c.   Where is the program going to be held? What are the facilities available?

_____ d.   Is this a preexisting group; will everyone know each other?

_____ e.   Are there specific teaching methods to be used?

2. Rank the following situations in terms of your level of excitement for each.

_____ a.   The curriculum packet you were promised six months ago, on a popular subject matter, finally arrives.

_____ b.   That program participant who "just didn't get it" finally "got it" in terms of a concept you have been teaching.

_____ c. You learn that you have the "honors" of being the first one to teach in the new classroom/laboratory facility, complete with updated equipment you have been struggling without for a number of years.

_____ d. The group you are teaching is interacting so well together that they hardly notice when time is up.

_____ e. The one method of instruction with which you have been most uncomfortable finally becomes "like second nature" to you.

3. When *planning* to conduct an education program, rank the following activities in terms of what you focus on the most.

_____ a. Learning about each individual's needs and skills.

_____ b. Obtaining and reading as much information on the subject as is available.

_____ c. Making a list and securing all needed equipment and arriving in plenty of time to arrange the room.

_____ d. Being sure that there are activities planned for each session that help people get to know one another.

_____ e. Planning to use the methods of instruction with which you feel the most comfortable.

4. If there were a particularly heated discussion in one of your educational program sessions, rank the following actions you would most likely take to "defuse" the situation.

_____ a. I would have planned ahead and arranged the room

(physical arrangement) such that discussion could be "controlled" when needed.

_____ b. I would exert my authority as the one in charge and ask that we "move on."

_____ c. I would speak individually with the persons involved to get a better perspective on the issues at hand.

_____ d. I would address the group to see what they preferred to do with the situation.

_____ e. I would call the group's attention back to the subject and have them refocus on the subject. After all, that's what they're there for.

5. When selecting curriculum materials for an educational program, rank the following criteria as to what is most (to least) important.

_____ a. The materials are the most comprehensive available.

_____ b. The materials are the most appropriate for the level of the group of learners.

_____ c. The materials use multiple approaches to various concepts.

_____ d. The materials were written by one of your most respected experts.

_____ e. The materials have high quality paper, print, and photographs.

6. When determining the *program objectives,* rank the following sources in terms of importance in your decision making.

_____ a. Direct input from the individuals who signed up for the program.

_____ b. Your knowledge of the kind of people who typically come to this type of program.

_____ c. Your opinion of what is important to learn in that particular program.

_____ d. The potential resources available (personnel, equipment, rooms) to engage the learners.

_____ e. The nature of the subject to be taught.

7. When selecting *methods of instruction,* rank the following sources in terms of importance in your decision making.

_____ a. Your particular expertise in using various methods.

_____ b. The learning styles of individual learners who are likely to participate.

_____ c. The nature of the subject to be taught.

_____ d. The kind of physical environment in which the program takes place.

_____ e. The expressed preferences of the group of learners.

8. You have been asked to teach a session for a group that you have never taught before. You have received the confirmation letter that gives you the specifics. When you arrive for the program, rank the following in terms of which would be *most bothersome* for you.

_____ a. The location has been changed; the room is not at all what you expected; the equipment you needed is not available for your use.

——— b.   The subject matter of the lesson has been changed.
         You are familiar with it but not prepared to teach it.

——— c.   The group of people shows up and to your surprise,
         they all know one another well—an element you did
         not expect nor plan for.

——— d.   The group of people shows up and they are not at all
         the kind of individuals you expected in terms of back-
         ground and demographics.

——— e.   The time frame you were given has been altered and
         you have significantly more/less time.

9. Picture yourself at the first session of a multiple session
educational program. The program is one in which you have never
taught. Rank the following in terms of what you would do first (to
last).

——— a.   Ask the individuals in attendance to share their goals
         for their participation.

——— b.   Conduct an activity to get people to know one
         another better.

——— c.   Introduce the subject matter of the session and try to
         get some enthusiasm going for the topic.

——— d.   Physically rearrange the room for maximum learning
         potential.

——— e.   Introduce yourself and share about your background
         and experiences.

10. Rank the following in terms of the impact each has on your decision-making as a teacher.

_____   a.   The subject(s) you teach.

_____   b.   The physical environment(s) in which you teach.

_____   c.   The needs you experience, as a teacher.

_____   d.   The nature of the typical group of learners.

_____   e.   The nature of the typical individuals you teach.

Code Number _____

Adult Basic and Literacy Education Version

Please respond to the following situations by *ranking* each of the five responses for each situation.

> Use the number one (1) for your *first* choice, two (2) for your second choice, and so on. If there is a response that you *completely* disagree with, please place a zero (0) in the blank but be sure to rank the others in the set.

1. You receive a telephone call from another teacher asking you if you would be able to fill in for him or her in a class (s)he is teaching tomorrow. Assuming your schedule permits your participation, in what order would you ask the following questions?

_____ a. What do you need me to teach?

_____ b. Can you tell me something about each learner in the class?

_____ c. Where is your class held? What facilities are available?

_____ d. How does this group of learners interact?

_____ e. Are there specific teaching methods to be used?

2. Rank the following situations in terms of your level of excitement for each.

_____ a. The curriculum packet you were promised six months ago, on your most important unit, finally arrives.

_____ b. That learner who "just didn't get it" finally "got it" in terms of a skill you have been working on with him or her.

_____ c. You learn that your class has been moved to a brand-new and well-equipped facility that is even closer (distance-wise) to your students.

_____ d. The group of learners you are teaching is interacting so well together that they hardly notice when time is up.

_____ e. The one method of instruction with which you have been most uncomfortable finally becomes "like second nature" to you.

3. When _planning_ to teach your class, rank the following activities in terms of what you focus on the most.

_____ a. Learning about each individual student's needs and skills.

_____ b. Obtaining and reading as much information on the subject as is available.

_____ c. Making a list and securing all needed equipment and arriving in plenty of time to arrange the room.

_____ d. Being sure that there are activities planned for each session that help people get to know one another.

_____ e. Planning to use the methods of instruction with which you feel the most comfortable.

4. If there were a particularly heated discussion in your class, rank the following actions you would most likely take to "defuse" the situation.

_____   a.   You would have planned ahead and arranged the room (physical arrangement) such that discussion could be "controlled" when needed.

_____   b.   You would exert your authority as the teacher and ask that they "move on."

_____   c.   You would speak individually with the persons involved to get a better perspective on the issues at hand.

_____   d.   You would address the entire group to see what they preferred to do with the situation.

_____   e.   You would call the group's attention back to the lesson and have them refocus. After all, that's what they're there for.

5. When selecting curriculum materials for your lessons, rank the following criteria as to what is most (to least) important.

_____   a.   The curriculum is the most comprehensive available.

_____   b.   The materials are the most appropriate for the level of the group of learners.

_____   c.   There are multiple approaches to various concepts helping to address each learner where he or she is.

_____   d.   The materials were written by one of your most respected experts.

_____   e.   The materials have high quality paper, print, and photographs.

6. When determining the *learning objectives,* rank the following sources in terms of importance in your decision-making.

_____   a.   Direct input from your current students.

_____   b.   Your knowledge of past groups of students who have participated.

_____   c.   Your opinion of what is important to learn in that particular lesson.

_____   d.   The potential resources available (personnel, equipment, rooms) to engage the learners.

_____   e.   The nature of the subject to be taught.

7. When selecting *methods of instruction,* rank the following sources in terms of importance in your decision making.

_____   a.   Your particular expertise in using various methods.

_____   b.   The typical learning styles of individual learners who are likely to participate.

_____   c.   The nature of the subject to be taught.

_____   d.   The kind of physical environment in which the program takes place.

_____   e.   The expressed preferences of the group of learners.

8. You have been asked to teach a special lesson for a group of learners that you have never taught before. You have received the confirmation letter that gives you the specifics. When you arrive to teach, rank the following in terms of which would be *most bothersome* for you.

_____ a.   The location has been changed; the room is not at all
             what you expected; the equipment you needed is not
             available for your use.

_____ b.   The subject matter of the lesson has been changed.
             You are familiar with it but not prepared to teach it.

_____ c.   The group of people shows up and to your surprise,
             they all know one another well—an element you did
             not expect nor plan for.

_____ d.   The group of people shows up and they are not at all
             the kind of individuals you expected in terms of back-
             ground and demographics.

_____ e.   The time frame you were given has been altered and
             you have significantly more/less time.

9. Picture yourself the first day of a new class. Rank the
following in terms of what you would do first (to last).

_____ a.   Ask the individuals in attendance to share their goals
             for their participation.

_____ b.   Conduct an activity to get people to know one an-
             other better.

_____ c.   Introduce the subject matter of the class and try to get
             some enthusiasm going for the topic.

_____ d.   Physically rearrange the room for maximum learning
             potential.

_____ e.   Introduce yourself and share about your background
             and experiences.

10. Rank the following in terms of the impact each has on your decision making as a teacher.

_____ a. The subject(s) you teach.

_____ b. The physical environment(s) in which you teach.

_____ c. The needs you experience, as a teacher.

_____ d. The nature of the typical group of learners.

_____ e. The nature of the typical individuals you teach.

Name/ID No. _____

Score Sheet

For each question, write the rank for each of the responses, A through E, below.

Then total each column and write the total in the correct blank below.

Question	Content	Environ	Teacher	Group	Student
1	A ___	C ___	E ___	D ___	B ___
2	A ___	C ___	E ___	D ___	B ___
3	B ___	C ___	E ___	D ___	A ___
4	E ___	A ___	B ___	D ___	C ___
5	A ___	E ___	D ___	B ___	C ___
6	E ___	D ___	C ___	B ___	A ___
7	C ___	D ___	A ___	E ___	B ___
8	B ___	A ___	E ___	C ___	D ___
9	C ___	D ___	E ___	B ___	A ___
10	A ___	B ___	C ___	D ___	E ___
Total	___	___	___	___	___

Now, transfer each of the totals to the appropriate blank below and rank the totals from one (1) to five (5) using the *lowest* score for number one, the second lowest score for number two, and so on.

Center	Raw Score	Ranking
Content	————	————
Environment	————	————
Teacher	————	————
Group	————	————
Student	————	————

Resource C

Focusing on Culture as a Characteristic of Learners

Directions for the Major Culture

You are to design an educational program for a group of single adults. Use the following questions as a guide. Be sure to describe the rationale for your decisions using characteristics of the target group (single people).

1. What is the topic of the program? Why did you choose it? Is it a topic that will interest "singles" and address their needs?

2. Develop a brief outline of the content and why each part has been included.

3. What will be the methods of teaching and why are they being used specifically?

4. Who will do the teaching? Why?

5. What is the title for the program and why did you choose it?

6. Describe the logistics (where, when, length, and so on) and the rationale.

Directions for the Mini-Culture

Discuss, as a group of single people, the answers to the following questions. You must come to consensus as a group. Use as your reference point the fact that you are all single.

1. What are some beliefs that single people hold about being single and that life-style?

2. What are some values that single people hold as extremely important? Are there key words that single people might share and would agree upon as representing the value system shared by "singles"?

3. What are the characteristics of a learning situation that might increase and enhance participation for single people? What about the topic, the teacher, the methods, and the marketing?

4. What are some beliefs held by single people about married people and how "marrieds" interact with "singles"?

5. What has been your history, as a group of single adults, with education as it directly relates to your single life-style?

Resource D

Representative Teaching Methods and Techniques

Author	Mode	Technique
Abella (1986)	Training	Role play Discussion Simulation
Adams (1973)	Control	Simulation games
Applbaum, Bodaken, Sereno, & Anatol (1974)	Group	Panel Roundtable Symposium-forum Dialogue Colloquy Brainstorming Buzz sessions Phillips 66 Posting
Bergevin & McKinley (1977)	Group	Participation Training

Brown (1987)	Formal	Lecture/explaining
Delbecq, Van de Ven, & Gustafson (1975)	Group	Nominal group technique
Dunn & Dunn (1979)	Motivated learner	Programmed activity
	Informal design	Contract activity
	Structured design	Instructional packages
		Visual/Tactual task cards
		Learning circles
Fluegelman (1976)	Group	Group games
		Team building
		Cooperative ventures
Gajanayake (1984)	Community education	Consensus
		Decision making
		Skill training
		Observations
		Audiovisuals
		Field trip
		Case studies
		Survey methods
Hill (1977)	Group	Learning through discussion
Howe & Howe (1975)	Decision making	Values clarification
Institute for Participatory Planning (1981)	Citizen participation	Working meeting
		Open meeting
		Forum
		Hearing
		Open house

		Town meeting Samoan circle Fishbowl Delphi
Jones (1989)	Group	Simulations
Lenz (1982)	Proactive	Individual study Reactive panel
Leypoldt (1967)	Teacher-learner	Lecture Symposium Demonstration Interview
	Learner-learner	Group discussion Seminar Quiet meeting
Loughran (1984)	Distance education	Correspondence Radio Television Video Interactive video
Lovell (1987)	Social settings	Lesson Tutorials Games Lab/practical work Projects
Lowman (1990)	Group	Discussion Integrating learning

O'Neill, Lamber, Lin-
   nell, & Warr-Wood
   (1976)
	Classroom	Drama

Pfeiffer & Jones (1981–1985)	Training	Icebreakers Team building Conflict utilization Group process
Reed & Loughran (1984)	Nonformal education	Fotonovelas Puppets Theater Study-action groups Peer learning
Schrank (1972)	Classroom	Discovery learning
Tough (1979)	Individual	Self-planned learning
Treat (1981, 1983)	Individual/small group	Analytic games
Verdun, Miller & Greer (1977)	Adult basic	Explanation Questioning Drill
Warren (1964)	Learning simulation Creative techniques	Debate Group interview Movie Roundtable Discovery discussion

References

Abella, K. T. (1986). *Building successful training programs.* Reading, MA: Addison-Wesley.

Adams, D. M. (1973). *Simulation games: An approach to learning.* Worthington, OH: Charles A. Jones.

American Association for Applied Psychology. Report of the Committee on the Contributions of Psychology to the Problems of the Preparation of Teachers. (1942). *Journal of Consulting Psychology, 6,* 165–167.

American Psychological Association Task Force on Psychology in Education. (1991). Learner-centered psychological principles: Guidelines for school redesign and reform, a proposal. Washington, DC: American Psychological Association.

Anderson, M. H., Elliot, M. E., & La Berge, J. (1972). *Play with a purpose* (2nd ed.). New York: Harper & Row.

Applbaum, R. L., Bodaken, E. M., Sereno, K. K., & Anatol, K. W. E. (1974). *The process of group communication.* Chicago: Science Research Associates, Inc.

Apps, J. W. (1989a). Foundations for effective teaching. In E. R. Hayes (Ed.), *Effective teaching styles* (New Directions for Continuing Education, No. 43) (pp. 17-28). San Francisco: Jossey-Bass.

Apps, J. W. (1989b). Providers of adult and continuing education: A framework. In S. B. Merriam & P. M. Cunningham (Eds.), *Handbook of adult and continuing education* (pp. 275-286). San Francisco: Jossey-Bass.

Archambault, R. D. (Ed.). (1964). *John Dewey on education: Selected writings.* New York: Modern Library.

Ary, D., Jacobs, L. C., & Razavieh, A. (1985). *Introduction to research in education* (3rd ed.). New York: Holt, Rinehart & Winston.

Axelrod, J. (1970). Teaching styles in the humanities. In W. H. Morris, (Ed.), *Effective college teaching: The quest for relevance* (pp. 38-55). Washington, DC: American Council on Education.

Bany, M. A., & Johnson, L. V. (1964). *Classroom group behavior: Group dynamics in education.* New York: Macmillan.

Barker, J. (1985). *The future . . . The business of paradigms* [Video], distributed by Video Publishing, 10740 Lyndale Ave. S., Minneapolis, MN 55420.

Bateman, W. L. (1990). *Open to question: The art of teaching and learning by inquiry.* San Francisco: Jossey-Bass.

Beard, R., & Hartley, J. (1984). *Teaching and learning in higher education.* London: Paul Chapman.

Beder, H. W., and Darkenwald, G. G. (1982). Differences between teaching adults and pre-adults. *Adult Education, 32*(3), 142-155.

Benedict, R. (1935). *Zuni mythology.* New York: Columbia University Press.

Bergevin, P., & McKinley, J. (1977). *Participation training for adult education.* St. Louis, MO: Bethany Press.

Best, R. (1989). *We've all got scars: What boys and girls learn in elementary school.* Bloomington: Indiana University Press.

Bidwell, C. E. (1973). The social psychology of teaching. In R. M. W. Travers (Ed.), *Second handbook of research on teaching* (pp. 413-449). Chicago: Rand McNally.

Blake, R. R., & Mouton, J. S. (1969). *Grid organization development.* Reading, MA: Addison-Wesley.

Bloom, B. S. (1956). *Taxonomy of educational objectives: The classification of educational goals by a committee of college and university examiners.* New York: Longmans, Green.

Bloom, B. S. (1976). *Human characteristics and school learning.* New York: McGraw-Hill.

Bonham, A. (1989). Using learning style information. In E. R. Hayes (Ed.), *Effective teaching styles* (New Directions for Continuing Education, No. 43) (pp. 29–40). San Francisco: Jossey-Bass.

Boone, E. J. (1985). *Developing programs in adult education.* Englewood Cliffs, NJ: Prentice Hall.

Borich, G. D. (1990). *Observation skills for effective teaching.* Columbus, OH: Merrill.

Bowes, S. G., & Smith, R. M. (1986). Directing your own continuing education. *Lifelong Learning, 9*(8), 8–10.

Briscoe, C. (1991). The dynamic interactions among beliefs, role metaphors, and teaching practices: A case study of teachers' change. *Science Education, 75*(2), 185–199.

Brookfield, S. D. (1986). *Understanding and facilitating adult learning.* San Francisco: Jossey-Bass.

Brookfield, S. D. (1990). *The skillful teacher: On technique, trust, and responsiveness in the classroom.* San Francisco: Jossey-Bass.

Brown, G. (1987). *Lecturing and explaining.* New York: Methuen.

Brown, G. M., & Atkins, M. (1988). *Effective teaching in higher education.* New York: Methuen.

Carlsen, M. B. (1988). *Meaning-making: Therapeutic processes in adult development.* New York: W. W. Norton.

Carter, G. L., Jr., & Kaitajarvi, R. S. (1983). A proposed starting point in designing learning experiences: What a study of education literature reveals. *Perspectives in Adult Learning and Development, 4*(1).

Cole, E. L. (1987). *Entering crisis and leaving.* Tulsa, OK.: Honor Books.

Conti, G. J. (1983, March). Analysis of scores on Principles of Adult Learning Scale for part-time faculty and recommendations for staff development activities. College Station: Texas A&M University. (ERIC Document No. ED 23535)

Conti, G. J. (1985). Assessing teaching style in adult education: How and why? *Lifelong Learning, 6*(8), 7–11, 28.

Conti, G. J. (1990). Identifying your teaching style. In M. W. Galbraith (Ed.), *Adult learning methods* (pp. 79–90). Malabar, FL: Robert E. Krieger.

Conti, G. J., & Fellenz, R. A. (1988, May). *Teaching and learning styles and the Native American learner.* Paper presented at the Adult Education Research Conference Proceedings, Calgary, Canada.

Conti, G. J., & Welborn, R. B. (1986). Teaching-learning styles and the adult learner. *Lifelong Learning, 9*(8), 20–25.

Cranton, P. (1989). *Planning instruction for adult learners.* Toronto, Canada: Wall & Thompson.

Cross, K. P. (1983). *Adults as learners.* San Francisco: Jossey-Bass.

Crouch, B. R. (1983). *The problem census: Farmer-centered problem identification. Training for agriculture and rural development.* Rome: Food and Agriculture Organization of the United Nations, United Nations Educational Scientific and Cultural Organization, and International Labour Organisation.

Darkenwald, G. G., & Merriam, S. B. (1982). *Adult education: Foundations of practice.* New York: Harper & Row.

de Carvalho-Neto, P. (1965). *The concept of folklore* (J. M. P. Wilson, Trans.). Coral Gables, FL.: University of Miami Press.

Deese, J., & Hulse, S. H. (1967). *The psychology of learning* (3rd ed.). New York: McGraw-Hill.

deGroat, A. F., & Thompson, G. (1949, September). A study of the distribution of teacher approval and disapproval among sixth-grade pupils. *Journal of Experimental Education, 18,* 57–75.

Delbecq, A. L., Van de Ven, A. H., & Gustafson, D. H. (1975). *Group techniques for program planning.* Glenview, IL: Scott, Foresman.

Draves, W. A. (1984). *How to teach adults.* Manhattan, KS: Learning Resource Network.

Dubos, R. (1968). *Man, medicine, and environment.* New York: Praeger.

Dunn, R. S., & Dunn, K. J. (1979, January). Learning styles/teaching styles: Should they . . . can they . . . be matched? *Educational Leadership, 36,* 238–244.

Ebel, R. L. (1965). *Measuring educational achievement.* Englewood Cliffs, NJ: Prentice Hall.

Eble, K. E. (Ed.). (1980). *Improving teaching styles* (New Directions for Teaching and Learning, No. 1) (pp. 1-6). San Francisco: Jossey-Bass.

Eble, K. E. (1983). *The aims of college teaching.* San Francisco: Jossey-Bass.

Elias, J. L., & Merriam, S. (1980). *Philosophical foundations of adult education.* Malabar, FL: Robert E. Krieger.

Ellis, S. S. (1979). Models of teaching: A solution to the teaching style/learning style dilemma. *Educational Leadership, 36,* 245-254.

Even, M. J. (1987). Why adults learn in different ways. *Lifelong Learning, 10*(8), 22-27.

Fairchild, H. P. (Ed.). (1970). *Dictionary of sociology and related sciences.* Totwa, NJ: Rowan & Allanheld.

Fessler, D. R. (1976). *Facilitating community change: A basic guide.* La Jolla, CA: University Associates.

Fischer, B., & Fischer, L. (1979). Styles in teaching and learning. *Education Leadership, 34,* 251.

Flanders, N. A. (1951, October). Personal-social anxiety as a factor in experimental learning situations. *Journal of Educational Research, 45,* 100-110.

Flanders, N. A. (1970). *Analyzing teaching behavior.* Reading, MA: Addison-Wesley.

Florini, B. M. (1989). Teaching styles and technology. In E. R. Hayes (Ed.), *Effective teaching styles* (New Directions for Continuing Education, No. 43) (p. 41). San Francisco: Jossey-Bass.

Fluegelman, A. (Ed.). (1976). *The new games book.* Garden City, NJ: Headlands Press.

Fraher, R. (1984). Learning a new art: Suggestions for beginning teachers. In M. M. Gullette (Ed.), *The art and craft of teaching* (pp. 116-127). Cambridge, MA: Harvard University Press.

Fraser, B. J. (1985). *Individualized Classroom Environment Questionnaire.* Melbourne: Western Australian Council for Educational Research.

Fraser, B. J. (1986). *Classroom environment.* London: Croom Helm.

Fraser, B. J., Anderson, G. J., & Walberg, H. J. (1982). *Assessment of learning environments: Manual for Learning Environment Inventory (LEI) and My Class Inventory (MCI)* (3rd ed.). Perth: Western Australian Institute of Technology.

Fraser, B. J., Trengust, D. F. & Dennis, N. C. (1984, November). *Development of an instrument for assessing classroom psychosocial environment at universities and colleges.* Paper presented at the meeting of the Australian Association for Research in Education, Perth.

Freire, P. (1973). *Education for critical consciousness.* New York: Continuum.

Freitag, H. (1991). Thoughts on the art of teaching. *Educational Forum, 55*(2), 167-172.

Gagné, R. M. (1970). *The conditions of learning* (2nd ed.). New York: Holt, Rinehart & Winston.

Gajanayake, S. (1984). Education for community development. In H. B. Reed & E. L. Loughran (Eds.), *Beyond schools: Education for economic, social and personal development* (pp. 73-96). Amherst, MA: Citizen Involvement Training Program.

Ganrose, J. T. (1980). Conscious teaching: Helping graduate assistants develop teaching styles. In K. E. Eble (Ed.), *Improving teaching styles* (New Directions for Teaching and Learning, No. 1), (pp. 21-30). San Francisco: Jossey-Bass.

Gauld, V. F. (1982). *A study of individual teaching styles in a noncredit, continuing education program.* Doctoral dissertation, University of Alabama.

Glasser, W. (1986). *Control theory in the classroom.* New York: Perennial Library.

Goodenough, W. H. (1971). Culture, language, and society. In *Current topics in anthropology* (Vol. 2, pp. 1-48). Reading, MA: Addison-Wesley.

Gordon, T. (1974). *T.E.T., teacher effectiveness training.* New York: Peter H. Wyden.

Govan P., Faber, T., Prins, S., & Mangold, B. (1972). *The use of sensory stimulation in teaching mentally impaired students.* Springfield, IL: Charles C. Thomas.

Greenberg, H. M. (1969). *Teaching with feeling: compassion and self-awareness in the classroom today.* New York: Macmillan.

Greenberg, H. M. (1974). *To educate with love*. New York: Macmillan.

Gross, R. (1991). *Peak learning*. Los Angeles: Jeremy P. Tarcher.

Haertel, G. D., & Walberg, H. J. (1988). *Assessing social-psychological classroom environments in program evaluation. New directions for program evaluation: evaluating program environments* (New Directions for Program Evaluation, No. 40). San Francisco: Jossey-Bass.

Hagan, K. L. (1990). *Internal affairs—A journal keeping workbook for self intimacy*. New York: Harper & Row.

Hamachek, D. (1975). Characteristics of good teachers and implications for teacher educators. In M. Mohan & R. E. Hull (Eds.), *Teaching effectiveness: Its meaning, assessment, and improvement* (pp. 239–251). Englewood Cliffs, NJ: Educational Technology Publications.

Hamilton, M. L. (1993). Think you can: The influence of culture on beliefs. In C. Day, J. Calderhead, & P. Denicolo (Eds.), *Research on teacher thinking* (pp. 87–99). London: Folmer Press.

Harmin, M., & Gregory, T. (1974). *Teaching is. . . .* Chicago: Science Research Associates.

Harris, S. (1981). Aboriginal learning styles and the Three Rs. In F. Darnell & P. Simpson (Eds.), *Rural education in pursuit of excellence* (pp. 191–206). Nedlands: University of Western Australia, Western Australia National Center for Research on Rural Education.

Heck, S., & Williams, C. R. (1984). *The complex roles of the teacher*. New York: Teachers College Press.

Hedges, L. (1989, July). *Educational mysteries that defy explanation*. Paper presented at the Ohio Vocational Agriculture Teachers' Conference.

Heimlich, J. E. (1990). *Measuring teaching style*. Doctoral dissertation, Ohio State University.

Heimlich, J. E., & Van Tilburg, E. (1988). *Subcultures and learning: Redefining the roles of educators and learners*. Columbus: Ohio Association for Adult and Continuing Education.

Hiemstra, R., & Sisco, B. (1990). *Individualizing instruction*. San Francisco: Jossey-Bass.

Highet, G. (1989). *The art of teaching*. New York: Vintage Books.

Highlander Education and Research Center. (1989). An approach to education presented through a collection of writings. New Market, Tenn.: Highlander Research and Education Center.

Hill, W. F. (1963). *Learning: A survey of psychological interpretations.* San Francisco: Chandler.

Hill, W. F. (1977). *Learning through discussion: Guide for leaders and members of discussion groups.* Beverly Hills, CA: Chandler.

Hill, W. F. (1981). *Principles of learning: A handbook of applications.* Sherman Oaks, CA: Alfred.

Hitt, W. D. (1973). *Education as a human enterprise.* Belmont, CA: Wadsworth.

Hodgkinson, H. (Ed.) (1973). *Alternatives to the traditional: How professors teach and how students learn.* San Francisco: Jossey-Bass.

Houle, C. (1961). *The inquiring mind.* Madison: University of Wisconsin Press.

Howe, L. W., & Howe, M. M. (1975). *Personalizing education: Values clarification and beyond.* New York: Hart.

Huelsman, J. M. (1983). *An exploratory study of the interrelationships of preferred teaching styles, preferred learning styles, psychological types and other selected characteristics of secondary teachers.* Doctoral dissertation, Ohio State University.

Humphrey, J. H. (1980). *Child development through physical education.* Springfield, IL: Charles C. Thomas.

Humphrey, J. H., Love, A. M., & Irwin, L. W. (1972). *Principles and techniques of supervision in physical education.* (3rd ed.). Dubuque, IA: W. C. Brown.

Hunter, M. (1976). *Improved instruction.* El Segundo, CA: Tip.

Institute for Participatory Planning. (1981). *Citizen participation handbook: For public officials and other professionals serving the public* (4th ed.). Laramie, WY: Author.

Ishler, R. E., & Ishler, M. R. (1980). Developing desirable teaching behaviors. In K. E. Eble (Ed.), *Improving teaching styles* (New Directions for Teaching and Learning, No. 1). San Francisco: Jossey-Bass.

Jackson, P. W. (1968). *Life in classrooms.* New York: Holt, Rinehart & Winston.

Jarvis, P. (1985). *The sociology of adult and continuing education.* London: Croom Helm.

Jersild, A. T. (1955). *When teachers face themselves.* New York: Teachers College, Columbia University.

Jones, K. (1989). *Simulations in language teaching.* Cambridge, U.K.: Cambridge University Press.

Jung, C. G., Von Franz, M. L., Henderson, J. L., Jacobi, J., & Jaffe, A. (1964). *Man and his symbols.* Garden City, NY: Doubleday.

Kearney, M. (1984). *World view.* Novato, CA: Chandler & Sharp.

Kern, J. (1990). *Build the fort . . . today.* Spring Branch, TX: Author.

Kettelhack, G. (1984). *The wit and wisdom of Quentin Crisp.* New York: Harper & Row.

Kidd, J. R. (1973). *Relentless verity: Education for being-becoming-belonging.* Columbus, OH: ERIC Clearinghouse on Adult, Career, and Vocational Education. (Microfiche No. TN:1757544)

Kilmann, R. H., Saxton, M. J., Serpa, R., & Associates (Eds.). (1985). *Gaining control of the corporate culture.* San Francisco: Jossey-Bass.

Kimloch, G. C. (1979). *The sociology of minority groups.* Englewood Cliffs, NJ: Prentice Hall.

Kline, L. W. (1971). *Education and the personal quest.* Columbus, OH: Charles E. Merrill.

Knowles, M. S. (1970). *The modern practice of adult education: Andragogy versus pedagogy.* New York: Association Press.

Knowles, M. S. (1980). *The modern practice of adult education: From pedagogy to andragogy.* Chicago: Follett.

Knox, A. B. (1986). *Helping adults learn: A guide to planning, implementing, and conducting programs.* San Franciso: Jossey-Bass.

Knox, A. B. (1987). *International perspective on adult education.* Columbus, OH: ERIC Clearinghouse on Adult, Career, and Vocational Education. (NIE-C-400-84-0011).

Koberg, D., & Bagnall, J. (1974). *The universal traveler: A soft systems guide to creativity, problem-solving and the process of design.* Los Altos, CA: William Kaufmann.

Kottkamp, R. B. (1990). Teacher attitudes about work. In P. Reyes (Ed.), *Teachers and their workplace.* Newbury Park, CA: Sage.

Kounin, J. S. (1970). *Discipline and group management in class-rooms.* New York: Holt, Rinehart & Winston.

Kozman, H. C., Cassidy, R., & Jackson, C. O. (1967). *Methods in physical education* (4th ed.) Dubuque, IA: William C. Brown.

Lenz, E. (1982). *The art of teaching adults.* New York: Holt, Rinehart & Winston.

Lewin, K., Lippitt, R., & White, R. K. (1939, May). Patterns of aggressive behavior in experimentally created "social climates." *Journal of Social Psychology, 10,* 271–299.

Lewis, K. (1991). Gathering data for the improvement of teaching: What do I need and how do I get it? In M. Theall & J. Franklin (Eds.), *Effective practices for improving teaching.* (New Directions for Teaching and Learning, No. 48) (pp. 65–82). San Francisco: Jossey-Bass.

Leypoldt, M. M. (1967). *Forty ways to teach in groups.* Valley Forge, PA: The Judson Press.

Lindenfeld, F. (1973). *Radical perspectives on social problems* (2nd ed.). New York: Macmillan.

Locke, D. C. (1992). *Increasing multicultural understanding: A comprehensive model.* Newbury Park, CA: Sage.

Long, H. (1983). *Adult learning research and practice.* New York: Cambridge University Press.

Loughlin, C. E., & Suina, J. H. (1982). *The learning environment: An instructional strategy.* New York: Columbia University, Teachers College.

Loughran, E. L. (1984). Community education in context. In H. B. Reed & E. L. Loughran (Eds.); *Beyond schools: Education for economic, social and personal development* (pp. 213–232). Amherst, MA: Citizen Involvement Training Program.

Lovell, R. B. (1987). *Adult learning.* London: Croom Helm.

Lowman, J. (1990). *Mastering the techniques of teaching.* San Francisco: Jossey-Bass.

MacGregor, J. (1990). Collaborative learning: Shared inquiry as a process of reform. In M. D. Svinicki (Ed.), *The changing face of college teaching* (New Directions for Teaching and Learning, No. 42) (pp. 19–30). San Francisco: Jossey-Bass.

Magendzo, S. (1990). Popular education in nongovernmental organizations: Education for social mobilization? (Cristina Cardalda, Trans.). *Harvard Educational Review, 60*(1), 49-61.

Malehorn, H. (1984). *Elementary teacher's classroom management handbook.* West Nyack, NY: Parker.

Merriam, S. B., & Caffarella, R. S. (1991). *Learning in adulthood.* San Francisco: Jossey-Bass.

Merrill, H., & Gregory, T. (1974). *Teaching is . . .* Chicago: Science Research Associates, Inc.

Mezirow, J. (1977). Perspective transformation. *Studies in Adult Education, 32*(1), 100-110.

Mezirow, J. (1978). Perspective transformation. *Adult Education, 28*(2), 100-110.

Miles, M. B., & Huberman, A. M. (1984). *Qualitative data analysis.* Newbury Park, CA: Sage.

Mocker, D. W., & Spear, G. E. (1982). *Lifelong learning: Formal, nonformal, informal, and self-directed* (Information Series No. 241). Columbus, OH: ERIC Clearinghouse for Adult and Vocational Education.

Moos, R. (1974). *Issues in social ecology: Human milieus.* Palo Alto, CA: National Press Books.

Moos, R. (1975). *Evaluating correctional and community settings.* New York: John Wiley.

Moos, R. (1976). *The human context: Environmental determinants of Beharin.* New York: John Wiley.

Moos, R. (1979). *Evaluating educational environments.* San Francisco: Jossey-Bass.

Moos, R., & Trickett, E. (1987). *Classroom environment scale manual* (2nd ed.). Palo Alto, CA: Consulting Psychologists Press.

Mueller, A. D. (1940). *Principles and methods in adult education.* New York: Prentice Hall.

Mueller, D. J. (1986). *Measuring social attitudes: A handbook for researchers and practitioners.* New York: Teachers College Press.

Myers, I. B., with Myers, P. B. (1980). *Gifts differing.* Palo Alto, CA: Consulting Psychologist Press.

Newcomb, L. H., McCracken, J. D., & Warmbrod, J. R. (1986). *Methods of teaching agriculture.* Danville, IL: Interstate Printers & Publishers.

Newcomb, L. H., & Trefz, M. (1987) Toward teaching at higher levels of cognition. *National Association of College Teachers in Agriculture Journal*, 26–30.

Niebuhr, H. R. (1951). *Christ and culture.* New York: Harper & Row.

Norland, E. (1992). *Instrumentation and data collection procedures for the social sciences.* Columbus: Ohio State University.

Norland, E. (1993). *Course Packet: Ag Ed 622.* Adult Education in Agriculture. Columbus: Ohio State University.

Norland, E., Budak, J., & Heimlich, J. E. (1993, November). *The relationship of selected elements of the teaching-learning exchange to student outcomes.* Paper presented at the annual Conference of the Association for Adult and Continuing Education, Dallas.

Norland, E., & Heimlich, J. E. (1990, May). *Clarifying theory through operationalizing construct: A look at sensitivity and inclusion in adult teaching style.* Paper presented at the Adult Education Research Conference, Athens, GA.

Norland, E. & Heimlich, J. (1991). *Course notes, Agricultural Education 795.01.* Columbus: Ohio State University.

Norland, E., & Heimlich, J. E. (1993) *Teacher Center Inventory* (instrument).

Nuthall, G., & Snook, I. (1973). Contemporary models of teaching. In R. M. W. Travers (Ed.), *Second handbook of research on teaching.* (pp. 47–76). Chicago: Rand McNally.

O'Neill, C., Lamber, A., Linnell, R., & Warr-Wood, J. (1976). *Drama guidelines.* London: Heinemann Educational Books.

Ott, J. S. (1989). *The organizational culture perspective.* Pacific Grove, CA: Brooks/Cole.

Parsons, T. (1966). *Societies: Evolutionary and comparative perspectives.* Englewood Cliffs, NJ: Prentice Hall.

Pfeiffer, J. W., & Jones, J. E. (1985). *A handbook of structured experiences for human relations training* (rev. ed., Vols. 1–10). San Diego: University Associates.

Pintrich, P. R., & Johnson, G. R. (1990). Assessing and improving students' learning strategies. In M. Svinicki (Ed.), *The changing face of college teaching* (New Directions for Teaching and Learning, No. 42) (pp. 83–92).

Postman, N., & Weingartner, C. (1969). *Teaching as a subversive activity*. New York: Delta.

Prather, H. (1980). *There is a place where you are not alone*. Garden City, NY: Doubleday.

Preece, C. (1987). *Teaching without tears: The classroom teachers' survival book*. Ann Arbor, MI: Braun-Brumfield.

Purkey, W. W., Cage, B., & Graves, W. (1973). The Florida Key: A scale to infer learner self concept. *Journal of Educational and Psychological Measurement, 33*, 979–984.

Purkey, W. W., & Novak, J. M. (1984). *Inviting school success: A self-concept approach to teaching and learning*. Belmont, CA: Wadsworth.

Queior, D. (1986). Teaching and empowering of lifelong learners. In E. H. Brady (Ed.), *Perspectives on adult learning* (pp. 23–30). Gorham: University of Southern Maine.

Rando, W. C., & Menges, R. J. (1991). How practice is shaped by personal theories. In R. J. Menges & M. D. Svinicki (Eds.), *College teaching* (New Directions for Teaching and Learning, No. 45) (pp. 7–14). San Francisco: Jossey-Bass.

Reed, D. B. (1939). *Keep fit and like it*. New York: Whittlesey House.

Reed, H. B. & Loughran, E. L. (Eds.). (1984). *Beyond schools: Education for economic, social and personal development*. Amherst, MA: Citizen Involvement Training Program.

Richards, M. C. (1980). *Toward wholeness: Rudolf Steiner education in America*. Hanover, NH: University Press of New England.

Robinson, R. D. (1979). *Helping adults learn and change*. Milwaukee: Omnibook.

Rogers, C. (1969). *Freedom to learn*. Columbus, OH: C. E. Merrill.

Rogers, C. (1983). *Freedom to learn for the 80's*. Columbus, OH: C. E. Merrill.

Rosenshine, B., & Furst, N. (1971). Research in teaching performance criteria. In B. Smith (Ed.), *Research in teacher education* (pp. 37–72). Englewood Cliffs, NJ: Prentice Hall.

Rubin, L. D., Jr. (Ed.). (1990). *An apple for my teacher: Twelve writers tell about teachers who made all the difference*. Chapel Hill, NC: Algonquin Books.

Ruediger, W. C. (1932). *Teaching procedures.* Boston: Houghton Mifflin.

Ryans, D. G. (1960). *Characteristics of teachers: Their description, comparison, and appraisal.* Washington, DC: American Council on Education.

Ryans, D. G. (1970). *Characteristics of teachers in relation to financial and cultural conditions of their childhood homes.* Washington, DC: American Council on Education.

Sanchez, M. J. M. (1987). *Natural elements: Abstractions and mental images.* Master's thesis, Ohio State University.

Schaef, A. W. (1985). *Women's reality: An emerging female system in a white male society.* San Francisco: Harper & Row.

Schaie, K. W., & Geiwitz, J. (1982). *Adult development and aging.* Boston: Little, Brown.

Schön, D. A. (1987). *Educating the reflective practitioner.* San Francisco: Jossey-Bass.

Schrank, J. (1972). *Teaching human beings: 101 subversive activities for the classroom.* Boston: Beacon Press.

Seaman, D. F., & Fellenz, R. A. (1989). *Effective strategies for teaching adults.* Columbus, OH: C. E. Merrill.

Seevers, B. (1991). *Factors related to teaching style preference of Ohio Cooperative Extension faculty and staff.* Doctoral dissertation, Ohio State University.

Senge, P. M. (1990). *The fifth discipline: The art and practice of the learning organization.* New York: Doubleday.

Sizer, T. R. (1973). *Places for learning, places for joy: Speculation on American school reform.* Cambridge, MA: Harvard University Press.

Skilling, H. H. (1969). *Do you teach? Views on college teaching.* (Narrative of a seminar for graduate students, Stanford University). New York: Holt, Rinehart & Winston.

Smelser, N. J. (1963). *Theory of collective behavior.* New York: Free Press of Glencoe.

Smith, J. A. (1966). *Setting conditions for creative teaching in the elementary school.* Boston: Allyn & Bacon.

Smythe, W. J. (1986). *A rationale for teachers' critical pedagogy: A handbook.* Victoria, Australia: Deakin University Press.

Solomon, D., & Miller, H. L. (1961). *Exploration in teaching styles:*

Report of preliminary investigations and development of categories. Chicago: Center for the Study of Liberal Education for Adults.

Solomon, I. D. (1989). *Feminism and black activism in contemporary America: An ideological assessment.* New York: Greenwood Press.

Solomon, R., & Solomon, J. (1993). *Up the university: Recreating higher education in America.* Reading, MA: Addison-Wesley.

Sommer, R. (1970). The ecology of study areas. *Environment and Behavior 2,* 271-280.

Sork, T., & Caffarella, R. (1989). Planning programs for adults. In S. Merriam & P. Cunningham (Eds.), *Handbook of adult and continuing education* (pp. 233-245). San Francisco: Jossey-Bass.

Spengler, J. J. (1961). Theory, ideology, non-economic values, and politico-economic development. In R. J. Braibanti & J. J. Spengler (Eds.), *Tradition, values, and socioeconomic development* (pp. 1-56). Durham NC: Duke University Press.

Stormzand, M. J., & McKee, J. W. (1928). *The progressive primary teacher.* Boston: Houghton Mifflin.

Strecker, E. A., & Appel, K. E., with Appel, J. W. (1962). *Discovering ourselves: A view of the human mind and how it works* (3rd ed.). New York: Macmillan.

Sudman, S., & Bradburn, N. M. (1982). *Asking questions.* San Francisco: Jossey-Bass.

Svinicki, M. D. (1990). Changing the face of *your* teaching. In M. D. Svinicki (Ed.), *The changing face of college teaching.* (New Directions for Teaching and Learning, No. 42) (pp. 5-15). San Francisco: Jossey-Bass.

Tarule, J. M. (1988). Voices of returning women: Ways of knowing. In L. H. Lewis (Ed.), *Addressing the needs of returning women* (New Directions for Continuing Education, No. 39) (pp. 19-34). San Francisco: Jossey-Bass.

Thompson, L. L. (1984). *An investigation of the relationship of the personality theory of Carl G. Jung and teachers' self-reported perceptions and decisions.* Doctoral dissertation, Ohio State University.

Tough, A. (1979). *The adult's learning projects: A fresh approach to theory and practice in adult learning* (2nd ed.). Austin, TX: Learning Concepts.

Treat, L. (1981). *Crime and puzzlement*. Boston: David R. Godine.

Treat, L. (1983). *You're the detective*. Boston: David R. Godine.

Turiel, E. (1983). *The development of social knowledge: Morality and convention*. Cambridge, MA.: Cambridge University Press.

Turner, J. H. (1974). *The structure of sociological theory*. Homewood, IL: Dorsey Press.

Twining, J. E. (1991). *Strategies for active learning*. Needham Heights, MA: Allyn & Bacon.

Van Tilburg, E. L., & DuBois, J. (1989, April). Literacy students' perceptions of successful participation in adult education: A cross-cultural approach through expectancy valence. In Proceedings of the 30th Annual Adult Education Research Conference, Madison, Wis.

Van Tilburg, E., & Heimlich, J. E. (1987). Education and the subculture: Incorporation versus inculturation concerns for the educator. *Lifelong Learning, 11*(3), 21–24, 28.

Verdun, J. R., Miller, H. G., & Greer, C. E. (1977). *Adults teaching adults: Principles and strategies*. Austin, TX: Learning Concepts.

Verner, C. (1962). *A conceptual scheme for the identification and classification of processes for adult education*. Washington, DC: Adult Education Association.

Verner, C. (1964). Definition of terms. In G. E. Jensen, A. A. Liveright, & W. C. Hallenbeck (Eds.), *Adult education: Outlines of an emerging field of university study* (pp. 27–40). Washington, DC: Adult Education Association.

Warren, V. B. (Ed.). (1964). *A treasury of techniques for teaching adults*. Washington, DC: National Association for Public Continuing and Adult Education.

Washington, B. T. (1965). *Up from slavery*. New York: Dodd, Mead, & Company. (Originally published 1900)

Weiler, K. (1988). *Becoming an effective classroom manager: A resource for teachers*. Albany: State University of New York Press.

Weimer, M. (1990). "Study" your way to better teaching. In M. Svinicki (Ed.), *Changing the face of college teaching* (New Directions for Teaching and Learning, No. 42) (pp. 117-130). San Francisco: Jossey-Bass.

Wilkinson, J. (1984). Varieties of teaching. In M. M. Gullette (Ed.), *The art and craft of teaching* (pp. 1-9). Cambridge, MA: Harvard University Press.

Witkin, B. R. (1984). *Assessing needs in educational and social programs.* San Francisco: Jossey-Bass.

Wlodkowski, R. J. (1990). Strategies to enhance adult motivation to learn. In M. Galbraith (Ed.), *Adult learning methods: A guide for effective instruction* (pp. 97-118). Malabar, FL: Robert E. Kreiger.

Zinn, L. M. (1983). Development of a valid and reliable instrument to identify a personal philosophy of adult education (Doctoral dissertation, Florida State University, 1982). *Dissertation Abstracts International, 44,* 1667-1668-A.

Zinn, L. M. (1990). Identifying your philosophical orientation. In M. Galbraith (Ed.), *Adult learning methods: A guide for effective instruction* (pp. 39-78). Malabar, FL: Robert E. Krieger.

Index

255